JOURNEY IN THE WILDERNESS

More Praise for *Journey in the Wilderness*:

"Gil Rendle has long been a reliable guide for leaders navigating change in our culture and the church. *Journey in the Wilderness* is another invaluable piece of the map to help mainline church leaders seeking to discern God's vision for our future amid disorienting change."

John Wimmer, Program Director, Religion, Lilly Endowment, Inc.

"Gil Rendle provides not only a descriptive understanding of how mainline churches got into the wilderness but also clues for their path forward. He does it with perceptive wisdom and hopeful steps for the journey. *Journey in the Wilderness* is a must read for leaders of congregations and denominational leaders who seek a new/ancient role for congregations."

John R. Schol, Bishop, the Washington, DC Episcopal
Area of The United Methodist Church

"This book is a gift of well-founded hope. Gil Rendle deftly describes the unique opportunities present within our wilderness experience and offers a clear perspective on the pathway for learning and relevant change we may find there."

Tom Locke, President, Texas Methodist Foundation

Journey in the Wilderness

New Life for
Mainline Churches

Gil Rendle

Abingdon Press
Nashville

JOURNEY IN THE WILDERNESS
NEW LIFE FOR MAINLINE CHURCHES

Copyright © 2010 by Abingdon Press

All rights reserved.

This book is printed on acid-free paper.

Library of Congress Cataloging-in-Publication Data

Rendle, Gilbert R.
   Journey in the wilderness : new life for mainline churches / Gil Rendle.
      p. cm.
   Includes bibliographical references (p.   ).
   ISBN 978-1-4267-1065-0 (trade pbk. : alk. paper)
   1. Mission of the church—United States.   2. Church renewal—United States.   I. Title.
BV601.8.R46 2010
262'.7—dc22

2010031010

Scripture quotations unless noted otherwise are taken from the New Revised Standard Version of the Bible, copyright 1989, Division of Christian Education of the National Council of the Churches of Christ in the United States of America. Used by permission. All rights reserved.

Scripture quotations marked *"THE MESSAGE"* are from *THE MESSAGE*. Copyright © by Eugene H. Peterson 1993, 1994, 1995, 1996, 2000, 2001, 2002. Used by permission of NavPress Publishing Group.

Sharing Stories, Shaping Community by Mike Mather. © 2002 by Discipleship Resources. Used with permission.

10 11 12 13 14 15 16 17 18 19—10 9 8 7 6 5 4 3 2 1

MANUFACTURED IN THE UNITED STATES OF AMERICA

CONTENTS

For Lynne

FOREWORD

Like most pastors starting out, I sought to offer my best leadership. Mentors taught me preaching, pastoral care, and administration, but I reached into the toolbox for more. I booked up on church growth, and we counted parking spaces, repainted signs, designed brochures, cleaned the nursery, and followed up with visitors. Soon we reached for more tools and expanded small group ministries, added worship services, and developed hands-on mission projects. We reached deeper and experimented with marketing, praise bands, and international mission teams. Next, we explored bilingual ministries, breakfast before worship, a visitor's center, and service evangelism. We expanded and built new facilities. We learned our way into these things, borrowing from churches of all types. We attended workshops, read books, trained laity, studied systems theory, hired consultants, restructured governance, visited churches, learned leadership, evaluated ministries, aligned staff, developed teams, adopted goals, wrote mission statements, and focused on results. By the grace of God and with a swell of favorable demographics, we inched forward year by year. We bucked the heavy trend of decline among mainline churches.

As a pastor, my leadership style was thoughtful, calculated, and strategic. We moved slowly, steadily, cautiously. We built consensus, aligned resources, and communicated thoroughly. We persistently focused on the mission, developed a clear identity, experimented carefully, and progressed in small steps. The scope of congregational ministry allowed me to focus on my own small field of influence. And yet I realized the toolbox no longer contained everything we needed. Each year we reached a smaller portion of the population.

Then I became a bishop, and the stakes were higher. I was assigned nine hundred congregations. Under the leadership of faithful bishops, pastors, and laypersons, the conference had lost eighty-five thousand members in forty years, closed two hundred churches, and watched the median age rise to fifty-eight. I saw the profound nature of the crisis, seemingly insurmountable and irreversible. Constituencies wrestled with the reality that we no longer had the people to fund ministry, as we did in previous generations. Denial and blame fed conflict. These staggering trends marked us as "average" among mainline judicatories.

We needed radically new understandings. The tools of the past took us only so far. From a slow and steady leader, I became an active risk taker, pushing for change and willing to experiment, explore, and learn in every aspect of our work. We tried to break through impenetrable structures, clarify identity and purpose, develop a common language, reward innovation, learn from success, start new congregations, highlight fruitfulness, embrace accountability, develop learning communities for pastors and laity, and lift our eyes toward the mission field around us. Even if we make all the best decisions, it may take a generation before we find our baseline and begin to see ministry that grows consistently each year. We persist even when there is no clear consensus about what will work. A few congregations thrive, an increasing number turn around, and we explore forms of church that would have been unthinkable a generation ago.

Gil Rendle is among the most influential people on my pathway of leadership development. Gil brings an extraordinary understanding of organizational dynamics to renewing the mainline denominations. His unmatched experience as a pastor, teacher, and consultant to congregations, pastors, bishops, conferences, dioceses, and synods has made him one of the most valued resources for denominational leaders. He is attuned to the larger trends, trained in systems theory and organizational leadership, and unusually helpful in processing how we take the next step. I have benefitted personally from his teaching and encouragement, spending several days with him each year working through case studies with colleagues.

In *Journey in the Wilderness*, Gil Rendle offers perspective, hope, and encouragement to congregational and denominational leaders. He picks up the pieces of the puzzle one at a time and holds them to the light at just the right angle for us to see how they fit together into a new narrative about our recent history, current challenges, and future possibilities. He reframes the church leadership conversation. Using the Hebrew wilderness stories, he describes our last forty years of experimentation as a time of necessary learning and preparation. Our dabbling in church growth, congregational transformation, leadership development, and endless restructuring has not been wasted effort. Rather, this has been a period of growing awareness, exploration, and testing through which we have learned much. We have been learning how to change people's lives rather than merely their membership affiliations. We are questioning assumptions of egalitarianism, representative democracy, scarcity, and harmony in church life. We have learned to draw our attention to the right things. We have formed better conversations. We are at a better place, and this has prepared us for a future yet unseen. This is necessary work for new responses to God's calling to emerge and new forms of Christian witness to take hold.

Journey in the Wilderness is part *textbook* on church leadership, part *field guide* for identifying organizational behaviors we have all seen but could never name, and part *instruction manual* on how to leave behind systems that are no longer conducive to our mission. Drawing on theorists such as Deming, Drucker, Collins, Heifetz, Friedman, and Miller, Gil Rendle offers insight on leading in organizations that demand new answers while also restraining innovation. He acknowledges the futility of merely trying harder or setting higher goals and describes the necessity of birthing new systems. He moves us toward organizational principles that support a way of life, with a clear identity and purpose. He reminds us of the underused power of agenda and of convening. He teaches us how to lead in systems where none of us have direct control over others. He presents a powerful analysis of what paralyzes us and challenges us to innovate, experiment, and explore. He helps us hold a wide array of congregational forms and diverse people together around a shared story and identity. His ideas stimulate hope for leaders searching to understand and act.

Wendell Berry said, "Now when hope sets out in its desperate search for reasons, it can find them." As leaders of mainline churches, what reasons do we have for hope?

Do we hope that God will miraculously revive our churches? It's time to stop asking God to do for us what God created us to do for God.

Do we expect God will work *around* us rather than *through* us? I'm not ready to concede that the way of life that marks our denominational heritage is no longer true or useful to God.

Gil Rendle offers reasons to hope. We see that other people are working on the same things we are. We accept all we have accomplished in our learning over the past forty years of wilderness searching. We see new life emerging from many corners and margins of the church. We practice exploration and experimentation. We see people doing the necessary work of learning. We see the first gleanings of fruit from the promised land. There is reason for hope.

Christianity began as a way of life, a movement with a clear identity and purpose. Most of our denominational families began with simple organizational structures that supported growth in Christ. My hope for those who read this book is that we gather encouragement, understanding, and strength for the tasks ahead. I pray we learn to lead in a way that communicates the way of life in Christ to future generations. I hope for better conversations. I pray for congregations that are clear about their mission and confident about their future. I pray for the courage to risk the change that is necessary to remain faithful to the message that has been entrusted to us.

Robert Schnase

Robert Schnase serves as Bishop of the Missouri Conference of The United Methodist Church. He is author of *Five Practices of Fruitful Congregations* and *Five Practices of Fruitful Living*.

INTRODUCTION
WELCOME TO THE WILDERNESS

People no longer join congregations because they want relationships or because they want to "belong." As far as relationships that serve as social friendships, increasingly people already have as many as their time and lifestyle allow. Rather than simply seeking social relationships for which there is less room in a harried contemporary lifestyle, people now come to congregations because they want a purposeful relationship with others who are seeking a purpose and meaning in response to the questions that they feel in their lives. For many the function of relationships in congregations has now shifted from being only social to being also purposeful. This shift that removes the congregation from its position as a central institution that provides friendships out of which members then shape a personal identity is difficult news to many congregations, which continue to think of their only strength as being warm and friendly relationship providers.

No longer the de facto centers of social connections, congregations must now learn to pick up their new/ancient role as a place where meaning is shaped for people's lives. This represents a difficult shift within congregations from being excessively focused on relationships (keeping members satisfied) to being much more focused on purpose (giving people meaning). Welcome to the wilderness. This central shift of institutional life for congregations is one of several that we will explore in this book. For many leaders the new reality feels like a wilderness in which the territory is suddenly foreign and feels dangerous.

The church is not the only one in the new wilderness. We are joined by a host of other organizations and institutions now living in a new world. In North America the years immediately following World War II began as an orderly time of building a new national postwar economy and organizing communities, businesses, schools, farms, industries, and family life in very structured and standardized ways. The new ordering of North America was enabled by lessons harnessed during the war from a scientific worldview that seemed, at first blush, to offer a secure future. But beneath the hopeful surface, the war had quietly taken its toll by weakening the hope and trust that people had in science and technology and the commitment they had to a worldview of rationalism that had developed over several centuries of discoveries that once seemed to promise that life could be controlled. The problem was that, applied to the battlefield, the same science and technology had proved lethal through new forms of weaponry, extermination camps as efficient and productive as any modern manufacturing indus-try, and the use of atomic power to destroy whole cities within seconds. While out-wardly appearing organized, the post-WWII generations were left with tumultuous internal questions. For many the world was becoming unhinged. The early, orderly postwar years of "the organization man" were quickly followed by a confusing array of events and movements from Woodstock to Watergate. Beginning in the 1950s, the neat and orderly postwar North American people experienced the fuller blossoming of the atomic age, "red" hunts for the insidious Communists who were thought to be hid-den within our own government, the civil rights movement, assassinations of national leaders, the drug culture, the free love movement, the emergence of rock and roll, a contentious war in Vietnam, the impeachment of a sitting president, the peace move-ment, the women's movement, urban rioting, and indeed, the list could go on quite a bit longer. The hope that science, technology, and the civilized human being could bring order to the world, making life safe, productive, and meaningful, was deeply dented and damaged. A simple, unquestioning trust in God and dependence on the church suddenly felt less secure. At the same time, new expressions of faith were tak-ing the stage, including evangelicalism, pentecostalism, and a fundamentalism that has continued to grow in all three of the monotheistic religions of Christianity, Judaism, and Islam.[1]

In the midst of this turmoil the mainline church was, along with a whole host of other North American institutions, the target of questions and confusions. Membership and attendance dropped in congregations, and the church found itself in new competition for the attention and participation of its members, let alone other people who might become new members. Clergy dropped in their ranking of the most trusted professionals, and the dominant and dominating presence of the mainline Protestant voice suddenly had to compete to be heard in the public square where it had once, and very recently, held unchallenged prominence. It was a wilderness where old assumptions and practices seemed no longer to work, where new assumptions and prac-tices had not yet been formed, and where there seemed to be more than enough self-doubt and blame to go around. An adage related to understanding systems states that when people don't know *what* went wrong, they want to know *who* went wrong. The search for the causes and the "causers" of our dismay was an active search. Fingers were pointed in multiple directions.

This was the time in which I grew up in the mainline church, felt called to ministry, was ordained, and began to serve as pastor and then later as consultant and teacher. It has been a wilderness journey for me and for my colleagues as well. I do have a deep conviction, however, that the time for pointing fingers has passed and it is time to get on with living in the wilderness and appreciating the hard-won lessons that we have already learned and that will sustain us in this foreign territory.

Like the Israelites who could yearn for the familiar fleshpots back in Egypt when the unfamiliar desert felt too disorienting, I too can, at times, drop into longing for older, steadier days. But it is time for all of us, self included, to recognize the change that the hand of God brings to those who are led, willingly or not, into the new land. It has been a very rich forty years since the mainline church first faced the challenge of the changed postwar world. We have tried many new ways. We have learned a lot of new things. But most important, we are being shaped as a new people with a new identity, fresh purpose, and if we allow, new hope.

This book is a reflection of my time in the wilderness shared with so many others. While it is a personal story, it will be told in an institutional and organizational way because this is the lens through which I do my work and practice my calling. Our time in the wilderness has been spent productively searching multiple paths that might lead us to our more purposeful future. We now stand on the shoulders of those who have led and gone before us in this wandering. We now can claim and use with confidence their lessons, particularly in explorations of church growth, congregational transformation, and leadership development.

This book will track the lessons that have already sustained us in the wilderness and also point to work still waiting to be done and lessons still to be learned. The journey through the wilderness that this book proposes is pretty straightforward. The first chapter will move more deeply into the metaphor of the wilderness as a way of understanding and being informed by our own "particular exodus." The new sciences commonly talk of chaos as order not yet discovered. To live in the changed culture, we need to accept the transformative power of the chaos that is found in the wilderness and the new order that it promises for our lives. The church needs to talk with the culture, a conversation that requires more of an interdisciplinary approach in which the church becomes more adept at the language of the culture while inviting the culture to learn the language of the church. In the case of this book the exterior lenses of organizational development, organizational psychology, and general systems theory will be identified as helpful tools to support this conversation.

In the following two chapters we will recall much of what we have already learned on our exodus. While many of our leaders and members in the mainline church are still cynical, discouraged, and adept at practicing our demise as denominations, the reality is that much has been tried, much has been learned, and there is a good body of both knowledge and practice that has and will sustain us into the future. Chapters 2 and 3 will describe the four critical paths of learning that we have already pursued: the paths of church growth, congregational transformation, clergy development, and understanding identity and purpose.

We will then go on in chapter 4 to explore changes in the culture that have had particular impact on the mainline church. The story of the cultural change that we have lived through in our lifetimes is complex, confusing, and unendingly interesting. It is a story that can be told in multiple ways through any number of lenses, each of which brings a different perspective to the change. The telling of the changing culture in chapter 4 will not seek to be comprehensive but will point to several particular shifts that require that the mainline church rethink its assumptions and practices. As we proceed, we should be mindful that much of the current behavior and practice in the mainline church was established in an earlier time in which that behavior and practice was appropriate. My generation of leaders inherited a church that was once effective and well built for an earlier day. Being able to be clearer about what has changed in North American culture to challenge the assumptions and practices of that earlier day allows the church to be more measured in its response and more appropriate in determining what must be changed.

Chapters 5 and 6 will then consider the deep change that faces our practices of leadership. Leadership itself has changed in the church, and we currently ask for results greatly different from what leaders were once expected to produce and different from what leaders, myself included, were trained to produce. Part of the current challenge for leaders in our mainline churches is the dual task of not only knowing what to do but also knowing what not to do, what to let go of. The final chapter will hazard some guesses about the changed mainline church as it begins to emerge from the wilderness. Futuring is more than guessing since it is based on current experience and learning. But it is also less than predicting since we do not control the land we live in and we worship a God of multiple surprises. Nonetheless, when we are tired from marching in the wilderness, our minds are drawn to the future that might be found in the promised land. There are things that we can already say about the reshaping of our church through efforts of futuring—as long as we are willing to be wrong.

We do not live alone in the wilderness, so it is important for the mainline church not to overly personalize the difficulties and challenges. Our wilderness has been prompted by a great sea change in both national and global culture. While the mainline church has its own particular variation, the theme of deep change is shared widely in North America no matter what expression of faith community I work with as consultant. Apart from the differences in details, the story does not appreciably change when I work with Jews and Roman Catholics. In addition, as I work with laity, I am told repeatedly that the issues of change we are working on as leaders of denominations and congregations apply equally to people's leadership in their families, friendships, and workplaces, whether in police departments, hospitals, law offices, manufacturing plants, high-tech communication companies, or schools and universities. It certainly is a mix of metaphors, but the reality is that in this desert wilderness of cultural change, "we are all swimming in the same water."

While reporting on our wilderness journey I want to acknowledge that I have been taught by the best instructors—the thousands of congregations that have invited me in to share their questions and their experiments as we walked together. I have been instructed by the many thousands of leaders, lay and clergy, who listened to my ideas and reflections and encouraged or corrected me with their responses as needed. In particular I have had the privilege of working for the past few years with the Texas Methodist Foundation Institute for Clergy and Congregational Excellence in Austin, Texas, which is the brightest example of a learning organization within the mainline church that I know of. Here I have learned more about how reflective conversation of leaders enables us to teach one another what cannot be learned in other ways. Here creative conversation is the currency used to explore the purpose of the church.

As a part of my work with the Texas Methodist Foundation Institute, I have served as facilitator for structured conversations with the eleven bishops and more than fifty district superintendents of the South Central Jurisdiction of The United Methodist Church for more than four years. Our meetings, two or three days at a time, multiple times during each year, have been pure learning conversations of leaders who might not be in love with the wilderness but are certainly learning their way. A number of sections of this book were initially prepared as monographs or presentations to these groups and were initially used to help focus their learning. The ideas and the shape of the story of our wilderness were then tested and deepened through continual consulting that I did on issues of denominational change with a number of mainline denominations, the American Roman Catholic Church, and the Reform Jewish movement.

To all of these people and places, I give my deep thanks. I have been aided by the fact-finding help of Amanda Black of the Texas Methodist Foundation in an effort to be clear about the early paths of our wilderness wandering that will be reported in chapters 2 and 3. And as always, I have been helped by the critical conversations with my friend and colleague Ian Evison, who consistently seeks to keep me honest. The countless conversations with Ian and others about the monographs that preceded this book have added to their depth in telling this story. This book is offered as my perspective using the tools and lenses that I find most helpful. Although errors in the telling are fully mine, nonetheless, this is our story—the partial story of a whole people who may not be fully happy to be living in a wilderness but who are changing and beginning to thrive. We are reforming and being reformed as a new people of God. The future will be different, but it will still be God's.

CHAPTER 1
OUR PARTICULAR EXODUS

It isn't that often that a whole people go through a religious wilderness together. Yet in North America that has been the case in my lifetime and in my experience. There have been historical instances, of course, all along the way, from the beginning of the European settlement of North America to the initial arrivals of religious people bringing their practices, followed by shifts, schisms, realignments, mergers, and inventions of groups, sects, and denominations. At some point or another there have been moments of discomfort in each of our religious bodies—Protestant, Catholic, and Jewish—that have required refocusing, restructuring, or restaffing. But rarer is the radical, rooted shift in a global culture that prompts and requires a whole people to question their practices and enter a prolonged wilderness in search of their future way of life. Ours has been such an exodus, an escape (or perhaps an expulsion) from a constraining past in search of a promised, and findable, future.

My personal experience in the church has been defined by this exodus. It has been a pilgrimage through a changed North American landscape. In reality the changed landscape is global rather than North American. The explosive growth of a new form of Christianity in the Southern Hemisphere, the global spread of Islam, the growing practice of Hinduism and Buddhism in non-Asian countries including the United States, and the essential disconnecting of postmodern people from modern and premodern religious practices all attest to a broad-based and wholesale change. Nonetheless, given the massive changes that have brought both turmoil and ferment to all religious communities, this book is about *our particular exodus* through the wilderness. "Our particular exodus" refers to the mainline church in North America, which is the church I have been a part of throughout my life. The word *exodus* is rooted in the Greek (*ex*—out of; *hodos*—way). It offers the image of a people who have been taken out of a way of life that was well known and deeply established. My experience was to be born into a North American mainline denominational church that was strong, confident, growing, and a dominant voice in shaping the norms of North American life. As a young seminary graduate, I was ordained into a mainline church

1

that was still able to live out of its assumptions of strength, confidence, growth, and dominance. However, my time as an adult working in the mainline church took me out of that earlier way and introduced me to a time of questioning, doubt, and searching. My time, along with that of many brothers and sisters across the mainline church, has been a wilderness experience, and I have been changed by the journey.

I do not despair of the fundamental connection between God and the people. The search for and interest in a relationship with God show no evidence of weakening in all their multifaith and personal spiritual dimensions. But I am the inheritor of a particular way to be with God—a Wesleyan inheritance through The United Methodist Church. Like my brothers and sisters in other mainline expressions of Christianity, I now ask, What do we bring to this relationship between God and God's people? Do we have a word to share? Can we shape a way to be that offers a current connection to God and to God's dreams for us and for our world?

I am encouraged. The longer I am in this wilderness, the greater my hope grows. For I have been witness to people all around me who have been open to learning new ways to live what were earlier and deeply established identities. Above all else the wilderness is a place to learn. The wilderness is where we learn again to live in a new way because old supports are gone, old assumptions no longer hold true, and old practices either fail or are no longer possible. To live, the people must learn anew even those most basic things that in the old homeland were hidden by our easy assumptions and learned behavior.

We have been learning. In fact, one question that this book seeks to address is, What have we learned by living in the wilderness for the last forty years that will sustain us in the future? In reality the question should be framed as, What have we taught ourselves? There are times and situations in which we must learn what no one can teach us. We cannot turn to others who have gone ahead because no one has been in front of us on the journey. We cannot point outside ourselves. We learn—teach ourselves—as a "community of practice."[1] We learn by doing. Getting clear and bringing to conscious awareness what we have learned will instruct us further about how we can live in our future. By my measure, we have learned much. The story of our exodus is rich, and we are already changed. Of course, there is much left to do, and not everyone will want to do it. There is little doubt that our mainline denominations will be changed in size and shape by the rest of the journey. There is little doubt that a good percentage of our local congregations, perhaps as many as 25 to 30 percent, will not live through the journey and they will close. There is little doubt that our denominational structures, staffing, and use of resources will continue to undergo deep change. Nonetheless, we are being helped and shaped by what we have learned, our trust in God has deepened, and we have sufficient bread for the rest of the journey.

This book is framed by the metaphor of exodus, thinking about the pilgrimage of the mainline church out of old ways and into a new and unknown territory. Walter Brueggemann points out that the usefulness of a metaphor is not in a search for a direct connection between one's reality and the images of the metaphor. The relationship between a metaphor and the reality it reflects is odd, playful, and ill fitting, which allows the metaphor to show us more than we would have otherwise seen in our own experience.[2] In this case the metaphor of exodus is meant to help us recognize ourselves as a displaced people who need to trust God for our future and who need to be willing to learn new ways and reshape our lives as we travel. The metaphor allows us to recall that without courage fear overwhelms, and the people will prefer to return to the old but deadly slaveries. We recall that in the wilderness old diets are replaced with new foods; old slave masters are replaced with new leaders, organization, and structure. We recall that there are times when the path ahead seems so clear it is as if lit by a pillar of fire; there are times when the path ahead is so unclear it is best to pitch tent and wait; there are times when some paths that seemed so promising peter out and steps must be retraced. We recall that at times the right hand and the left hand get disconnected and disorganized so that at the key moment that new commandments are received on the mountaintop, the same commandments are being broken at the mountain base. We recall also that through such a messy and oh-so-human exodus, the people are changed from those who were slaves in the old land to become a new nation for God, called to live in a new place.

I suggest that in our dominant North American bias toward orderliness, we perhaps expect too much from an exodus. We expect that the trip can be scheduled on a clear time line, that leaders will know the right direction to walk every day, that faithfulness will not be challenged, and that everyone will willingly take the trip together without argument. Were such an orderly trip even possible, the fact remains that neat, tidy trips produce little learning and perhaps, in the end, no change.

We've Been Here Before

One idea that sustains me on our particular exodus is that we will manage this deep transition as God's people because we have been here before. We are the people of the original Exodus and the Exile. We have been displaced before. We have learned to sing the Lord's song in a foreign land before. Despite our best efforts to escape hard and, at times, distasteful work, we have been delivered up on the shores of Nineveh before and been given new directions. And through it all, we today have received an inheritance from those earlier people who faced the wilderness and responded with deepened theology, richer hymnody, and more authentic community. It has been messy, but we've done it before.

Beginning in January of 2006, I was invited to provide primary leadership at two large gatherings of Roman Catholic priests in the Midwest, each of which met for four days to learn about how to lead change. Faced with deep challenges within the Roman Catholic Church, of changing membership, changing attendance patterns, and the need to merge weakened but deeply ethnic parishes into new merged cross-ethnic parishes, these groups of about 250 priests met with me, a Protestant teacher, in gatherings along with their bishops and archbishops to consider their leadership in regard to such changes coming from the ground up. These were unprecedented gatherings in a church with a heritage where change is usually introduced from the top down and where there is a well-established practice of working only with teachers of their own faith.

On the second afternoon of each event Father Thomas Tifft presented a historical perspective of change in the Roman Catholic Church. Tom is rector and professor of church history at Saint Mary Seminary and Graduate School in Ohio and, as such, offered both a pastoral and an academic review, tinged with humor. His task was to identify other times when the church faced such deep change as in this present moment. He identified six periods that are worth our review. They are in very abbreviated form because of the summary of learnings that Tom distilled. The six periods are as follows:[3]

1. *Acts 6:1-7*: Having received complaints about the distribution of resources, the apostles recognized that they were dealing with a very changed situation. They responded by rethinking their community, clarifying roles, and realigning the work. The first deacons were appointed and the apostles were given the task to preach the word. Acts 15: The apostles were faced with the question of including Gentiles without requiring them to embrace Mosaic law. The Council of Jerusalem listened to both sides and in its decisions changed the church from a local community to a global movement.

2. *Emperor Constantine granting tolerance in 313*: The first persecutions beginning with Nero continued for 250 years and eventually awakened the emperor Constantine to the Christian message. The persecutions ended with his conversion, yet Constantine's acceptance was a double-edged sword recognizing and supporting Christians, on the one side, and putting the church in an inferior position under the power of the ruler, on the other side. The early monastic movement was a protest against—a withdrawal from—state alignment.

3. *Gregorian reform (ninth through eleventh centuries)*: The Norman and Viking invasions provided a dark period for the church. The church lived under almost total control of the state to the point that local lords rather than the church appointed the priests. Strong Italian families took over the papacy as their own personal tool and misused it, prompting a deep need for reform. The movement of reform headed by monks enforced celibacy as the rule for clergy in order to correct misbehaviors from the popes on down, ended lay authority over clergy, reestablished papal authority, and resolved disputes vertically through authority rather than horizontally through power.

4. *The Reformation and the Council of Trent (sixteenth century)*: Never before had so many priests and religious women abandoned the church, with as much as 50 percent of Europe embracing Protestantism. The response, twenty to thirty years later, was the Catholic Reformation, which did not try to reestablish relationships or reunite with Protestants but set out Catholic doctrine in the areas of papacy, episcopacy, and the pastoral role. The church responded by going back to what was essential.

5. *The emergence of liberalism and the rise of individualism (nineteenth century)*: The secular impact of the French Revolution in areas such as civil divorce, civil marriage, and public education attacked the role of the church. Liberalism, which introduced the freedom of the individual, stressed human dignity and autonomy while also demonstrating hostility to a church aligned with old political forms. The liberal Catholicism of the nineteenth century sought to reestablish a relationship between church and culture.

6. *The Second Vatican Council (1962–1965):* The council debated the importance of continuity or discontinuity with the past and whether authority was only top down or could be more inclusive. (Should attention be given to collaboration and the vocabulary of the servant?) Changes with lasting impact were made: liturgy was revised to make it more intelligible to laypeople; the church understood itself as the whole people of God, and attitudes toward and practice with other Christians were shifted; and the church called for a new dialogue with the modern world.

This informative review of Christian history from a skilled historian captured the essentials out of complexity. It was further proof that we have been here before, and rehearsing the preceding times of deep change should, by itself, help us deal with the anxiety we feel in our present uncertainness. But further support comes from identifying ways that the church found to address such wilderness experiences. Tom concluded with seven general lessons drawn from the past times of deep change faced by the church. His summary follows with my brief observations:

1. Things move slowly in the church. (*This conclusion surprised no one and prompted group laughter that comes from self-recognition, which we Protestants can share with our Roman Catholic brothers.*)
2. Because things move slowly in the church, we need to be a people of great patience who resist the temptation of cynicism. (*Connecting patience with resistance to cynicism was a new and important insight to me.*)
3. The church has a long tradition of making decisions collaboratively through councils, and top-down authority is not always the best. (*This observation offers a new perspective on what feels to be unending and iterative motions, debates, and studies that come out of general conferences, general assemblies, and regional and global conferences of our denominational church bodies.*)
4. The church responds best when it recognizes what is essential, what is primary. (*Indeed, the conversation about what is essential has been at the heart of our wilderness experience of the past forty years. Much of this book focuses on the leadership task and the skills necessary to claim the essentials while dealing with the confusion of an accretion of established practices and the conflicting preferential voices of people and groups with competing needs.*)
5. The church needs to constantly discern and stay in touch with people. (*This point is essential. What makes it difficult is that the people the church needs to connect with are not necessarily the people already in the church but the people who are not yet in the church and for whom the church is now called. How can one be an evangel to those who cannot understand what is spoken? How can one be a missionary to those whose language is not understood? The tasks of discernment and connection are today greatly complicated by a people whose generational styles shift and multiply quickly and a people whose global character holds competing claims.*)
6. Our God is a God of surprises. (*Indeed, this may be one of the most difficult lessons. We can never allow ourselves to believe that we are in control and to miss seeing God as capable of surprising us. But neither can we risk directing our resources and*

attention to those places that hold little potential and will live only if they are a surprise from God. Discernment is a complex task of leadership that always requires wise decision making in order to direct resources and is accompanied by a willingness to be wrong when surprised by God, who moves in different directions.)

7. We live in constant hope. History teaches us that we have seen worse, we have survived, and we have been renewed. *(Perhaps the most important lesson is to risk trusting God in the wilderness. While we want to find our hope in the clear decisions and decisive directions that we expect from leaders, hope may be better found in the skills of anger, courage, and laughter practiced by leaders willing to learn what is not yet fully understood.)*

However one tells the story, we are clearly in a wilderness moment. Some call it a paradigm shift or postmodernism or an emergent moment. Robert William Fogel calls it "the fourth great awakening," connecting the swells of American religion with progressive economic and political change.[4] Perhaps the most inventive is Phyllis Tickle's description of the present time as a giant rummage sale when the church cleans out its attic to rid itself of what no longer serves.[5] The descriptions of the depth of change that we now face have been multiple and creative and are reported from a wide array of disciplines and perspectives.

Whatever the description, we need to remember that we have been here before, we have managed change before, and what will emerge at the end will be more vibrant and will serve better than what we knew in the past. Pointing back to her list of times when the church has encountered its deepest moments of change, Tickle notes, "It is especially important to remember that no standing form of organized Christian faith has ever been destroyed by one of our semi-millennial eruptions. Instead, each simply has lost hegemony or pride of place to the new and not-yet-organized form that was birthing."[6]

Using the Language at the Wall

When King Hezekiah reigned in Judea and King Hoshea reigned in the northern kingdom, the king of Assyria sent troops to Jerusalem and threatened King Hezekiah (2 Kings 18–19). The Assyrian king's Rabshakeh, or "cupbearer," traveled to the wall of Jerusalem and mocked the Israelites inside because of their trust in God. He said, "You're living in a world of make-believe, of pious fantasy. Do you think that mere words are any substitute for military strategy and troops?" (2 Kings 18:19 *"THE MESSAGE"*). The Rabshakeh then offered a challenge to the Israelites and threatened to destroy them.

The response of Eliakim from within the city of Jerusalem was to demand that the Rabshakeh change the language that he used in his threats: "Please speak to us in the Aramaic language. We understand Aramaic. Don't speak Hebrew—everyone crowded on the city wall can hear you" (2 Kings 18:26 *"THE MESSAGE"*). Eliakim asked to be addressed in Aramaic because he did not want the people to understand the threat and he wished to protect the people from their fears. He hoped that the leaders within Jerusalem could address the threat without panicking the people.

Too often the church has protectively withdrawn into its own language, insisting that faith can be approached only by using the certain words and practices of the interior language, not wanting to hear the threats and the opportunities that come from outside the walls. And yet our particular exodus in the present wilderness is driven by the need for the mainline church to connect with the fast-changing culture and people that surround it right outside the heavy walls of tradition, learned behavior, and assumed cultural dominance that have held the church captive. The choice for the church is not which of the languages (the language of the church or the multiple languages of other disciplines of the culture) is correct. This is not a moment to examine the postures of Christ for or against culture. For the church to stand against North American culture using only an interior language that is understood only by itself is to be dismissed as irrelevant by a people who search for meaning and a connection with God wherever they can be found. Conversely, to stand only with the culture is to be captured by values and practices not necessarily of the faith. Indeed the challenge now is not either/or but both/and.

"People of faith must be bilingual," says Walter Brueggemann. "They must have a public language for negotiating at the wall. And they must have a more communal language for processing behind the gate, in the community, out of sight and range of imperial negotiators."[7] Being bilingual is more than learning another person's words for your own experiences. Being truly bilingual means being able to think and experience in multiple and different ways. Being bilingual forces us not only to understand the new but also to revisit and reclaim the native language that we once saw as sufficient. The deep challenge for the mainline church is not only now to learn a new cultural language such as marketing, technology, or postmodernism (or other new languages from outside the wall). The challenge is also to revisit, revalue, and learn once again to use the faith language from inside the wall.

In a presentation to a small group of leaders from across the nation, hosted by the Texas Methodist Foundation, John Wimmer, Program Director, Religion, at the Lilly Endowment Inc., pushed the issue that we miss a part of the task when we think only about leading change. Leading change is only half the task, he noted. The real challenge is to lead both continuity and change.[8] As a consultant to congregations and denominations who has spent several decades consulting, teaching, and writing about change and the challenges of leadership, I can only say that John is much more accurate than I may have been. There is a language and practice of tradition and heritage from our past that carries the riches of the faith. Multiple current languages of change carry tools and opportunities to shape mission and ministry. And there is a need for bilingualism at the wall that provides a platform for negotiation by being able to use interior and exterior multiple languages. As leaders, we are responsible for both continuity and change, for mastery of internal and external languages that allow for negotiating at the wall where church and the new people of a changing culture come together to meet.

The Interior Language

Turning first to the interior language, the communal language of the church, we do well to recognize the appropriately renewed attention being given to preparing leaders for excellence in ministry. Such excellence depends on a deep, solid theological grounding using the texts, the traditions, and the discipling experiences from within the walls of the church. In their book on resurrecting excellence within the church, Jones and Armstrong ask, "How do we calculate the effect of reconciling forgiveness, the value of deepened prayer life, the impact of passing on the faith to a child, the quiet presence of sitting with a dying parishioner or hammering nails to help provide housing for a homeless family?"[9] In order to pursue these, which are some of the most important gifts of faith, leaders from inside the church need to honor and value the words, ideas, and experiences that are already held in the tradition and practice of the church.

I love Richard Lischer's memoir of his first sojourn as pastor of a country church because it is such a wonderful example of a pastor being so thoroughly grounded in the interior language of the church that it casts new meaning on people's common experience. For example, because of his intimate familiarity with the church's theology, he recasts gossip that is so often regarded as the bane of the church.[10] His training and life in the teachings of the church taught him that "the word *gossip* originally implied a spiritual relationship. A gossip was a sponsor at a baptism, one who spoke on behalf of the child as it grew in years. . . . Gossiping was speech within the community of the baptized."[11] Where standards of secular community behavior and concerns for public civility would otherwise denounce and hope to end all gossip, Lischer was able to see a deeper sense of community at work in people's conversations about one another. He came to realize that his ministry among the people would suffer, indeed would be almost impossible, without the gossip within the church. Deeply grounded in the communal language of the faith "inside the wall," Lischer helped the people reshape idle gossip into the care of community as people sought forgiveness, into a deepened prayer life, into the importance of offering quiet presence with others in need, and into the helping hand that would bring a difference to a life, which could not be found in the exterior languages of politeness, consumerism, individualism, or ambition. Using the interior language of the church inside the wall, Lischer was able to understand and help his people use conversation about one another to build community and extend care. The church needs leaders to be so imbued with the interior language of the church that they can help others find a relationship with God and find community with one another that offers insights, options, and experiences that can't be found outside the walls.

The Exterior Language

Other languages outside the wall are multiple and confusing and can often be experienced as evaluating the church as behaving with, as Rabshakeh described it, "make-believe and pious fantasy." They are the languages of a culture that has become highly technical and technological. They are languages that are less communal, more individual, and more preferential, such as the languages of the advertising and marketing industries that have underscored our understanding of ourselves as individuals. They are languages of a changing economy that is global in character while locally unsympathetic, pulling people, regions, and nations between the poles of scarcity and overabundance. They are the languages of the hard sciences that we now understand as failed if seen as the certain path for continued progressivism but that nonetheless remain dominant as a way of understanding the material world.

What is needed is an ability of the church to be grounded through its own internal language but to have the facility to use public languages by which we can negotiate at the wall—Brueggemann's bilingualism. All inside the church is not good and sufficient. All outside the church is not bad and unserving. What is needed is a practiced bilingualism that allows a blending at the wall. To manage our particular exodus and to find our way in the wilderness are to negotiate this interior/exterior tension facing the church.

This book seeks to help this bilingual negotiation at the wall. As noted earlier, this book addresses the question, What have we learned (what have we taught ourselves) so far on our exodus that will aid our future? The languages upon which this book heavily depends to address this question and to negotiate at the wall are the languages of the human social sciences, particularly the languages of organizational development, organizational psychology, and general systems theory.

The insights and directions that come from organizational development and organizational psychology help us become more faithful, focused, and effective. These languages can help us identify what is central to the future effectiveness of our congregations and denominations. Pursuing effectiveness of our congregational and denominational institutions is not a bureaucratic exercise—although it must be admitted that organizational leadership in the church can become bureaucratic if practiced without regard for the interior language of God's purpose. At its best, effective organizational leadership is spiritual leadership. From the very beginning, when Jesus called the disciples, Christianity has been experienced in organized forms of community. If groups, organizations, congregations, and denominations are at the base of how we encounter God, then it matters how we use those forms of groups, organizations, congregations, and denominations. It matters a great deal. Organizations are primary tools of spiritual leadership, and one would hope that we have emerged beyond an earlier dismissiveness aimed at "church administration" or the "running of a church" that was once assumed to be so simple as not to require training, reflection, and discipline. There is much to learn about leadership from the theories, constructs, and practiced behaviors of organizational sciences, which can inform the decisions and choices that congregational and denominational leaders make in the wilderness.

The insights that come from general systems theory and group theory can even more powerfully help us by offering the freedom that comes from recognizing the greater portion of what we currently experience in the church as normative and natural. Yes, of course, there are individuals in our congregations and denominations who are troubled or limited and who create havoc. Yes, of course, we can be described at some level as a hard-hearted people resistant to the evidence of God in the change about us. But it does not serve us well to always assume that what we see in the congregation or in our denominations is improper, problematic, or pathological. Having served as consultant to several thousand congregations, many thousand leaders, and a broad spectrum of denominations, denominational offices, and denominational leaders, I continue to assert that most of what I experience in the church is normal human behavior. We may not always be pleased with what we find, and we may wish that our best efforts were better, but what we encounter is routinely common and natural. One dilemma of negotiating change is that we commonly personalize the discomfort, assuming that we are alone when having difficulty in dealing with difficult people and coming up short with no clear answers. A general systems perspective allows us to see that we do not need to personalize much of our experience and that what we encounter is most often commonly shared. One of my favorite notions from humorist Garrison Keillor's monologues on the NPR *Prairie Home Companion* radio program is that winter is not a private experience. Keillor's recurring observation is that in Minnesota everyone is cold in winter and it is of no help for anyone to complain about the cold. It is a normal, natural, and widely shared experience, and his comedic conclusion is that, therefore, people should "get over it" and just keep going. Realistically it may not be particularly helpful in times of deep change to tell people to just get over it. But it is important for people to understand that they are sharing in a common experience, and concluding that something is wrong, or even more debilitating to conclude that something is "wrong with us," may be an unnecessary and unhelpful personalized response.

In particular, too much effort and energy during our exodus have been given to control or fix normal and natural responses of healthy systems. I will argue that our anxiety in the wilderness has caused us to be overcontrolling, overworried, and overactive. I have joked with many people, saying that I have worked with a great number of congregations that are dying of terminal seriousness. The leaders are so worried about survival that they try to control everyone else and they place a stranglehold on the very thing that they are trying to keep alive. A stranglehold allows no space for breathing. Overcontrolling assumes that we can do this alone, that only we can do what needs to be done and do it right. Overcontrolling allows no room for the hand of God or the movement of the Spirit. Spiritual communities that can't breathe (and therefore can't relax and laugh) cannot feel the movement of the Spirit and the excitement of purposefulness, and so they die.

Consider my first Sunday as the new pastor in my first appointment in Philadelphia. At the appropriate time in worship I took the offering plates from the altar, turned, and walked *down* the chancel steps to deliver the plates to the ushers as I had done for two years in my student parish in New England. Too late I noticed the ushers were *walking past me* and going *up* the chancel steps where they were accustomed to receiving the plates. There we stood back-to-back on two separate levels of steps. If you can't laugh at such wonderful moments that come when learning one another in community, what hope is there? But then consider the large church where I worked years later as a consultant to address a deep conflict between the senior pastor and the church leaders. The senior pastor was the new leader recently called to follow a beloved retiring pastor who had served this church for twenty-nine years. The retired pastor was most famously known throughout the city and beyond as an exceptional preacher, indeed as a pulpiteer. A master in the pulpit, this man also practiced his own form of humility. Although he processed down the center aisle of the sanctuary following the choir at the beginning of worship, he did not follow the choir back out the center aisle at the end of worship. Instead he recessed down a side aisle by himself so as not to call attention to himself and his preaching as the center of worship. Participants at the church knew this practice well because the pastor had called public attention to it numerous times. No one told his successor, who was a good but much more moderate preacher, about this practice of his predecessor. On his first Sunday there, the successor followed the choir at the end of the service and walked right down the center aisle where, in a congregation without humor, he was pronounced arrogant and unacceptable. The troubles two years later that would finally force his termination could be traced, in part, to the end of his first hour of public ministry there and the inability of the people to be less than terminally serious.

Much in our congregations and denominations is difficult and can be disturbing to leaders, but most of this behavior that we find difficult is also normal and natural behavior easily found in other settings. If we seek to control and fix all that we don't like or that doesn't meet our preference, our congregations and our denominations become increasingly rigid and we have no life. We need a language from beyond our community that will help us identify and understand natural systems behaviors and thus negotiate our expectations and purpose at the wall. Being able to see the normal and natural within our communities as living systems in the midst of change allows anxiety to transform into energy and worry to turn into hope.

Reclaimed Purpose and Identity

I have already claimed that we have made great progress in our particular exodus, having moved both far and faithfully from our starting place in the 1960s when many mainline denominations first had evidence of their changed reality by the shrinking numbers of members. As I will describe in the next chapter, the exodus has required us to follow distinct paths of learning where we have accomplished much as we explored the three paths of church growth, congregational transformation, and clergy develop-ment. The fourth path, which will be explored in depth in chapter 3, engages us in the need to reclaim our purpose and our identity, difficult work indeed for a people who had for so long easily and unthinkingly assumed their purpose and identity.

Now, having been ordained for more than thirty-five years, having served congre-gations as pastor for more than sixteen years, and having served as part-time and full-time consultant to congregations and denominations for more than twenty-five of those years, I have observed that the longer we are involved in an exodus, the harder the work becomes, the more difficult the questions—and the richer the results, the deeper the hope. Having done so much of the easier and necessary technical work in those early years, our leaders are now addressing the much more adaptive and much more difficult questions of the purpose and identity of our denominations and congre-gations. Consider my own United Methodist denomination.

In November of 2007 the United Methodist denomination hosted a historic gath-ering to which the bishops, district superintendents, and key conference executive staff were invited. Meeting at Lake Junaluska in North Carolina, this gathering of 850 denominational leaders from around the globe had not happened previously for more than forty years. The purpose was to recall and to rehearse the story that now lives at the center of the denomination. It was a story meant to be strong enough to hold this group of people together in all of their substantial diversity—global, theological, polit-ical, regional, and generational. It was also a story strong enough to point forward to a new life in a changed culture. It was an initiative of purpose and identity. Consider how difficult the work is:

- Purpose: "The mission of The United Methodist Church is to make disciples of Jesus Christ for the transformation of the world." This newly reframed mission statement of the denomination is the culmination of work over a number of years and debates that have taken place over several general conferences. It has been carefully thought out, energetically argued, and prayerfully shaped. However, familiarity with this mission statement will quickly give it a resonance that will allow it to be reduced to a denominational tag line and, at the least, be a tool to explain the denomination to a consumer-conscious people. Over time such familiarity hides the original difficulty of coming to terms with the radical shift of understanding ourselves anew. Making disciples who will transform the world as the purpose of the church is a significant statement. Making disciples is different from making members. When first entering ordained ministry, I was not trained or asked to make disciples. I was trained to make members. Like that of our mainline brother and sister denominations, our track record over past decades of making members has not been good, yet we know more about making members than we do about making disciples. We know more about changing people's affiliations than changing their lives. The United Methodist Church now willingly claims that its purpose is to do the much harder work of changing people's lives and in changing people's lives to also transform the world. The purpose goes beyond membership. The purpose goes beyond helping people find richer and more meaningful personal lives. It is a transformation of people who, being changed, will transform their relationships, their families, their work, their world.

  This mission statement is much more than a change in language. The shift from members to disciples is a paradigmatic shift—a deeply rooted change that requires rethinking and re-creation of all things. When a paradigm shifts, all goes back to zero. Assumptions cannot be trusted, all must be learned anew, and new ideas need to be translated into new behaviors.[12] The mainline church is now engaged in such a paradigm shift, a reconstruction from new (or perhaps newly reclaimed but ancient) fundamentals. Such paradigmatic change is exceptionally difficult because all things need to be questioned, all practices evaluated, all norms challenged.

- Identity: Distinct among Christians, United Methodists follow John Wesley's three general rules: "Do no harm. Do all the good you can. Stay in love with God." In preparation for the historic 2007 gathering at Lake Junaluska, a team of theologians, historians, and church leaders prepared the paper "The United Methodist Way," which was intended to help frame the conversation among the participants.[13] The paper centered on three general rules from John Wesley as a means to bring to focus what is unique about the identity of The United Methodist Church, the United Methodist "way." Along with other mainline denominations, we within the United Methodist denomination are a theologically, politically, regionally, racially, and ethnically diverse group of people. Where once in an earlier age we had a much clearer shared practice that held us in community, our breadth of differences now often makes the people within our mainline denominations uncomfortable with themselves and one another. We are left wondering what we now hold in common, what holds us together. Without a clear sense of identity it is hard to stay in community with one another in order to address our purpose. Without a clear sense of identity it is difficult to be in the world of competing identities.

Recapturing a lost identity is challenging. In the case of United Methodism the reframing of a denominational identity around three general rules does not say enough, and certainly does not say all that can be said about the denomination's contributions and distinctions. However, in the hard work of reestablishing organizational identity, clarity serves where comprehensiveness obscures. While the academic discipline of history serves us well in capturing and charting our past as a way of keeping us connected to our origins, over time that same academic discipline of history, along with the plethora of differences that live in a mature global organization, tends to diffuse a denominational identity by recalling and recapturing too much information. Tracking too much detail and cataloguing too many regional and subgroup differences can eventually hide what is at the center. One task at the heart of the current challenge of our mainline North American denominations is to remember what is essential and to remember what shared identity and purpose hold the denominational group together for the present and particularly for the future. Newly shaped groups, movements, and denominations do not have the challenge of an unfocused identity. Clear identity and purpose give birth to new groups, movements, and denominations. The need to recapture and reclaim a central and functional identity is the unique challenge of a long-established denomination that is rich in history and practice.

We will explore the challenges of reestablishing purpose and identity more deeply later in the book. For the moment it is sufficient to note that over time in a difficult environment where it has been increasingly hard to operate from strength, it is natural that our mainline denominational identity and stories have become both safe and weak. Our stories, our identities, become safe and weak because we have learned to tell only the more comfortable, less challenging parts of the stories so that we are not demoralized. Consider what happens naturally in an established congregation over time. For example, a congregation tells its story about how warm and welcoming it is to the people of the congregation and how members reach out to one another in times of need. Indeed, the story is quite often true. But this is also a safe and weak story because of what is left unsaid. Missing in this story may be the congregation's fear of the changed community that now surrounds its building and how it tends not to welcome and naturally include the neighborhood people who might join in a worship service. Because it tells only the safe and weak parts of its story in this all-too-common scenario, the congregation robs itself of a new future that can come from the strength of remembering who it really is as a community of faith and what can happen in the neighborhood if members of the congregation come to terms with their discomforts and fears. Like local congregations, our mainline denominations have been held captive by the safe and weak stories they have been willing to tell themselves while there is much more that could be said.

Within long-established groups, organizations, or institutions identity may become assumed and rigid. Essentially long-established denominations risk carrying forward an older identity that once served but is no longer accurate or effective. Recalling, reclaiming, and risking to live into a newer, fresher identity as a people of God are essential tasks of our particular wilderness experience.

Living into the Wilderness

In all of this we have great reason for hope. Not only are we who are of Christian heritage a people who have been in this kind of change before but at another organizational and institutional level, we also are not the only ones in this wilderness. In his work on organizational change, Robert Quinn writes about a level of change that he identifies as "deep change," and he states that many organizations are now at a point where there is only one choice left—either deep change or slow death.[14] Quinn was not writing for the church, although this point of deep choice is clearly felt by the mainline church. He was commenting on the level of change that all organizations, corporations, and businesses need to address in order to learn how to stay alive and thrive in the newly shaping world about us. Thomas Friedman described this newly shaping world as "flat"—a global world in which geography and time no longer separate nations, people, or opportunities and in which an increasingly large portion of the global population has a chance to reach a level playing field through technology.[15] As an example of how such global shifts create a need for established institutions to negotiate deep change, consider the plight of the U.S. Midwest where the economic mainstays of farming and automobile manufacturing have been threatened by globalization. A central point of the study done by Richard Longworth is that the Midwest is constrained in its response because of old and established boundaries of states, counties, cities, and municipalities.[16] Where these governmental boundaries once served the area well by delineating responsibilities in established areas and by keeping local services close to the people being served, such governmental segmentation no longer serves a part of the country that needs to learn how to mount a *regional* response to globalization that has affected a whole region, not discrete governmental regions. It is a very fundamental question of identity: who are we and how do we best respond? States, counties, cities, and municipalities notoriously find it difficult to cooperate and align their efforts because of competing interests. Yet the case can be made that unless deep change is engaged and governmental bodies and agencies learn how to reshape their identity and purpose in order to behave regionally, the Midwest will remain ineffective in its response to globalization. Such examples of the need to learn the wilderness and discover new ways of living are widespread across corporations, banks, universities, and health-care systems—in fact, everywhere one looks. While the mainline church is clearly in the mix, the need for change among organizations is broad and demanding. We are not alone.

The level of change that all organizations face in this moment has spawned an array of images that seek to capture the challenge involved. They are creative ways of catching both the radical nature of the change and the spirit necessary to meet it. Consider some favorites: the change we negotiate today is like . . .

- building a bike while riding it,
- changing a tire on the bus while it's moving,
- laying track in front of a moving locomotive.

One of my favorite images seems to particularly fit the wishfulness of the church. This image of change suggests that negotiating the wilderness is like building a new prison using the bricks from the old prison, without losing the prisoners. This image seems to fit the church because, despite the difficulty involved and despite what is required of all involved, the church still wishes that everyone will eagerly take the trip and still be involved, invested, and engaged when the dust settles. We want to cross whole wildernesses and address all the necessary changes without losing anyone. But such an ideal outcome can't happen. You can't go through a wilderness exodus and not lose some people. You can't wait each day for everyone to be ready and eager to move. To try to go through deep change yet to also remain unchanged so that everyone currently involved in the congregation or denomination remains connected and satisfied is an unreasonable goal. To go through change requires that we ourselves be changed— that is, after all, what a wilderness is for. Self-change is one of the greatest gifts of an exodus.

It is all right that not everyone makes the trip on this particular exodus. However, leaders need to be clear about why they are moving on without others and what calls them to value purpose over relationship as change takes us into new directions and practices. Such clarity of leadership is part of what we will explore here, because this, too, is some of what we have already learned on our journey. We are already in the process of being reshaped by our exodus. We are already experiencing change and the cost that comes with it. We are already learning much from this experience of the past four decades that will sustain and direct our future faithfulness.

So, where is this exodus taking us? Certainly the Israelites on that original Exodus did not get up each morning ready for the day's hike without speculating and arguing about what the promised land they were headed for would look like when they got there. Similarly the people in our particular exodus would like to know where we will end up and what it all will be like. With what we have learned so far, we can project and begin to outline what our mainline denominations might look like in the future— as long as we are willing to be wrong. Telling the future is a frightful task if taken too seriously. If, however, the pictures drawn of the future are held loosely, based on what is now seen, and kept open to what will yet be learned, we can now reasonably guess at some changes that will last, and they are the subject of the last chapter. But keep in mind that the wandering is not over. If much has been learned, there is still more to teach ourselves and more godly surprises to discover. God's promises do not come with well-marked maps, known paths, and guaranteed destinations. Neither do God's promises come cheap. Nonetheless, we are no longer in captivity. We have already traveled far, and we have more evidence of the new life that awaits us.

CHAPTER 2
A MAP OF MULTIPLE DIRECTIONS
In Search of a Costly Promised Land—Part 1

The first time that The United Methodist Church registered a net loss of members was 1965. It was difficult in that first year or so to understand that The United Methodist Church and other mainline denominations in North America were taking the first steps into their own wilderness, their own particular exodus. At first the membership loss must have appeared as an aberration, an anomaly in a denomination that had for so long experienced prolonged growth in numbers, in resources, and in influence. As a new seminary graduate appointed to my first church in Philadelphia in 1972, I remember how the generation of pastors who preceded me continuously told their stories of working ceaselessly to keep up with growth. They told of times when they knocked on a door to greet new arrivals to the neighborhood only to discover another Methodist minister already inside talking to the family. Just as in times of fish spawning or salmon working upstream, there seemed to be plenty for all to catch their fill. Membership swelled. Budgets grew. Buildings were built.

Those earliest years of national membership loss no doubt prompted arguments that characterized the more recent early speculations about global warming—are the numbers part of a natural self-correcting cycle or the beginning of a long-term shift that will change our daily reality and threaten our future? Forty some years later it is clear that the membership trends of mainline and established denominations were being deeply set in those first years. No aberration, the change has been long term and of great concern. Some journeys through the wilderness take longer than others.

As difficult as the subsequent years have been for our denominations and congregations, I would argue that the sky is not falling, all is not lost, and our leaders have not failed us. I prefer to tell the story as a trip through our particular wilderness that is the product of our changed culture. With a natural mix of courage and fear, of insight and ignorance, of clarity and bewilderment, and a wish for answers in a time when we should be asking questions, we have been wandering in a new cultural wilderness that challenges our churches. Day after day, year after year, leaders within mainline denominations have actively and faithfully been seeking our way. Far from being passive or ineffective, despite all of our grumbling against our congregations and our leaders, we have been on a long, demanding, and rich learning curve. We have come far over the past forty years, and the learning, as well as the wilderness journey, is not over.

I can most easily track what we have been learning by reflecting on my experience, first as a local church pastor in urban settings, and then as a full-time consultant with Protestant, Catholic, and Jewish congregations and denominations. My first appointment, as noted earlier, was to a small congregation in the northwest section of Philadelphia in 1972. Although the generation of pastors who preceded me still told stories of running to catch up with the growth that was exploding around the city, I was soon aware that such growth was not naturally happening in the city and that there was anxiety among younger clergy and in church literature focused on the developing trend of denominational membership loss. From the earliest days as a young parish pastor, I was aware of denominational efforts to both understand and respond to the changing reality surrounding our churches. In those earliest days I lived through any number of initiatives developed by my denomination that hoped to change me and my congregation in ways that would "make more members." Looking ahead in that earlier time did not offer much perspective, and it seemed reasonable for denominations to urge their leaders to work harder for wanted results.

Looking back over almost forty years as an ordained minister, however, I now have an appreciation for how our journey through our wilderness has taken us on four different but fundamental paths of initiatives and experiments. They have been paths following multiple directions, all on the same journey, hoping to recapture a strength that seemed missing. As one would expect in the wilderness, the paths have not been neatly organized, one tidily following the other. The paths have overlapped and intersected, some starting before others, but all contributing either helpful insights or insights that come from failed initiatives. Like the Israelites who, according to the map at the end of our Bibles, did a lot of wandering and who at times had to correct and even reverse their direction, we have been wandering in a wilderness of rich but complex experiences that are deeply changing us. I often point to the map at the back of the Bible as one of the best reminders that there are few sure and dependable paths into a new future. Like the Israelites, we too have been building our map of multiple directions. We have followed learning paths that, at first, seemed a promising way out of the wilderness, only to discover that we needed to pitch our tents or retrace our steps. There are few straight steps in the wilderness, which is why it is called a wandering. We have wandered in multiple directions—never lost but never quite getting to the promised land. We were always learning more about being faithful and effective, however. We were learning more about trusting God. Each path contributed to progress and gave new hope.

I want to be clear that what follows is a recounting of the wilderness paths and the subsequent learning curve as told through the lens of my experience. It is a recounting of what I was asked to learn as a parish pastor and what initiatives and conversations I was invited to join, first as a participant and then as a leader and teacher. There is certainly more to our particular exodus that I know or can recall, and there are ways that others might tell this story through their own experiences. The telling of the story here is simply meant to capture the spirit of the time spent in our particular wilderness. Our present time of leadership within the mainline church does not evidence failure of either nerve or effort. Instead, ours is a story of denominational and congregational leaders continuously walking with and toward God through a confusing landscape.

Path 1: Church Growth

The initial path of learning focused on church growth. This first set of initiatives set about to answer questions of how churches grow or, conversely, what keeps churches from growing. Anchored first in the work of Donald McGavran, founder of the Church Growth Institute at Fuller Seminary, the church growth movement gave much attention to understanding how congregations "worked" in a changing cultural landscape. McGavran's insight was that evangelism and the exercise of the Great Commission could be measured by their results. He relentlessly pursued whatever worked to achieve clear missional ends. The focus on ends and the openness to explore what helped or hindered reaching results spawned a church growth movement that brought new focus to how congregations worked. As early as 1973, an ecumenical initiative of the church growth movement, known as "Key 73," tried to help congregations attend to the initial learnings. Intended as a year-long evangelical campaign that began as a meeting between Billy Graham and Carl Henry, it moved forward as an interdenominational and interfaith effort. Although the campaign suffered financially, it accomplished the distribution of fifty million Bibles and scriptural excerpts, promoted a new kind of interdenominational cooperation, and introduced a new generation of leaders to church growth ideas and tools. This early path through church growth had a number of layers:

- Passive barriers: Leaders learned that several conditions or practices may live beneath the radar of the local church and block people's connection to a congregation. We learned that there is a natural limit to space; when a sanctuary is 80 percent physically full, it appears 100 percent psychologically full to a visitor who would not comfortably sit too close to an unknown person. Pastors could be found in their sanctuaries measuring their pews, dividing by the appropriate number of inches of acceptable personal seating space, and getting much clearer about how many people their sanctuaries could actually seat. Leaders also went out to their parking lots and counted parking spaces to determine how large an attendance their parking lot could support at 2.4 persons per car. Leaders learned that visitors actually needed to be able to find the nursery in order to use it. Congregations with a parking lot behind the church, from which all members entered the building through a back door, learned to unlock the front door to accommodate visitors who didn't know "the rules."
- Theological correctness: Early in this learning cycle there was a rich and competitive debate about which form of Christian theology was most "correct" and "faithful." The lines were drawn between doctrinal distinctions described variously as liberal or conservative, as mission oriented or social gospel oriented, as personal (focused on the individual) or social (with implications for the community or world in which the person lived). Much was said about a wide and

growing gap between the leaders of mainline denominations and the people in the pews. The gap reflected the assertion that the agenda of the regional or national church was not aligned with the agenda and needs of the people in the local church. During this stage when the effectiveness and faithfulness of the mainline church were challenged, strong voices advocated a conservative theology with a focus on a person's individual relationship with Christ and with particular attention on a select number of moral issues.

- Denominational identity: There was also an extended conversation about whether denominational identity was an asset or a liability for a congregation in this new wilderness. Since mainline congregations were losing members while evangelical congregations and megachurches (which initially were mostly evangelical or independent) were gaining members, it was reasonable to question whether a mainline denominational identity was a barrier to ministry. Some mainline congregations removed or changed public signage that connected them to a denomination. Church letterheads and newsletters appeared either without denominational names or with denominational connections printed in greatly reduced font size. Pursuit of this experiment in the new wilderness stemmed from the ongoing quest for a single cause that might lead to a quick solution. In many congregations it became clear that while the clergy and a relatively small percentage of the congregation might be sensitive to or uncomfortable with their denominational connection, visitors and new participants had neither sufficient background nor awareness of denominations to be either encouraged or discouraged by denominational affiliation. The greater lesson was that the search for a singular cause hides the complex interplay of a matrix of variables that might also have an impact on the congregation—such as the physical location of the congregation, the demographic growth and profile of the area served by the congregation, the clarity of the mission of the congregation, or the giftedness of the leaders to be externally and future focused in their mission. In the wilderness wanderings this question of denominational identity proved less helpful, and leaders who were on this path had to "pitch tent" and wait for new directions to explore.

- Congregational expectations (high and low thresholds of membership): Explorations in church growth included an anecdotal exploration of congregational membership expectations as a leverage point of ministry in the new wilderness. Strong public voices suggested that high-demand congregations were more suited to ministry in the new culture. In essence, high-demand congregations that required more, rather than less, of their members were seen as having an advantage.

All organizations that are voluntary associations, such as congregations, have low thresholds of belonging. They are easy in and easier out. People can decide to show up or not show up as a purely personal decision. Compared to other organizational types, such as employment-based organizations where the process both in and out is formal and highly structured, congregations are rightly seen as having low thresholds and porous boundaries. The new cultural landscape was proving that new people were not coming to congregations simply looking for a place to belong, as people did generations earlier. The new reality was that most people already belonged to too many organizations and groups, and had too many commitments. Once again, viewed as a single cause that could lead to simple problem solving, this path was disappointing.

In this case we may have turned our attention away too quickly and missed rich insights, however. It may seem counterintuitive, but congregations that place higher demands on formal membership also have a higher tolerance for people who want to participate without being members. Presumably if it takes more to claim the formal relationship of "membership," the congregation has to develop more skills to work with participants who choose to be involved in the congregation but are not (or not yet) members. Today learning to include people in the congregation who participate without joining is a new and necessary skill to address within our changed mission field.

High-demand congregations allow a wider range of alternatives to people who want to engage Christian community—some fully at the center of the congregation through membership and leadership, others farther toward the edges of the congregation but engaged nonetheless. In the 2003 statistical report of United Methodist churches, nineteen of the two hundred largest churches posted an average attendance at worship that was larger than their official membership. Surely, as one goes down the list of congregations according to size, more examples of congregations with attendance in excess of membership can be found. It is not clear that we understand how these congregations manage their multiple, rather than singular, membership/participant relationships with people in their congregations. Yet there is generational evidence that these congregations may hold clues to help us live in our current wilderness.

- Marketing and generational niche ministries: One of the more uncomfortable steps on this learning path was the exploration of marketing as applied to congregations. The ideas and tools of the marketing industry were helpful to congregations in understanding the new language of our changed culture and the way to live in the new culture. No longer could congregations simply say (passively), "You all come now," and expect a response from their communities. To be heard in this new world, congregations now needed to be much clearer about to whom they were talking and much clearer about what they were offering to these people. The exploration of marketing and generational niches (a primary segmentation of the marketing industry) was uncomfortable because of the deeply appropriate theological questions that were stirred up. Do we invite people to the demands of the gospel or are we being asked to mold the gospel to fit the preferences of the people? Is Christian community inclusive without boundaries or do we follow marketing principles of homogeneity in which community is narrowly defined so the gift of commonness in Christ is lost? As uncomfortable as this stage of our learning proved to be, it nonetheless provided rich and valuable insights to congregations and leaders who were trying to learn the new language of the culture. Just as earlier missionaries to foreign lands learned, an immersion in the culture was necessary to learn the language, traditions, and habits of the people before the gospel could be announced. But now the foreign land came to us and

21

surrounded our long-held assumptions and practices right where we lived. The need to learn the new language, traditions, and habits of the culture was just as important whether we go to the foreign land or it comes to us.

- Large churches and megachurches: One of the most valuable learnings along the way was that large congregations are most comfortable in this new culture. We North Americans now seem to like our organizations and institutions to be either very large or very small. We continue to simultaneously build large regional public school systems and small charter schools; large multinational full-service banks along with small neighborhood personal service banks; large national food chains and small boutique ethnic food shops; large regional medical centers and small single-purpose surgery or diagnostic centers. Large congregations offer what these other large institutions offer—choice, activities, and services specifically tailored to a wide range of needs, personal control, anonymity, and diversity. In the large congregation individuals can appreciate the full range of options and the wide diversity of the people but still choose what is most meaningful to them and then move on. Control of the level of engagement is left to the individual. All of these factors are reversed in smaller congregations.

- Large congregations have come to dominate our landscape not by their number but by their influence. According to Mark Chaves, director of the National Congregations Study, the average congregation has a worshiping attendance of seventy-five people, while the average person who attends worship now goes to a congregation where the average attendance is four hundred people.[1] More to the point, of the estimated 350,000 congregations in the United States, a very large number of small congregations do ministry with a small percentage of the people who go to congregations, while there are a very small number of very large congregations with a large percentage of the people. The smallest of our congregations, which together make up 50 percent of the total of all congregations, do ministry with only 11 percent of the people who go to congregations. Conversely, only 10 percent of all congregations that are the largest include 40 percent of all the people. In the 2003 statistical report of The United Methodist Church the largest two hundred churches (by membership) represented only 0.5 percent of all United Methodist churches but held 9.5 percent of the national membership of the denomination.

However, the error made on this segment on the church growth path was the assumption that the practices of the large congregation could and should be transported to small and midsize congregations as a benchmarked ideal that, if practiced in the smaller churches, would produce growth. We have mistakenly leaned toward evaluating a congregation's value by its size and done a disservice to many other congregations and their leaders by asking them to be who they are not and have not been called to be. There is growing evidence that the number of very large churches and megachurches will plateau as the next generational cohorts focus on and prefer smaller and more intimate communities. Again, the hoped for relief of the denominational problem proved disappointing and elusive.

Path 2: Congregational Transformation

As the church growth path, the first of the paths on the map of multiple directions, was developing a set of new insights about congregations, a concurrent conversation developed among those who quickly realized that the question facing many congregations was not just one of growth but of change. Congregations have historically been tradition-based organizations. The liturgical seasons of a congregation's life center on the traditions of worship and practice that follow the rhythm of holidays and holy days. Beyond the holy days, the common days of the congregation are similarly formed with lesser traditions—the norms and standardized practices that develop in all long-established groups and organizations. All ongoing groups and organizations develop a set of practices and behaviors that become deep-seated norms so that in any given congregation there is a particular way to hold a meeting; a particular agenda that is allowed; a particular way to care for the building, with permissions about who can and cannot use the building; a particular way in which leaders are elected, decisions are made, and budgets are developed. The norms and traditions of the congregation develop, in part, for reasons of efficiency. To have an established practice means that leaders do not have to stop and continuously ask themselves how to celebrate Christmas or how to elect and train leaders. The practices are already established, so leaders and members are free to move ahead without lengthy discussions of how to do things each time. Over time, however, the norms that develop for reasons of efficiency and effectiveness become deeply embedded and resistant to change.

A basic principle in systems theory is that vital, vibrant organisms must learn how to be *steady in purpose* but *flexible in strategy*.[2] For example, one of the primary purposes of any bird species includes being able to gather food for survival. To exist and be vibrant, birds of that species need to be constant in pursuit of that purpose. Yet the birds must be flexible in their strategy so that if their woodland is developed into a tract of new homes by a developer, they must learn to change strategies for gathering food by either relocating or accommodating the changed environment. The dilemma is that long-established congregations, like all long-established systems, develop norms that make them so *steady in strategy* that they *lose focus on purpose*.

Fairly early in the learning cycle that accompanied being displaced into a new cultural wilderness, it was clear that growth depended on change and that change was not a strength of established congregations. The question facing leaders on this second of the multiple paths of learning changed people's attention from understanding *what* to change in the congregation to *how* to change the congregation. This reframed question posed a whole new body of work for leaders. The question of how to change had a very organizational side to it, so many of the issues and insights in this arena of the work followed the lead of organizational literature and the work of the social sciences as applied to organizations.

- Mission and vision statements: One of the earliest steps of organizational strategy was to be sure that every church had a mission statement and a vision statement. A good deal of literature and teaching was directed at the congregation to help leaders understand a mission statement (classically defined as a statement of identity and purpose: who are we and what are we called to do?) and a vision statement (defined as a description, a "picture," of what it will look like if we are faithful in our mission).

In this earliest exploration of purpose the work was slow going. The conversations about mission and vision sought to push congregations to be clear about what they did and what they were trying to accomplish. However, mainline Protestant congregations were coming from a long history of being the established Christian tradition that lived at the heart of the culture and had not had to ask the question of purpose for a very long time. Good questions of identity and purpose are hard to answer because in established congregations the answer already seems obvious. For example, one of the critical leadership questions that leads to understanding purpose in the congregation is, Who are we? (the question of understanding our identity, which is closely linked to purpose). The question needs to be constantly addressed because in the answer is embedded an awareness of the gifts and strengths that the congregation holds and the passion for ministry that drives it. This question proves difficult to answer in many congregations, though, because leaders already think that they know who their congregation is.

In the earliest efforts of the work on mission and vision the task was to try to help the congregation move from axiomatic to unique understandings of its mission. Congregations often had or created generic mission statements—some variation of this: "The mission of ___(name)___ Church is to provide worship, Christian education, care for our members, and service to our world." In the "Order for Confirmation and Reception into the Church" found in the 1964 edition of *The Methodist Hymnal* there is a generic purpose statement for the church:

> The Church is of God, and will be preserved to the end of time, for the conduct of worship and the due administration of his Word and Sacraments, the maintenance of Christian fellowship and discipline, the edification of believers, and the conversion of the world. All of every age and station, stand in the need of the means of grace which it alone supplies.[3]

This statement in the ritual of the church almost seemed to be the template of many mission and vision statements of congregations in that earlier time. The description of purpose, of course, was true. As mission statements, these early attempts were fully axiomatic and offered no direction of what the *particular* congregation was called to do beyond providing the basic and assumed programs and practices of all congregations.

- Congregational studies: During this time, there was a burst in the effort to observe and understand congregations as a separate and discrete target of study. While much was known about American Christian faith and denominations, the lenses most often used up to this point were of history, theology, polity, and ethnicity. Until the 1970s the congregation itself had not been seriously viewed as an object of study so relatively little was known about the normative behavior of congregations as organizational or social structures. Consequently, little was known about how to help them change. This new avenue of inquiry did not have a location in the established disciplines of the seminary, so much of the initial learning happened in early parachurch organizations such as the Alban Institute under the leadership of Loren Mead and through the efforts of independent consultants and others who worked with congregations. For example, attention was given to the size typology of congregations, recognizing that the most dominant characteristic that would determine the behavior and strategies of a congregation was its size measured by average attendance at worship.[4] Using applied social sciences, consultants and denominational executives began to develop constructs and tools to help leaders in congregations describe, measure, and understand the organizational dynamics of their congregations. In a similar way the application of personal and interpersonal social sciences in forms such as family systems theory, introduced to congregations through the work of Ed Friedman,[5] provided ideas and tools for leaders to understand personal behavior in congregational organizations. This new path of organizational and behavioral learning in the wilderness helped leaders understand, and at times even measure, what was normative, healthy, unhealthy, or even pathological in the behavior and practices of congregations and their members.

• Descriptions and measures of vital congregations: The exploration of congregations along this particular wilderness path of congregational transformation also precipitated a conversation about (or argument over) how to identify a "vital" congregation. Appropriately people recognized that if we wanted vital congregations, we needed a way to measure vitality. How else would leaders know what they were trying to achieve? This part of the work set numerous consultants and researchers on the path of identifying variables of vitality. Some argued that congregational vitality required small-group ministries, or contemporary worship, or welcome centers near sanctuaries, or emphasis on evangelism, or . . . . The potential list of priorities, practices, programs, services, or choices identified as necessary to vitality became extensive and well beyond the capacity of most congregations to address. Books were written by consultants, self-report congregational inventories were developed so that church leaders could check off whether their congregation had this program or that priority, and arguments ensued over whether a particular constellation of variables of vitality was more effective than others.

During this time, the Alban Institute was asked to participate in a study of church growth and vitality, sponsored by the then Aid Association for Lutherans, involving the Evangelical Lutheran Church in America, the Lutheran Church-Missouri Synod, and the Wisconsin Evangelical Lutheran Synod. The research-based study focused on the dual questions of vitality and growth: how do leaders make vital congregations, and how do congregations grow? Two helpful insights were produced in this work. The first was that there was no consensus on the variables of vitality. As a part of the study, Alban senior staff member Speed Leas searched more than fifty resources winnowed down from a list of more than one hundred books, articles, and unpublished studies addressing church growth or

vitality. While there was obviously considerable overlap in the variables identified by the many authors, there was no consensus. In fact, the variables identified
in the literature could not be conclusively correlated with growth, but in each
case the variables identified with the writer's vision or model of what a vital congregation looks like. If the writer assumed that congregations with small-group
ministries were vital, then small-group ministries became a variable of vitality.

The second insight, which became a hard-won foundational conclusion in this
study, was that when seeking growth and vitality, "solutions are found within
individual, motivated congregations taken one at a time."[6] In other words, there
was no single answer and no single group of actions or programs that, if adopted,
would make all, or even many, congregations vital. At first this appeared to be a
rather disappointing conclusion from an extensive and very costly study of congregational vitality among these Lutheran denominations. Wisely, however, the
Lutheran executives, researchers, and consultants stayed with their work to
explore the implications, chief among which was that if congregational vitality
and growth were a congregation-by-congregation proposition, then denominations and helping organizations needed to stop trying to develop codified generic
programs of church growth or continuing education events for leaders that would
present "the answer" to growth. Attention needed to be shifted away from providing standardized answers for congregations and their leaders and toward helping leaders identify the processes and conversations by which their individual
congregations might recover vitality and grow. The critical learning was that if
vitality was an issue that could be addressed only congregation by congregation,
then denominational efforts and consultant help needed to be structured in ways
that looked at each congregation individually.

This part of the path in the wilderness was draining because of the amount of
time, attention, and resources the leaders gave to trying to identify the critical
variables of vitality that all congregations needed to possess. The search for and
the long and inconclusive conversations about variables of vitality produced endless sheets of brainstorming newsprint but no agreement. The false search for the
conclusive list misdirected a considerable amount of time and resources to
explore a path that offered significant insights to living in the wilderness but did
not have the way out of the wilderness.

- Strategic planning: In the shift from developing generic turnkey programs for
congregations to developing new initiatives of individualized approaches to help
congregations, attention turned to strategic planning with new importance.
Influenced by work in the business and corporate community, strategic planning
offered ways to help leaders describe or measure their congregations and assess the
surrounding communities in order to have necessary conversations about the mission of the congregations. At the heart of much of this work was the effort to help
established congregations shift what, in many cases, had become a singular internal focus on the people who were already in the congregation to a shared focus
on those already in the congregation, those not yet in the congregation, and the
missional needs of the larger world, defined as anywhere from the immediate
neighborhood to the global community.

Strategic planning represented a significant shift for congregations that had more commonly approached planning as a half- or full-day exercise of gathering leaders on a Saturday morning or Sunday afternoon to brainstorm a list of ideas of what the members would like to do next. Such early forms of planning often produced a long brainstormed list of activities, all of which could be seen as good things for the congregation to do in the coming year. What was missing was purposeful conversation about the *right* things for the congregation to give itself to.

More formal strategic planning invited leaders into a structured and sustained conversation about mission that included the gathering of information from books, church records, small-group meetings with members, and community demographics to inform richer conversations and the development of larger and more purposeful goals. Since this deeper and more sustained strategic planning prompted larger missional goals, which in turn prompted a perceived need for the congregation to change its practices, it was natural that the work done by a small group of select leaders would meet resistance from the larger body of leaders and members. Some or all of the larger active membership of the congregation who were more distant from the planning conversation saw only the resulting recommendations, which suggested that things were to be different in the future. This predictable response of resistance was a new experience in the wilderness that required even more learning from leaders. But the people were grumbling against Moses as the hurdles of change began to feel higher and higher.

Like other paths of wandering and learning in this new wilderness, the emphasis on strategic planning started mechanistically with programs of planning following corporate models in which steps and stages were offered in formulaic ways. If leaders gathered congregational data (step A), then gathered community information (step B), and then had small-group listening sessions with church members to receive their input (step C) and included Bible study and reflection in the work (step D), then the congregation would end up with a strategic plan with action steps (end product E). This is not to trivialize the earlier efforts in strategic planning by using such a linear description; nonetheless, this initial stage focused more on the technology of planning than on the purpose of planning. We were still learning.

Through continued learning, leaders began to be aware that there were different forms of planning (problem planning, developmental planning, and frame-bending planning),[7] each to be used appropriately to address the planning needed by the individual congregation. It also became clearer that effective planning was not about mastering the tools of planning as much as about applying the tools of planning (however well or poorly) in order to help the congregation have a discerning conversation about its identity, purpose, and context of ministry. Unlike the tools and methods of planning applied in employment-based organizations from which the church was learning, the tools and methods needed to be reshaped to fit the voluntary association structure of congregations, which have very short attention spans for prolonged processes. Models of strategic planning were reshaped so that leaders of congregations could learn to use new tools and new information appropriately in the congregation, moving away from efforts to solve old problems toward conversations that undergirded a discerning search for God's purpose for the congregation. This change from problems to purpose represented a fundamental paradigm shift for leaders and prompted a cycle of new exploration and learning that we are still exploring and trying to understand.

- Connection to neighborhood and region: Another path in the wilderness was greatly helped by a resource that had previously been unavailable to congregations but had come to live at the center of businesses, corporations, institutions, and other nonprofits. Demographic and psychographic regional reports were available to businesses to offer deeply descriptive and highly accurate information about any target area of interest to them. Demographic information is statistical information about the population in a designated area. Psychographic information results from adding a rich and extensive source of financial and economic information to the demographics of an area, allowing a detailed description of the dominant lifestyles (values, behaviors, needs) of the people in the area. As early as 1990, Equifax Marketing Decision Systems, one of the primary providers of information, worked from an incredible database covering 95 percent of the American population, a database updated 65 million times per day.[8] The new information was a product of the marriage between the marketing and the advertising industries, made possible by an advanced data-based technology.

This highly accurate information was expensive and stayed beyond the reach of congregations and denominational offices until the Percept Company established itself as a secondary research group in the late 1980s,[9] buying primary research from Equifax and repackaging the information for use by congregations. The repackaged research was both user friendly and affordable for congregations and quickly became a resource for planning and strategy in congregations and regional judicatory offices.

It took some time for leaders to understand that the exceedingly helpful demographic and psychographic reports were, once again, tools, not answers. A common but flawed assumption is that answers can be found in data, and these reports were some of the most data-rich resources that congregational leaders had ever seen. Some congregations and leaders mistakenly chased the populations described in the reports without regard for the gifts or sense of call of their congregations, prompting defeating strategies of being all things to all people. Rather than providing answers, these valuable resources were—and are—critical tools in the wilderness to help leaders stay on the path of mission.

Path 3: Clergy Development

During this time in the wilderness, it became clearer that the leadership of congregations—especially clergy leadership—was of critical importance. Rarely does any organization dream more boldly or perform more effectively than its leaders. Attention to leadership development, clergy development in particular, shaped the third path in this wandering in multiple directions. Not only were the called or appointed ordained leaders of the congregations seen as the critical links in renewal and change, but the certification and deployment of these people were also the strongest leverage point that the denomination could find for change in congregations and in the denomination itself. If congregations were to find new ways to live in this changed world, then leaders with the training, spirit, ideas, and boldness to see new things would be required. Again multiple paths were followed in the search for "making" better leaders.

- Continuing education: A natural starting point on this path was the continuing education of clergy beyond seminary training. Congregations were urged to include identified funds in their annual operating budgets to pay for resources and experiences of continuing education of their clergy. Quite naturally the recognition of the need for continuing education prompted a normative systems response to discover whose fault it was that clergy were unprepared for the challenge of leadership that they faced. A common response of systems under stress is that when people don't know *what* went wrong, they turn to ask *who* went wrong. For example, blame was ascribed to congregations for not challenging "the brightest and best" young people to consider the call to ordained ministry.

  Perhaps the greatest blame was ascribed to the seminary for producing students ill prepared for congregational leadership. This assignment of blame prompted a deep and ongoing conversation about the contemporary role of a seminary in developing leaders for congregations. The exploration of the proper role and responsibility of the seminary led to the more helpful conversations about the appropriate role of each of the parts of the denominational system to train, support, and encourage ordained leaders. People began to ask about the appropriate role of the seminary, the local church, the regional denominational structure, and the national denominational offices and how their various efforts might be aligned to train and encourage the leadership needed.

  One way to view the separation but necessary coordination of institutional roles can be described by using the five stages of learning a profession, developed by Hubert and Stuart Dreyfus.[10] The first stage, the "novice stage," focuses on learning the "rules of the game." Key to this stage is learning the theory and tools of professional practice. The theory thus engaged at this initial level is context-free information that can be understood at the most basic level without experience. This is the province of seminaries. But as the next stage of learning is approached, the "advanced beginner stage," connecting theory to experience is critical. Fieldwork and clinical pastoral education provided through a seminary presented limited opportunity to connect theory and experience for this level of learning, but it became clearer that more was needed. Regional denominational offices stepped forward to provide follow-up mentoring through required probationary programs meant to help people in the transition from seminary to congregations. Newly ordained clergy continued their advanced beginner work in a more supportive environment by being connected with more experienced clergy rather than through the isolated trial-and-error individual work of testing how things were done by guessing how to do them for the first time. Moving to the third stage of "competent to proficient" and to the further two stages of learning a profession required clergy to connect theory and experience at increasingly intuitive levels. This continued professional learning required environments of ideas and support sometimes made available through regional denominational efforts or parachurch organizations but often were missing for clergy who experienced their role in isolation with insufficient links to other people or experiences that could help them shape their practice.

Once again this was highly valuable learning and experience to provide better-prepared and better-performing ordained leaders for congregations. But once again it was only a partial advance and could not fully address the perceived problem of being lost in the wilderness. There were systemic and motivational limitations to what could be accomplished through continued education. The systemic issue centers on the reality that it does not help to change the leader if the system in which the leader operates does not also change. Focusing only on educating the leader amounts to a strategy of "fixing" the person when actually both the person and the system need to learn and change so that different outcomes may be achieved.

Simply sharing information, even if it is new or better information, is not what continuing education is all about. Information is a critical component of learning, but learning requires the full engagement of the individual learner. Ed Friedman stated this in his wonderful observation that "the unmotivated are notoriously invulnerable to insight."[11] The limitation of "force feeding" information was regularly encountered as regional denominational offices—districts, conferences, synods, presbyteries—began to use their resources to provide *mandatory* workshops for clergy. Often felt as an imposition by many clergy, mandatory continuing education was experienced as a denominational effort to answer questions that the clergy weren't necessarily asking—another invitation to resistance. At such denominationally mandated learning events clergy often showed up late, left early, and tried to skip the portion of the workshop that did not provide presentation of additional ideas but focused on what participants might actually change in their own practice. The path of continuing education was one of the richest advances for addressing the change facing congregations, but there was continually more to learn about the content that was most helpful, the way in which clergy were invited to participate in learning experiences, and the way in which information and practice needed to be integrated in order for change to be produced.

- Personal and spiritual renewal: The time in the new cultural wilderness also required that attention be paid to the personal and spiritual renewal of the clergyperson. Largely because of the changed culture and the new multitude of competing and conflicting expectations on both the person and the performance of the clergy, leadership in a congregation was seen as an increasingly difficult challenge and an increasingly unlivable lifestyle. During this period, the Reconstructionist Jewish movement commissioned a study to explore why so many people valued spiritual training and completed seminary but then chose not to serve a congregation in the rabbinic role. The conclusion was that many viewed the life and lifestyle of clergy as too demanding and unlivable.[12] Protestant, Catholic, and Jewish clergy were being perceived as an increasingly belabored, joyless, and less-than-healthy professional group. Denominations and parachurch organizations set about to help renew clergy personally and spiritually, again with the assumption that vital congregations needed vital leaders.

The single largest effort of renewal has been the Lilly Endowment National Clergy Renewal Program begun in 2000.[13] Based on the assumption that "[giving clergy and congregations a chance] to engage in mutual renewal will have an important impact on their churches, their individual members, and their communities," Lilly offered a competitive grants program for an award of up to $50,000, of which up to $15,000 could be spent for congregational support during the renewal absence of the pastor. Renewal was not understood as study or continuing education, and applicants were challenged to dream boldly and plan experiences of travel, reflection, health care, or any of a variety of experiences that would actually lead to a feeling of renewal. Since 2000, the endowment has offered more than fourteen hundred individual grants. That Lilly is continuing the program into its tenth year is evidence of the conviction that the program is promoting the desired result.

If the Lilly National Clergy Renewal Program has been the largest single initiative in this growing area of care for personal and spiritual renewal, there have been a host of other efforts and offerings that have ranged from denominationally based employee assistance programs to provide confidential lifeline help to clergy through the health-care system, to parachurch organizations such as the Samaritan Pastoral Counseling system, the Shalem Institute, and the Alban Institute that have provided information and training on self-care and spiritual leadership practices. Clergy were encouraged to participate in peer support groups, which like continuing education experiences proved to be more effective when clergy made conscious choices to participate rather than when denominational offices required their participation. Clergy were also encouraged to find and use other supports from beyond the congregation, such as spiritual directors to enable them to remain spiritually grounded and growing, and therapists to enable them to remain balanced and emotionally healthy persons.

There is still a fourth path in the wilderness, a fourth direction on our map from which we have been learning the importance of clear purpose and identity. This direction is the subject of the next chapter. Standing on the foundation formed by the first three paths of church growth, congregational transformation, and clergy development, the fourth path holds our primary attention for new learning now required for living in this present wilderness. This wilderness of the past several decades has had a deep sense of rootlessness that comes from a people who feel dislocated. It has been a time of necessary grieving that allows for letting go of the old church and the old world so that the new may be grasped with open hands. Our particular wilderness has required the same trust in God that is needed whenever answers and directions are not easily found.

Above all, these decades in our particular wilderness have not been a time of desolation and loss. Instead our story suggests that our time of pursuing multiple directions on our wilderness map has been marked by exploration, hard work, new learning, multiple mistakes, and worry mixed with hope. It has been a time rich in discovery through what Ed Friedman invitingly calls "the willingness to encounter serendipity,"[14] which is the product of searching for new paths. The way has not been sure, but I have always been reassured and encouraged by what was once shared with me as a Native American saying: "Stumbling is moving ahead faster." Being surefooted and correct in the wilderness is not the issue, but being in motion is a critical issue. A consultant friend of mine often pointed out that you can't steer a parked car. There has to be some motion, some direction, even if wrong or inadequate. For when we stumble on the path currently being followed, it is not hard to catch ourselves and redirect our searching in more promising ways. I suggest that this searching and stumbling, along with its rich discoveries and learnings, is much more descriptive of the past decades than any hand-wringing description of despair over what has happened to the church. Rather than blame, it is much more appropriate to appreciate and give thanks to the present and prior generation of clergy, denominational leaders, and exceptional lay leaders who have endured the stress and insecurity of the journey thus far to bring us to this point.

Writing about the Exile, another of the deep wilderness experiences of the Israelites, Walter Brueggemann noted that the Jews were not led to abandon faith, settle for despair, or retreat into private religion in the time of dislocation and wandering. "On the contrary," he wrote, "exile evoked the most brilliant literature and the most daring theological articulation in the Old Testament."[15] In the wilderness the people of God reform and reframe themselves and their practices in order to be a new people. The reforming and reframing are enhanced, not delayed, by having to explore multiple directions. So, we push on, knowing that the journey in our particular wilderness is instructive, faithful, and transformative.

CHAPTER 3

THE FOURTH PATH OF IDENTITY AND PURPOSE
In Search of a Costly Promised Land—Part 2

Working with congregations on planning, I sometimes invite leaders to discover what part of the biblical story they believe their congregation is presently living.[1] I put leaders into small groups and ask them to identify a biblical story that captures a clear sense of their congregation. The results are often stunning in the way in which the chosen story can focus and clarify the issues or challenges facing the church.

In perhaps the most unusual example, the leaders discovered that they were not so much living out a biblical story but were captured by the biblical image of soaring on wings like eagles ("But those who wait for the LORD shall renew their strength, / they shall mount up with wings like eagles, / they shall run and not be weary, / they shall walk and not faint" [Isa 40:31]). Of course whenever leaders return with the results of their search for a biblical story or image, the natural question is, why does this image fit their church?

Let me share their answer in two parts. The first part of the explanation was, "Because we believed that we were called to soar like eagles." I suspect that they were reacting to the image of the eagle that is often connected with courage and risk as it is in the way in which we Americans use the eagle as our national symbol. In fact, this image fit this congregation quite well. Their neighborhood had changed around them over the past generations so that these primarily white, Anglo people now found their church surrounded by a neighborhood that was 40 percent African American, 40 percent Hispanic, and 20 percent older white. The neighborhood also suffered deeply from the constellation of problems that accompany urban poverty.

Over the years that their section of the city changed into a landscape of stark need, these people committed and then redoubled their commitment to remain in place and minister to the corner of the kingdom where God had set them. They built a coalition of local churches to address various neighborhood problems. They started a clothing bank to provide people with adequate clothes. They set up a food pantry, and learning that some people visiting the pantry did not have the tools to open cans or the means to heat food, they added a soup kitchen where warm, nutritious meals were available.

They were the leading voice to provide emergency shelter to homeless men in the southern section of the city. Wisely they tried to be careful to be more than a distribution center for charity, and they worked at building relationships with the neighborhood people, inviting them into roles as leaders and volunteers in the community programs and inviting them into the life of the congregation. If the image of a soaring eagle is one of risk and courage to do what is right despite the cost, then these folks fit the bill.

Over the past few years, however, the work became increasingly difficult, and not just because of the need to find sufficient resources of spirit, time, people, and dollars. The congregation also met the city's growing opposition to their efforts. While they were determined to meet the needs of the neighborhood, voices in the city preferred to make the city inhospitable to homeless men, with the hope of forcing them to relocate to other cities. There were groups that wanted to gentrify the neighborhood around the church to rebuild property values, which would require relocating the present residents without providing additional low-cost housing in other areas of the city. The church leaders were faced not only with a very difficult path of continuing a costly neighborhood ministry but also with the opposition of their city.

Recognizing the opposition, they added the second part of their reason for choosing their biblical image. The full explanation was, "Because we believe that we are called to soar like eagles—but sometimes we feel like we chicken out." They were feeling the stress of opposition from the city. Soon the conversation turned to the idea that if they didn't always soar like an eagle, they could at least be a flying chicken. The laughter changed to deep insight, and their identity became crystallized. They emerged from their planning with the image of a flying chicken. They had pictures of a flying chicken mounted in their building, and they used the image on their documents. For the next several years, which were difficult for the leaders of this church, their new image and their new identity gave them strength and purpose. When the leaders faced challenges, they reminded themselves in their meetings that they were starting to chicken out—and that God had always intended that they soar. Their purpose and their identity were secure. They knew who they were. They knew what they were about. The next chapter of their life as a congregation was strong, and they made a deep difference.

The Fourth Path

In the previous chapter we briefly tracked the initial three paths of discovery and experimentation that leaders of the mainline church pursued in our particular wilderness: church growth, congregational transformation, and leadership development. I have tried to be clear that these explorations and new learnings have made a significant difference in the mainline church's ability to live in the wilderness and adjust to the changed mission field. These paths, however, did not lead directly to answers and solutions as hoped. In fact, much of this earlier learning fit the category of "technical work," which according to Ron Heifetz of Harvard University is the search for the application of known solutions to known problems.[2] Technical work seeks solutions that can be acted on; it moves directly from problems to solutions. While much was gained by the technical work accomplished on the first three paths, the disappointment was that the connection between perceived problems and the actions to resolve those problems didn't get us all the way to where we wanted to go. Congregations still struggle to live in the new culture, and the denominations remain unchanged.

It takes time to realize that the application of known solutions to known problems is a limited strategy when the conditions of life are not fully known and when those conditions don't actually have solutions, as in the case in the wilderness. The good news is that discoveries on the first three paths, while not leading to solutions, did lead to better questions that require new learning. This new learning fits Heifetz's understanding of adaptive work—work that is much more difficult than technical work because it doesn't move to quick problem-solving action but requires changes in the beliefs, behaviors, and assumptions of people. *Technical work* leads directly to *action* that resolves a known problem. *Adaptive work* requires *learning* that can help people change their beliefs, behaviors, and assumptions in order to face into the questions that lie in a wilderness. It is much harder work. For example, Judith Ramaley, president of the University of Vermont, offers a telling description of the adaptive work that faces leaders across industries and institutions, including the church. In her role as president, Ramaley described herself as grappling with issues

> for which no precedent has prepared me, situations in which several significant and sometimes equally important values clash . . . cases that have too many variables, most of them problematic in several ways at once . . . an "ill-defined mélange of topographical, financial, economic, environmental and political factors" often, in my experience, changing shape even as they come into focus.[3]

Such a description of the situation in which institutional leaders today find themselves certainly qualifies as a wilderness—a wilderness shared by congregations and denominations alike. Dealing with such situations certainly goes well beyond the application of known solutions to known problems, which was the strategy followed on the first three paths.

The good news is that the technical work on the first three paths now brings us to this fourth path of the much more adaptive work of understanding and reframing identity and purpose. Identity is the question of *who we are*, and purpose is the question of *why we are*. Answers to these questions are necessary to negotiate the kind of wilderness described by Ramaley. They are interrelated questions that need to be addressed together and demand deeply adaptive and more difficult work than figuring out the next step. We are now at the deeper work that requires much more from our leaders. We have already discovered that following this fourth direction will require our leaders to learn and use a completely new set of skills, and they will need to engage a mindset quite different from what is typically used in the problem-solving mode. A major theme of this book is the exploration of this new leadership required of all leaders of the mainline church at both denominational and congregational levels, both clergy and laity. But first it is important to explore some of what we already know of this fourth path and why this new work is of a different order—more difficult and less connected to immediate action.

Identity, Purpose, and the Stories We Tell

In Thomas Long's research on worship,[4] as well as in the earlier research done by Roy Oswald and Speed Leas,[5] which focused on what attracts people to congregations, it became clear that identities of healthy congregations tended to be very different all over the map. What was critical in these healthy congregations, however, was that their identity was clearly understood and communicated to others. As we saw in the earlier paths of church growth and congregational transformation, where there was an ongoing argument about the "right" identity (should a congregation be evangelical, fundamental, charismatic, Pentecostal, liberal, or oriented toward social justice?), experience and observation now more strongly point not to the "rightness" but to the "clarity" of the identity. Evangelical and liberal, charismatic and social justice congregations share an equal potential to attract and engage people in their ministry if their *identity and purpose are clear enough and communicated well to people*. Oswald and Leas speak of identity as the "we" that endures.[6] They connect a clear identity with "accrued confidence" and necessary boundaries—the ability to say yes to some things and no to others. There is no right way to be a congregation. There are multiple gifts, all parts of the same whole. The important point is that the congregation is clear about its identity and gifts and learns to live from its authentic center.

What can be said about congregations is equally true of denominations. Attention to the story that carries the identity of the denomination makes it more attractive to people who seek to participate.[7] A clear denominational identity also provides a significant connection tying the local congregation to the denominational tradition.[8]

Identity and purpose are tied to the way in which the leaders and people tell the story of the congregation or the denomination. The story has to be true and strong and indicate a future if the organization is to thrive. No group realistically thrives on a pessimistic story.[9] If the story must be true and strong and hold a hopeful future, then it is the leader's task to learn how to help the people shape such a story. This is new leadership work on the fourth path and requires new narrative skills of leaders. While exceptional leaders have intuitively used this narrative leadership throughout history, the new attention being given to narrative leadership at this time in our wilderness underscores its importance for our mainline transition.

Before going too much further, a specific congregational example of narrative leadership that shapes identity and purpose gives some sense of the power that comes from learning this fourth path in the wilderness. What follows is a story from an individual congregation, written and told by the pastor, Mike Mather.[10] It is a true and strong story from the life of this congregation. By itself the story does not give identity and purpose to the congregation. However, in the hands of a creative leader like Mike, it is a story that can lead a congregation to purpose and identity, offering new life and new reason for people to participate. First, consider the story itself:

A Story of Broadway Church
During Advent and Lent we have weekly evening prayers at Broadway. A few years ago during Advent a strange thing happened. It had been snowing that Wednesday evening, so when we gathered for evening prayers, only six of us were

there. As we got near the time when we would be praying together, there were loud sounds of teenagers at the side door of the church. As people were reflecting on the Scripture reading in silence, I got up and moved to the door. A young man no older than thirteen who was standing at the door asked me what was going on. I told him we were having evening prayers. He asked if he and his two friends could come in. I considered that for a moment—I wasn't sure it would be a good idea. But of course I said, "Sure."

The young man and his buddies came in and sat down. We continued in silence for another few seconds and then moved into the hymn "Standing in the Need of Prayer." I heard the side door of the church open again, and more young voices. As the gathered body sang, I moved back to the door. There were three more young men. "Are our friends here?" they asked. "Yes," I answered. "Would you get 'em and tell 'em to come out?" they asked. I considered it, but then said, "No. But you're welcome to join them if you wish." Honestly, I was hoping a little bit that they would say no. But they didn't. They followed me into the sanctuary. They came and knelt down next to the first young man who had spoken to me and whispered hurriedly. Clearly, they were asking him to leave. But he shook his head, and the others sat down, not particularly any happier than I was.

I explained how our prayer time worked: Anyone could offer a prayer; and when a person finished offering a prayer, he or she would say, "Lord, in your mercy," and everyone else would say, "Hear our prayer." The prayer time began. I invited prayers for people in the congregation. There was silence and I heard the young people start to chatter. I was almost at the point of saying something when one of the Broadway members offered a prayer and closed with "Lord, in your mercy," and everyone said, "Hear our prayer." I must confess that my eyes were open and on the young people. When they heard everyone say, "Hear our prayer," I noticed that their open eyes got very wide. They started to offer prayers. "For my cousin Booder, who was killed last year," one of the young people said. He rushed to the words, "Lord in your mercy," and everyone said, "Hear our prayer."

Now all the young people were offering prayers for people in their families—many of them people who had been killed. The teenagers were all noticeably eager to hear everyone joining them with "hear our prayer." We prayed for the world, and people offered prayers for places of violence around the world. We prayed for our community; one of the young people prayed "that the schools would stop expellin' people!" and everyone said, "Hear our prayer." The time of prayer reached a height, though, when the young man who was the leader said, "For me and for my grandma, 'cuz my dad is tryin' to take me away from her." And everyone said, "Hear our prayer."

I invited people to turn in their hymnal to where the Lord's Prayer is printed, and we prayed it together. Then we sang "I Want to Walk as a Child of the Light." Those young people stayed and exchanged signs of peace along with everyone else. And then they left—much quieter than they had come.

While this is a good story, the story itself does not supply identity and purpose to the congregation. Instead, a good story like this provides the *opportunity* and the *tool* for leadership—narrative leadership. Consider "the rest of the story" as Mike continues to write, because the rest of the story points to what Mike did with the story:

> A year and half later, when we had all noticed that our ministry with young people had expanded dramatically, we received a grant from the national church to expand and build on our work with young people. At least in my mind, we were able to trace it back to our openness in worship that snowy evening in Advent.

To get from a snowy Advent prayer meeting to a financial grant to work with young people takes a good leader who is able to see the value in the story of a people and then tell the story in such a way that people can see more in themselves and their purpose than they did before. It would have been easy for this established congregation of older adults that had become somewhat disconnected from their community to talk about that strange night and then to go on with their fears of the neighborhood and their fears of the young people in the neighborhood. But as leader, Mike was able to see the congregation in a different way and to use that night as a way of talking to people when they were captured by fear, telling them that they were better than the way they thought about themselves. Mike helped people see that they could talk with the youth, that they had something to offer, and that what they had to offer was needed. Mike used the story to help the people reconnect to the neighborhood where their congregation lived. Whether, as in this story, the focus is the congregation or whether the focus is the denomination, this fourth path in the wilderness is teaching us the importance of story, of narrative. People need a good story, a strong and true story, to give them purpose and identity.

A challenge that remains in the mainline church is overcoming weak and safe stories. I often tell leaders that we in the mainline church have been "practicing our demise" for a long period as we remember and rehearse our declining membership and attendance numbers beginning in the 1960s. Over the past two decades almost every middle judicatory strategic planning document that I have seen began with several pages detailing how weak and small the churches of the judicatory had become compared to a period of thirty years earlier. When congregations are asked about themselves, they too slip into a rehearsal of weakness, often pointing to the photo of the sanctuary filled to overflowing with formally dressed men who were the men's Bible study group a hundred years ago and then describing how they can't have committee meetings anymore because the few people involved are afraid to come out at night. When congregations are asked to describe themselves, they often restrict themselves to safe adjectives such as *warm* and *friendly*, descriptions that are hardly purposeful. Weak and safe stories are comfortable and unchallenging; they are the stories that people tell from what philosopher Iris Murdoch refers to as the "safe middle."[11] She suggests that we work from the safe middle of who we are because it demands so little of us. If we go beyond thinking of ourselves from the safe middle, we have to name both our real strengths and our real limits. The dilemma is that if we actually name a limit, we need to do something about it. If we name a real strength, we actually have to use it. So we remain in the safe middle where our description of ourselves is much more comfortable . . . we are warm and friendly . . . we have good music . . . we like food and are like a family around the kitchen table.

In this context it is easy to understand Howard Gardner's assessment that a prime task of leadership is to give people a better story to live. Gardner is professor of education at Harvard and professor of neurology at Boston University School of Medicine. He argues that leaders achieve their effectiveness through the stories they use and that the most basic story that influences people and organizations has to do with issues of identity.[12] In his work he categorizes leaders in terms of the innovativeness of their stories: the *ordinary leader*, who relates the traditional story of his or her group as effectively as possible; the *innovative leader*, who takes a story latent among the people and gives it new attention or a fresh twist; and the *visionary leader*, who actually creates a new story.[13] In our time in the wilderness we have learned that a strong, positive story is needed in order to live with courage and purpose in the present landscape. We need strong, courageous leaders to help congregations and denominations live into new identities and purpose. Strong, positive stories cannot be manufactured. They must be claimed, shared, and then actively pursued until people discover that they are actually living their new story.

When shaping a people's story in an age of marketing and political posturing, it is important to make a distinction between manipulation and spin. The leader has primary responsibility for manipulating (finding and shaping) the identity of the people, but the story must be authentic and appropriate. Though this suggestion often surprises people, I believe that manipulation is a positive responsibility of leadership that shapes and aligns people around identity and purpose. The word *manipulation* has the word *mano* (hand) at its root. The original meaning of manipulation referred to having one's hand on the tiller—a reference to steering a boat, providing direction. This is, in fact, a good image of leadership for a wilderness experience in which direction must be constantly sought and constantly corrected as we learn. The role of the leader is to direct the attention of the people. Manipulation, the telling of the authentic story of the people's identity in order to direct their self-understanding and align their actions with missional purpose, is a powerful tool to help people shape and live an identity worth living, even if it comes with sacrifice. Mike Mather's story of an Advent prayer service, used to help his congregation find strength they did not know they had, was a leader's act of creative manipulation. When their fear captured people, Mike reminded them of that snowy Advent evening, told them that they were better than their fears, and told them they already knew how to talk with the people in their community. Mike helped his people see their experience in a new light that connected them to a purpose larger and more worthwhile than worrying about the survival of their church.

Compared to this healthy understanding of shaping the story of the people by manipulation (offering direction) is the darker side of shaping the story that we have come to identify as "spin." Spin infers shaping a story in a particular way for some benefit—especially for the benefit of the leader or the leader's constituency. Spin is the shaping of identity for gain rather than for the health or the fulfillment of the mission of the group. Spin is the recognition that "if we tell the story this way" there is some gain to be realized or damage to be minimized rather than if the story is told another way. Spin is connected with fabrication; it commonly lacks authenticity, thereby giving false identity. Living in a time when public communication has become public relations through marketing, Hugh Heclo points to what he considers a paradox: "The more professional and adept our leaders have become in plying the persuasive arts, the more distrustful their audience has become."[14]

Helping mainline denominations and congregations find their next chapter in their history that will sustain them in the wilderness is not a matter of marketing in which we try to make our traditions and practices more attractive to more people. It is a matter of remembering who we have been in our relationship with God, and who we are now called to be, in such a way that people are connected to God and to what Tom Locke, president of the Texas Methodist Foundation, calls "God's dreams"—the "more" that God sees in us and in our world.

Stories (narrative leadership) are a primary tool of shaping identity and purpose because they engage people in conversation about right things. Through conversation, we are changed. In her work on systems and change Meg Wheatley points out that every revolution that changed the world started as a conversation between two people.[15]

It matters what people talk about. As senior staff at the Alban Institute, Alice Mann and I had responsibilities to consult with churches and denominations on strategic planning and also to teach leaders how to do planning. We knew the mechanics of planning—forming the team; gathering data; doing analysis; setting mission, goals, and objectives; and working with the board. But our experience taught us that it was not the mechanics of planning that brought life to the people. Rather, life, energy, and mission were framed by using the mechanics to help leaders have conversations about the "right" things that would reshape them. The tough work of doing the homework of planning was still necessary and could be draining. But finding the "right" things to talk about (which changed from system to system) provided the power of change and purpose. Strategic planning in congregations and denominations is actually an act of discernment of God's call rather than an effort at organizational effectiveness. Alice and I eventually reframed our planning work as "holy conversations" and recognized that at least three essential and fundamental questions shape this work:[16]

- *Who are we?* This is the question of identity in which leaders need to move beyond tacit assumptions to more clearly understand who we are now as a people who hold particular gifts and particular limitations.
- *What has God called us to do?* This is the question of purpose in which leaders need to ask what specific difference they are now called to make in people's lives and in the world within the next three to five years. This question of purpose is different from questions of activity (what should we do next?) or questions of satisfaction (what do the people of our church want?).
- *Who is our neighbor?* This is the question of context. Once again this is the work of moving beyond tacit assumptions to relearn the community and the world in which the people now live. Leaders need to constantly relearn the "corner of God's kingdom" given to their responsibility, and they need to decide how best

to use the gifts and the resources of the people to make a difference in that "corner," both locally and globally.

The task of leaders is to guide the people to have conversations about right things. In the work of the Texas Methodist Foundation, Tom Locke refers to this as getting the right legs under the right table to talk about right things. The leader then helps the people shape a new story about themselves and about their purpose. It is a search for a story that is worth living.

Narrative leadership that engages conversations about identity and purpose changes us because it is a way of learning what no one can teach us. The dialogue of conversation allows us to see beyond what we know. One of the foremost thinkers of the twenty-first century, physicist David Bohm, identifies *dialogue* as the means to create something new.[17] Consider his description of dialogue:

> When one person says something, the other person does not in general respond with exactly the same meaning as that seen by the first person. Rather, the meanings are only *similar* and not identical. Thus, when the second person replies, the first person sees a *difference* between what he meant to say and what the other person understood. On considering this difference, he may then be able to see something new, which is relevant both to his own views and to those of the other person. And so it can go back and forth, with the continual emergence of a new content that is common to both participants. Thus, in dialogue, each person does not attempt to *make common* certain ideas of information that are already known to him. Rather, it may be said that the two people are making something *in common*, i.e., creating something new together.

Because holy conversations about identity and purpose put us into dialogue with God and with one another, such conversations introduce us to those empty spaces between what I say and what you hear. It is in those empty spaces that the Holy Spirit is given room to move and we and our stories are reshaped through the progression of our conversation.

There are four stages of the progression of dialogue that can be instructive in helping leaders understand what is appropriate to help people rediscover their identity and purpose.[18] The first stage is *a time of politeness*, which can be identified as "shared monologues." In this stage people don't deeply engage one another in dialogue but learn about one another by telling stories of themselves that they already know. This is where we so often repeat our safe and weak stories with one another. We rehearse our safe middles. We practice our demise.

The second stage is *a time of breakdown*. In this stage the leader helps the people deconstruct their safe, weak stories. This is where a leader like Mike Mather listens to the stories of his people in which they rehearse their fears about their neighborhood, and Mike responds by saying, "Come on, people. You're better than that. Do you remember that snowy Advent night when you made a difference for four young neighborhood boys?" This is where a bishop listens to people talk about their concerns for survival and responds by saying that God used this congregation in the past to provide programs for children and families in the neighborhood and it is now time for the people to ask what difference God will use them to make this time. Deconstructing a people's weak or safe story is difficult and potentially dangerous work for a leader because it involves challenge and discomfort. Doing this work requires new forms of leadership in the wilderness, which we will begin to explore in chapter 5.

The third stage is *a time of inquiry* marked by reflective dialogue. In this stage leaders invite people into conversations about what could be. It is the search for the better story to live, a story that will replace tacit assumptions that once limited life, energy, and ministry because the assumptions were unquestioned. *At this stage it is not necessary that people actually know how to live their new story.* Rather it is sufficient that people see their story as worth living and feel called to learn how to live it.

Knowing how to live into the new story comes in the fourth stage of generative dialogue in which the fresh, potential story is explored and people, step by step, teach themselves how to live. Again, it is a wilderness journey.

In the current time of the mainline experience we are still deeply into the second and third stages of dialogue and discernment to reframe the story that God would have us live. We are finally challenging old weak and safe stories of ourselves. We are beginning to claim a new life that we don't yet know how to live. Perhaps some of our congregations and some of our leaders may be in the fourth stage of discovery and learning, and they lead the way for others. For many, however, it is still a time of breakdown, of challenging the weak and safe stories that worry about survival and talk of vitality only in the past tense. The best of our denominational and congregational leaders do not understand themselves as caretakers of an inherited institution experiencing weakness. The best of our leaders begin to dream of what could be, challenge the weakness of the stories that hold us back, and then engage people in conversations about the new future. This new leadership is not an exercise of authority to tell people what to do. It is the use of leadership to give people a better conversation to have and then to be patient to see how God's hand will move in the empty spaces of our holy conversations.

A Single Identity and Purpose or a Shared Center

A temptation on the fourth path is to seek identity and purpose that will fit everyone's needs and expectations and produce full agreement. One mistake of leadership that we have been learning about through trial and error in our wilderness journey is the desire of leaders to seek too much agreement and uniformity. We have overlearned the managerial habits of orderliness and tidiness from the past that require agreement as prerequisite for participation. We think everyone must agree before we can move forward. Over time, however, our mainline denominations have not only experienced disestablishment but have also experienced diversity and inclusiveness that were embraced nationally and regionally, if not always congregationally. In any of our mainline denominations the voice heard in the mid-Atlantic states is different from the voice heard in the northwestern, the south central, or the southeastern states. Our denominations are a union of regional churches with all the differences that suggests, including the differences in the political map of red and blue states. In any region there are differences of economy, ethnic makeup, levels of education, and dominant industries. In any town or city of a given region multiple congregations of the same denomination frame their ministry by offering alternative styles of worship, styles of programs, or priorities of mission from their neighboring sister congregations of the same denomination. In every area there are sister congregations of the same denomination that attract different generational cohorts, which, by definition, means that they do not agree with one another on practices of worship, programs, structure, or decision making. Such differences and diversity that now live embedded in both mainline congregations and denominations make full agreement on identity and purpose impossible.

Nonetheless, having lost our denominational unity and agreement through the growth and diversity of a changing culture, leaders entering the fourth path naturally responded by trying to install a singular new identity that everyone would agree upon and that would bring us all back together as well as attract and welcome newcomers. Much of the internal contest in our mainline denominations over the past decades revolved around arguments of what *all* Methodists or *all* Presbyterians or *all* Episcopalians should look like or should care about. A major learning of the wilderness, however, is that the opposite of multiple, and often competing, differences that have now divided us in our denominations is not a singular identity but a shared center.

Beginning in 2002, I began to shape my congregational consulting practice to focus on our large and very large congregations (average attendance of five hundred or more) out of a conviction that these congregations had much to teach us about our identity, purpose, and denominational issues. In many ways these large congregations are microcosms of a denomination. They are large systems with central leadership and structure but with multiple expressions of ministry held by widely diverse constituencies, whether measured by the highly visible differences of age, race, or gender or by the more subtle measures of socioeconomic status, level of education, or political persuasion. Yet in the most vibrant of these large congregations, these differences live side by side with one another but are united in ministry.

To get a hint of the diversity and uniqueness that can live in a large system, consider a favorite story from my consultation with a large congregation when I was doing a series of individual interviews with leaders to support the congregation's holy conversation planning work. On the second day of the interviews my first conversation of the morning was with the leader of a woman's group in the church; her group's singular agenda was to attend to the status of women and empower women in the congregation, in their homes, their marriages, their work, and their friendships. After a pleasant conversation with her, my second interview was with a thirty-year-old professional male who led a weekly morning breakfast Bible study for a group of men his age. The primary focus of this group of men was to understand and to be faithful to their role as provider and head of the home. It was curious to find two agendas so different, even oppositional, living side by side. Both leaders knew of the other leader and the other group but were able to be held together to share in the ministry of the same church. I was told that each of the two leaders had a conversation with the senior pastor, who told them that as long as their group supported and stayed connected to the mission of the congregation there would be room and resources for them. A shared identity linked them to their congregation, which depended not on agreement but on connection—connection to the story of mission of that congregation.

Here is another example from a consultation with a very large Presbyterian congregation. I began the project by interviewing the senior pastor, clergy and program staff, and key lay leaders. The purpose of the consultation was to help this congregation prepare for the retirement of its long-tenured, high-profile, beloved senior pastor and the reception of his successor. At the end of the interview with the senior pastor, I asked a final question: "What do I need to know most about this congregation?" The answer was, "Gil, you need to know that this is a centrist church with a thick culture." I asked for an explanation, and the senior pastor explained that it was "centrist"—it lived at the center of its Presbyterian theology and practice. He said that there was a full range of theologies and moral perspectives among the members and participants of the congregation. All were welcome, but in this church, mission was to be shaped, programs were to be developed, worship (in its various forms) was to be connected, and decisions were to be made from their traditional Presbyterian center. Second, the congregation had a "thick culture," that is, it moved intentionally and strategically into change and did not necessarily seek to be innovative or agile but moved "thickly" with purpose. By being centrist with a thick culture, this very large church served its community and the wide surrounding region by being a solid base of Christianity. The senior pastor was telling me the story (the identity and purpose) of this historic congregation that was quite a bit more than the sum of its programs, services, missions, and aspirations.

As I continued through each of the fifteen interviews, I concluded each one with the same question: "What do I need to know most about this congregation?" Almost every one of the people interviewed, staff and lay leaders, offered the same answer: it was a centrist church with a thick culture. When asked to explain, each person offered the same definitions as the senior pastor. This church's story lived and operated effectively because it was known and shared, living visibly in the actions and telling of leaders. Indeed, the story held all of the differences within the congregation in balance.

The balance that held disparate voices together in this large congregation was most visible as it began to weaken when the senior pastor finally announced both his retirement and the need for a search committee for his successor. Suddenly the once balanced voices held in place by the church's story surfaced in new and oppositional ways as people sensed an opportunity to seek more attention for their preferences. For example, a few people became much more active, seeking attention and resources for programs with gays, lesbians, and transgendered people, while some other people pushed the church to take a stand against the ordination of gays. Some wanted more in the budget for social justice ministries, while others wanted new budget dollars for mission programs. With story and storyteller in place such diverse congregations as this large historic church live from their center, and the relationships with members and participants remain balanced. The point is that everyone in the congregation does not need to live at the center. But the story of the congregation that does live at its center is known, and people, from whatever their particular perspective or interests, can see themselves in the story and stay in connection and in balance around the story. Multiple and different relationships are managed by allowing individuals their differences but inviting them to connect to the same core identity and purpose.

Older and more naive ideas of harmony and agreement that live in many congregations and denominations force us to seek a false sameness as if we all are, or should be, alike. The reality in a highly complex culture where people encounter differences with great regularity is that community is built through acknowledging and negotiating the differences. It is not the differences that keep us apart; rather, they enrich us. False harmony and enforced intimacy are not needed. Individuals understand that they are not alike, do not choose to be like everyone else, and do not necessarily even enjoy everyone else. Tom Long describes a congregation (and perhaps by inference a denomination) as the place where a person goes in order to be with people he or she may not want to be with under other circumstances. He then explains that what we need to always remember as participants in that congregation is that those other people feel exactly the same about us.[19] Differences do not dissuade us in a congregation or in a denomination and do not block a diverse people from being in community while connected to a shared central faith. Our common and shared identity and purpose connect and use our differences in enriching ways.

The fourth path in the wilderness is built on what we have learned so far on the three earlier paths. However, this search for the new center of identity and purpose that will hold us together is new, different, and more difficult work. In my United Methodist Church we are now clear that we have a common mission to make disciples of Jesus Christ for the transformation of the world. We are getting clearer that there is a Methodist way built on three principles: doing no harm, doing good, and staying in love with God. We are clear that there are four primary paths or foci (new church starts and congregational redevelopment, leadership development, elimination of poverty, and global health) that will be the priority places where we will first give our time, attention, and resources in this initial stage of ministry for the next decade. The meeting of the global United Methodist leaders at Lake Junaluska in 2007, mentioned earlier, brought a historic gathering of people together to rehearse those basic and foundational pieces of the identity of the denomination that will move this denomination into the future. This gathering did not direct the leaders of the church on how they were to make this happen. Steps and strategies were not laid out. Rather, the story was rehearsed, and people were asked to affirm that this was what would hold them together. They were then invited to take the story back to their places of responsibility and to invite others to discover ways to focus their prayers, attention, and resources in whatever way possible to bring this ministry to life. Is there full agreement that this is who The United Methodist Church is and full agreement on the foci as the places of greatest priority? Is there not more to the theology of this church and its history and tradition? Do not others bring issues of passion and preference that they would rather see as the denomination's priorities? The answers are obvious. The new story that is shaping is not neat and tidy with full agreement all around. But it is the beginning of a reshaping of this large and diverse denomination to move into the future. We are more deeply learning this new path in the wilderness.

The Importance of Learning the Work of the Fourth Path

The fact is that the work of identity and purpose on the fourth path is not just more difficult; it is work of a different order. Mainline denominations and congregations lived with an inheritance that was without need of a clear identity separate from the national identity, which was assumed to be Christian. As the national character has changed, it has precipitated a crisis within the established mainline church far deeper than can be addressed by techniques or solutions. The importance of the fourth path is that it is rebuilding an identity that was once closely attached to a national identity that has now disappeared. Several years ago I had numerous conversations with congregational consultants from the South African University of Stellenbosch who were seeking help in learning how to engage congregations of the Dutch Reformed Church of South Africa in visioning. Their congregations did not know how to raise questions of purpose or discern a sense of call. Directing the congregational leaders into such conversations was proving to be a hard task. The consultants recognized that the congregations of the Dutch Reformed Church struggled with conversation about vision because they had not had the need to raise such questions in the remembered past. In many, if not most, congregations of that denomination in that place and at that time, the established cultural system of apartheid defined the purpose of a congregation as the place where cultural and colonial values were to be maintained and undergirded. That was all the purpose that many congregations needed, and it was unquestioned. People simply belonged to a congregation because they saw themselves as like one another and were part of—and wanted to ensure that they would continue as a part of—the underlying power system that directed the culture. The Dutch Reformed Church was a part of the established voice of authority that maintained the doctrine of separation—apartheid. When apartheid was dismantled, however, congregations for the first time had to ask the foundational but unfamiliar and disorienting questions of identity and purpose: Who are we now? What are we called to do? Who is our neighbor? The Dutch Reformed Church had been removed from its position as the established voice of religion in South Africa and in its disestablishment was forced to rethink itself. It proved difficult for many congregations because the changed environment required a fundamental paradigm shift in which leaders needed to actively form—rather than assume—a purpose and identity.

At some level the South African experience may be instructive for the mainline churches of North America. Particularly in the United States, we tell our history as framed, in part, around the ideal of separation of church and state. We claim there is no established religion in the United States, no religious group that speaks for the people or the values of our nation. Yet the practical reality is that the mainline church functioned as the established church throughout our earlier history. Mainline Protestantism was a dominant, if certainly not the only, religious voice in the development of North America, and the story of other faith traditions in the United States is a story of their need to claim their space alongside Protestantism. A part of my memory as I was growing up in the 1950s includes the articles published in wide-circulation magazines like *Life* and *Look* that regularly identified the ten greatest preachers in the United States. It was a list on which white, male, mainline Protestant clergy were routinely and heavily overrepresented. If not fully established, the voice of the mainline church and the mainline clergy was certainly dominant.

Add to this early established nature of mainline Protestantism the fact that religious affiliation was most often determined by birth—one followed the family path of faith practice. The family connection was most often determined in those earliest days by ethnicity through which a Scandinavian or person of German lineage kept the family connected to one of the Lutheran denominational lines, a person of English descent kept the family connected to the Episcopal Church, or one of Scottish lineage kept the family connected to the Presbyterian Church. Location, therefore, also provided a connection to congregation and denomination as ethnic groups immigrated to determined regions of the United States. In fact, the American experience of denominations continues to be a regional history in which particular denominations, like their early immigrant members, settled into particular regions of the country and brought their religious identities with them. Denominations developed historic regional strengths through their concentrated presence, which continue to dominate sections of the country today with different religious identities and values and which, in fact, influence the contemporary cultural practices of the respective regions. Within those regional concentrations the denominations of strongest local strength had clear centers of identity, which supported their shared history, theology, polity, ethnicity, and values. Ongoing regional studies offer a fascinating exploration of how the early concentrations of people continue to influence contemporary regional religious and political values and experience.[20]

The experience of the Dutch Reformed Church was that, having stood at the center of cultural values and identity for so long, any sustained conversations about identity and purpose proved to be difficult because the answers were already assumed. To a great extent, the established mainline Protestant denominations in North America also stood at the center of cultural values and identity for a long time, creating similar difficulties when wrestling with questions of identity and purpose. Assumptions often prove to be difficult to challenge because they operate at a hidden, tacit level. Why spend time on a question if one believes that the answer is already known?

The Disestablishment

Being disestablished creates internal crises that are experienced as self-doubt and confusion. Consider a fairly common pattern in congregations that experience a schism. In a congregational split where one group of people leaves over a controversy in order to form a new and separate congregation, the "daughter church" that separates from the established mother church initially fares best. After all, the daughter church has the clearer identity. The members know who they are by what they stand against in the theology or practice of the mother church. The clear sense of identity gives the daughter church energy, and the clear sense of purpose in needing to locate, staff, and fund the new church gives that energy direction. The people of the mother church, however, commonly sink into a depression precipitated by having established assumptions about themselves challenged and by having friends who no longer want relationships with them. The mother church can no longer think of itself as it has in the past. Repeated behaviors and practices no longer achieve the same results. A sense of abandonment leaves the mother church feeling powerless and operating out of self-doubt and confusion.

The initial three- to five-year period is difficult for the mother church, and it overcomes the difficulties only if and when it begins to ask questions of identity and purpose: If these other people left us, who are we now? If we can't think of ourselves as we once did, what is important for us to do now? Through wrestling with such difficult questions, which initially did not need to be asked and whose answers could be easily assumed prior to schism, the mother church can begin to build a new identity and purpose that reclaims self-confidence and restores energy. Mother churches that are unable to seriously ask the questions of identity and purpose more frequently flounder, caught by their sense of being abandoned, not knowing who they are, and only knowing that they aren't who they once were.

I would argue that this common pattern observable in congregational schisms where the authority of the mother church is disestablished can be instructive in understanding the disestablishment and the accompanying disempowerment of the mainline denominations in North America. In fact, the mainline church has experienced three disestablishments in America.[21] The first came as part of the democratic spirit that merged with the influence of free church ecclesiology around the time of the Revolutionary War. The second came in the early 1900s when the Protestant voice lost its prominence of place in shaping the broader culture to New Deal politics and the repeal of Prohibition. The third disestablishment began with the serial upheavals of the 1960s and 1970s, leading to the current wilderness. The sense of abandonment and displacement in each case has given the mainline church an additional heavy burden among all contemporary expressions of Christianity that have been struggling to find ways to continue to talk to a fast-changing culture. Over the past several decades the disestablishment of the mainline church has confronted leaders with a number of fundamental shifts that need to be understood in the work of establishing a new identity and purpose.

The Four Cultural Shifts of Disestablishment

The full story of the most recent disestablishment of the mainline church is appropriately complex. For the purpose of our discussion here, I point only to four cultural shifts that have been key drivers to the most recent disestablishment influential in our particular exodus. The first is the secularization of the culture that has led to an individualization and privatization of the religious experience. Robert Bellah and his team of sociologists noted this shift early on when, in the 1980s, they described an individual approach to spiritual searching exemplified by "Sheilaism," the approach of a young woman named Sheila who expected that her religious identity and participation specifically address her personal needs and questions rather than connect her to membership or the needs and questions of any group.[22] The shift to individualism as a way to live in the changed North American culture, as well as a way to search for meaning, is a key part of the new landscape of the wilderness we now experience. Chapter 4 gives us an opportunity to explore some particular cultural shifts that churches and denominations need to understand and navigate in order to address the new mission field that has been shaped around us by this individualism. For the moment it is sufficient to note this shift as a critical contributor to the current disestablishment experienced by the mainline church since the old paths of family and geography, which led so directly to membership in the past, were weakened and the old need to be a part of a dominant institution no longer served the individual in the same way. Individualism and secularization went hand in hand as other voices outside religion competed to offer answers of purpose and identity in the lives of individuals.

The second shift in disestablishment is an accompanying distrust of institutions. The generational distancing from institutions that happens in adolescence is now well understood. The adolescent task of establishing a personal identity apart from the parent often means separating not only from the parent but also from the meaningful institutions that are strongly identified with the parent. The church is one of those institutions, and the disappearance of adolescents from the church following confirmation (and the later reappearance in young adulthood when marriage and family reintroduce life questions) is well known and well documented. In this time of secularization and accompanying individualism, however, the distrust of institutions goes well beyond the explanation of individual maturation and is experienced wholesale across the ages and stages of people's lives.

In his work on understanding institutions, Hugh Heclo points to two important reasons people currently mistrust institutions.[23] The first he identifies as a performance-based mistrust. We don't trust institutions because they routinely served us badly and disappointed our trust. Consider the experience in politics over the past four decades in which there has developed deep suspicion about the questionable causes and reasons for going to war that surround our multiple experiences in Vietnam and the several wars of the Middle East; where presidents are publicly examined for what they knew, when they knew it, and what they did (which led to both attempted and successful impeachments); and where elected officials are regularly seen to betray their public trust for personal gain. The institutional church has its own history of earned distrust that can be seen in examples such as high-profile televangelist episodes and the Roman Catholic sex scandal. The latest institutional earned distrust involves a full range of banking and investment institutions. Earned institutional distrust is widespread.

More important to this discussion, however, is Heclo's identification of culture-based distrust, which finds its full bloom in an individualized culture. Heclo identifies a "moral polestar," a pervasive cultural norm, which rests at the heart of the understanding of our personal freedom. This norm states that "the correct way to get on with life is to recognize that each of us has the right to live as he or she pleases so long as we do not interfere with the right of other people to do likewise."[24] Although not a recent invention, this early and deeply embedded principle of American democracy and personal freedom resonates with our individualized culture. But then Heclo points out that at the very foundation of any institution, in contrast to the desired freedom, are requirements and boundaries—instructions of how to live, if you will—which stand in opposition to an individualized culture that prefers a freedom restricted only by the rights of other individuals. Institutions, by their very nature, limit personal freedom by their requirements of how to live. Schools have requirements of what should be learned. YMCAs have requirements and expectations of how to stay healthy. Banks have requirements and regulations about gaining and managing financial resources. In similar ways churches have requirements and disciplines for living in relationship with the Creator and with other people. While people today are more than willing to search for and follow personal disciplines that address their individual questions and needs, older institutional church requirements that include membership and the care of the institution of the church, which once lay at the heart of the mainline institutional involvement, no longer resonate with and attract people. The change of the place of institutions in people's lives has had a major impact on the disestablishment and trust of institutions that once rested at the heart of the culture, including the mainline church.

The third shift that has had a profound and powerful effect on the disestablishment of the mainline church is the simple, direct impact of demographics. The gift of time provides a perspective to see and reflect on the powerful cultural drivers of past years that are difficult to perceive and measure while being experienced. There is increasing evidence that along with the great social change of past decades, there have been quiet but unstoppable demographic shifts that have powerfully altered the reality of the mainline experience. While much has been said and accepted about what is wrong with the theology and practice of the mainline church that would cause it to lose market share to the evangelical and fundamental expressions of Christianity in the United States, there is growing evidence that demographics have been more at the heart of the changes. The general causes of mainline decline are not theological or organizational, asserts Anthony Healy, president of Visions-Decisions, Inc.[25] Instead Healy points to the changes in fertility and marriage among mainline adherents. The level of education among mainline adherents compared to evangelical adherents has traditionally been higher, resulting in later marriages and fewer children. (Level of education correlates with a later age of marriage; a later age of marriage correlates with having fewer children. Level of education also correlates with mobility as children leave home for education and then pursue careers that do not return them home where church membership in the family denomination is expected.) This fundamental difference and its significant impact are confirmed in sociological research. According to sociologists Michael Hout, Andrew Greeley, and Melissa Wilde, evidence from the General Social Survey indicates that higher fertility and earlier childbearing among women from conservative denominations explain 76 percent of the observed trend of evangelical denominational growth for cohorts born between 1903 and 1973—conservative denominations have grown their own. A recent rise in apostasy also added a few percentage points to mainline decline. Conversions from mainline to conservative denominations have not changed, so they played no role in the restructuring.[26]

If major national trends of levels of education, marriage, and fertility account for a large portion of the change within the mainline church, local movements of shifting populations have produced a compounding effect. Researcher Roger Stump gives evidence to the influence of migrating populations surrounding mainline congregations, which generally were founded in an earlier time and are more often located in areas that have undergone the greatest, if not most continuous and disruptive, demographic change.[27] For example, in eastern Pennsylvania, where I live, incorporated towns and cities have lost population over past decades while surrounding townships have gained. The United Methodist Church has been long established in much of this area of the mid-Atlantic states, with congregations historically located in the prime town and city areas. We had a history of planting churches wherever people held still, resulting in multiple congregations inside cities, towns, and villages. These are now the very areas from which people are moving away. In some areas the people leaving are not being replaced, resulting in the impoverishment of towns and cities. In some areas the people leaving are being replaced in smaller numbers by immigrant populations with different practices and expressions of faith. These large and exceptionally powerful demographic drivers are repeated in nuanced versions throughout the United States, producing changes over which mainline congregational and denominational leaders have had little influence.

It can be argued that living in the midst of such powerful cultural changes that are difficult to perceive and impossible to influence can lead to feelings of "surplus powerlessness," a description of a situation identified by Michael Lerner in which a set of feelings or beliefs makes people think of themselves as even more powerless than they are and leads them to act in ways that actually confirm their powerlessness.[28] The presence of powerlessness is not an excuse for the leaders of long-established mainline congregations and denominations to escape being accountable for their reticence and recalcitrance to change or lead change. The feeling of surplus powerlessness, however, removes the sense of agency from leaders who have come to believe that they have failed and that they are helpless to change in ways that will make a difference. One of the new tasks for denominational and congregational leaders is to reshape the agenda of the mainline church to escape this surplus powerlessness. This task calls for leaders to normalize and depersonalize the experience of so many of our congregations and leaders so that guilt and self-doubt no longer disempower people and then to shape the theological conversation about God's purpose in such a situation. Not being held responsible for overpowering forces over which they have no control frees leaders from the sense of failure over the past and powerlessness over the present. The theological task is to set leaders free to face risk in areas where they do have influence and control. Without a sense of personal, congregational, and denominational agency free from self-blame there is little hope of a fruitful reestablishment of presence of the mainline church.

The fourth shift that has heightened the impact of the disestablishment of the mainline church is the new presence of other world religions and faith orientations in North America. According to the research posted on adherents.com, the United States has a greater number of religious groups than any other country in the world.[29] While still the largest religion practiced in the United States, Christianity now has a longer list of religious neighbors competing for and challenging the once dominant position of an established Christian value system. The eight largest religious groups in the United States, in descending order, are Christian, nonreligious/secular, Jewish, Muslim, Buddhist, agnostic, atheist, and Hindu. In her study, Diana Eck wonderfully documents the new public appearance of world religions in the United States. Where these other world religions started with very low profiles and very low numbers as religious neighbors in the United States, they have now taken their very visible place in the public square as legitimate institutions and faith practices as part of what she describes as the "marbling of civilization."[30] In actuality, however, the disestablishment of Christianity goes beyond the new presence of world religions as described by Eck. Note that in the list of the largest religious groups, there are new religious influences such as nonreligious, secular, agnostic, and atheist value systems that also take their place in addressing the needs and questions of people. According to the American Religious Identification Survey conducted in 2008, the number of Americans who claim no religious affiliation has nearly doubled since 1990, from 8 to 15 percent; the number of people willing to describe themselves as atheist or agnostic has increased about four-fold in that same period, from 1 million to 3.6 million; and the percentage of self-identified Christians has fallen 10 percent, from 86 to 76 percent.[31] It is appropriate to understand these changes of the expansion of both world religions and competing value systems as a product of, and supported by, globalization in which the dominance of any people, institution, or mind-set is challenged.

The Difficulty of the Work of the Fourth Path

The work of shaping a new and clear identity and purpose as mainline congregations is critical in the midst of the disorientation of the disestablishment. However, we are still at the beginning of this fourth path with much to learn. It is likely that this part of our wandering will take a considerable amount of time and effort because we need to understand and address a number of confounding issues.

The first of these issues is the difficulty of challenging and changing tacit assumptions, a difficulty that the mainline church shares with all other long-established institutions, corporations, or organizations in a time of deep change. One way in which the human psyche has been explained is using a three-level model by which consciousness is described. The three levels are the *conscious*, the *unconscious*, and the *tacit*. The conscious level is, of course, the part of ourselves and our world of which we are aware. We see it, smell it, and feel it. It is the world of our five senses as well as the constructs we built with our senses to integrate our experience of the world into a coherent whole. The unconscious is the part of ourselves and our awareness that we cannot access. Information at this level escapes us, although it still influences and directs our experience of the world. In between the conscious and unconscious levels is awareness at the tacit level. Where information at the unconscious level remains beyond our easy access, the tacit level holds information that routinely remains hidden from us until we give it attention. We can access our tacit awareness rather directly by simply paying attention. One early model used in the human potential movement was the Johari Window, a construct to help people understand how to use personal feedback as a way of expanding an accessible but tacit conscious awareness of themselves.[32] The Johari Window helped individuals see that other people actually had information about the individual of which he or she was not aware because it was hidden (tacit within the individual). The way in which we perceive ourselves creates personal blind spots, which limit our self-understanding, but does not stop what others can see. Using the Johari Window, individuals were taught safe and responsible ways to seek feedback from others in order to move tacit information about the self, easily observed by others but hidden to the self, to the conscious level where decisions about behavior could be made.

Access to tacit information allows us to make decisions that were previously unavailable because the assumptions controlled by tacit information prevented the questions from being asked. Consider the experience of a congregation (or a denomination) that regularly engages differences from a contentious position. Rather than listen, people argue. Rather than try to understand, people try to persuade. What commonly lives at the tacit level within such a congregation is the dominant North American assumption that whenever there is a challenge, it is important to win. We are currently in a cultural cycle of incivility that prompts people to confront one another in order to win as a form of expected behavior.[33] Although we don't necessarily think of ourselves as contentious, people in congregations and denominations commonly behave this way. If we choose, it is fairly easy to call attention to this part of our behavior in congregations by differentiating between behavior regularly seen in the culture and the disciplines of behavior needed in a faith community. By giving attention and raising our behavior to a conscious level, we can invite a different response from leaders and participants. My book on behavioral covenants in congregations offers models by which assumed norms and behaviors can rather easily be brought to awareness. For example, people within a congregation can be invited to rethink and change their contentious behavior into more collaborative, community-building practices.[34] There have been initiatives in denominations, such as the behavioral covenant theme in the United Church of Canada a few years ago and the current holy conferencing emphasis in The United Methodist Church, that are designed to work with such tacit assumptions challenging them to change at denominational levels.

The critical issue with the tacit assumptions and norms that constrain change is that they cannot be addressed if not questioned and brought to awareness. The primary dilemma of any organization with an assumed identity and purpose is that it is difficult to question the identity and purpose because people believe that they already have the answer. Sometimes I ask leadership groups how many of the participants think of themselves as younger than they actually are. The question prompts chuckles as a good number of participants usually raise their hands. I then point out that this suggests that we tend to know more about who we *were* than about who we *are*. This is true of our congregations and denominations as well. Most congregations with which I have worked as a consultant knew much more about who they were than about who they currently are. Indeed, I often point out that it is common for the last twenty-five to fifty new members or participants to know more about who the congregation currently is than do the board members with thirty-five years of membership tenure. Long-tenured leaders tend to see what they remember rather than what is, and this is equally true of denominations. Consider the impact of the overwhelming percentage of denominational leaders who have thirty to fifty years of experience within the same denomination. The level of tacit and unquestioned assumptions for such individuals is exceptionally high. We don't easily ask the question of identity because we assume we already have the answer.

Tacit assumptions do not get challenged until they are proved not to work. "It is when the organization wants something, when it seeks help, that the psychological dynamic is set up for finding out what is really going on," writes Edgar Schein.[35] Schein notes that the external help of someone like a consultant can be critical for an organization because it is a way in which the organization allows itself to ask questions. Using someone to help ask questions allows what previously remained hidden to be brought to awareness, providing a more accurate description of the current reality. While much of the work of the first three paths in the wilderness was productive and necessary, it did not provide the relief sought because it focused so heavily on solutions and problem solving. However, this earlier work brought the mainline church to the ability to ask the better adaptive questions of purpose and identity where help is needed to challenge assumptions of who we think we are and what we think we are called to do. The need has finally been great enough (and the hope sufficient) that tacit assumptions are now being challenged.

The second of the three central issues that make this work particularly difficult for the mainline church can be found in an observation about purpose and relationship made by sociologist Peter Takayama.[36] Let's start with a basic premise of all organizations. All vital and viable organizations are built on the two pillars of *purpose* (sometimes identified in organizational literature as *task*) and *relationship*. Groups, organizations, and institutions must first be very clear about their purpose and then form relationships among people and segments of the organization to pursue that purpose with aligned efforts. Both purpose and relationship must be present for the organization to thrive. Takayama's insight is that given the presence of both of these pillars in religious organizations, denominations routinely give preference and priority to the issues of purpose while local congregations routinely give preference and priority to relationships. He identifies denominations as purposive while congregations are solidarity or communal organizations. What can perhaps be described as an overattention or sensitivity to relationship at the congregational level is an inheritance of the history of congregations in which leaders have always been subject to the pleasure of members. In his study of Christian clergy in America, Brooks Holifield observes that as early as the 1640s, parishes set the terms of clergy leadership through annual contracts.[37] Contracts protected the clergy but empowered the congregation. Clergy were given clear authority within a parish but only up to the limits of the satisfaction of those who could make decisions about their employment. Continued evaluation based on the satisfaction of members would make any leader highly sensitive to relationships.

This major difference in preference between the denomination and the local church makes it even more difficult to address identity and purpose at the denominational level despite the fact that, at this point in our wilderness exploring, clarity of identity and purpose is critical. The dilemma is that progress on identity and purpose made at the denominational level will encounter an initial affirmation at the congregational level, followed by a passive or active resistance based on the importance of relationships. Consider the situation of my United Methodist denomination, which is getting increasingly transparent about our purpose of making "disciples of Jesus Christ for the transformation of the world." We no longer make members but now commit to making disciples—changed people. The denomination has worked hard to be clear about this purpose and about what is to be different in the lives of individuals and in the world because of people who are shaped in a belief and relationship with Christ. In response the leaders and people of the local congregation routinely applaud the clarity and support the making of disciples. In many long-established congregations, however, the unspoken response also includes a strong feeling of NIMBY—not in my backyard. Many want their denomination to make disciples but would not want to get their congregation too deeply involved in such a denominational goal. Making the current people of the congregation into disciples (changed people) or reaching out to new people to make disciples is deeply disruptive of the balance of relationships currently maintained within many local church congregations. If these congregations worked to make "changed people," new decisions might need to be made, new voices would need to be heard, all of which would destabilize the learned behavior of the congregation, upsetting people and requiring leaders to manage differences and disgruntled people.

We are learning that one of the deeply difficult tasks on this fourth path is the rebalancing of the two pillars of purpose and relationship in many established congregations. A large percentage of our established congregations within the mainline church have been so centered on relationships with the intent of satisfying the preferences of the people who are already in the congregation that a significant push (perhaps even an overemphasized push) toward the pillar of purpose is required. In many ways the task of this fourth path of learning is to help congregations move from membership organizations to purposeful organizations. Membership organizations are relationally preferential, and it is very important to know who is in and who is out. Those who are in, having been members for longer periods of time, get preferential treatment and have more access to decision making. For example, the babies who are grandchildren of those who are in the congregation get baptized even if the babies and their families have no connection, or even want no connection, to the church or a life of faith. The babies are baptized as a way that the relationally sensitive congregation and its members claim that this baby is "one of us" by family connection, if not by intent. Relationships with or among the members of the congregation and their family and friends trump any purpose in the connection.

It is a difficult task to help rebalance the pillars of the congregation so that the congregation is able to do ministry out of a sense of purpose. Rebalancing the pillars puts the clergy at risk because they live with a foot in both the denominational world (which gives preference to purpose) and the congregational world (which gives preference to relationship). It should not be a surprise that clergy, when attending a denominational meeting or conference session, will strongly support a denominational initiative that is purposeful because they are, at that moment, standing within the purposeful boundaries of the denomination. However, when returning to the parish, those same clergy might not actively represent the denominational initiative or seek to get the congregation's support and alignment in the initiative because the clergy are then standing within the relational boundaries of the congregation. Clergy feel themselves at risk because they are evaluated by both levels of their denominational system, and each level evaluates them by the different standards appropriate to it. The middle judicatory evaluates the clergy on their performance around denominational goals and initiatives and the change that is evident in the congregation. The local congregation evaluates the clergy on the satisfaction of the people already involved in the congregation, a satisfaction commonly measured by minimal change. In fact, the shift from a membership organization to a purposeful organization requires significant change that might be measured, in part, by the questions that the leaders are willing to ask. A membership organization will ask if the members are satisfied. A purposeful organization will ask if people's lives are being changed.

If clergy in a local congregation feel caught in the tension between the poles of purpose and relationship, middle judicatory executives and staff live in a similar tension. Persons working in middle judicatory positions are expected to represent the purposeful preference of the denomination, but they do their work with the relational leaders and structures of the local congregation. Middle judicatory executives and staff, if you will, live their whole lives on the boundary between the competing preferences of purpose and relationship and, like clergy, suffer when caught between the two different evaluations of denomination and local congregation.

The third issue that makes the work of identity and purpose particularly difficult for the mainline church is related to the age and established nature of mainline denominations. In his work on "deep change" Robert Quinn recognizes that long-established organizations are a collection of subgroups within the larger organization, each with its own needs and preferences (a constituency of constituencies). Over time such organizations develop two different missions—a public and a private mission.[38] The public mission is what the organization openly claims as its purpose; the private mission is where the organization actually directs its attention and resources. The private mission is the satisfaction of the most powerful of the constituent subgroups in the system. Quinn uses the example of a school system. The public mission of a school system is the education of students, and there is much talk about this public mission. Over time, however, in well-established schools the private mission becomes the satisfaction of the most powerful of the constituent voices, which are the teachers, the administrators, and the parents. It is conceivable for a school system to behave in a way that the constituent voice of the students is marginalized or not even recognized.

Mainline denominations clearly fit the category of old and long-established institutions, which are constituencies of constituencies, a group of subgroups. There are multiple competing voices within each denomination, and each voice is careful to try to capture and keep as much of the attention and resources of the system as possible. Certainly it is a generalization, but an argument can be made that the strongest of the competing constituent voices in denominational systems are the clergy, the congregations, and special interest groups.

Clergy deployment—getting the right clergy into the right congregations—has long been understood as a primary responsibility of the middle judicatory, whether through a call or an appointment system. Clergy deployment is perhaps the largest of the denomination's primary leverage tools to affect and influence the life and ministry of the congregation. If following the *private* mission of the denomination, the satisfaction of the dominant constituent voices of clergy and congregations, then deployment will give a good deal of attention to the needs of clergy—salary level and size of congregation based on tenure as well as the needs of the congregations—clergy who can satisfy members and not cause conflict in our congregation. However, if following the *public* mission of the denomination (the capacity to make disciples), then clergy are deployed on the basis of their past performance or future potential. Under this circumstance, effective younger, less tenured clergy may be deployed to more effective churches of greater size with larger salaries and resources. Congregations that have demonstrated their effectiveness or that are located in areas of greatest potential, rather than congregations with survival needs, will have greater claim on the most effective clergy. The standards of clergy deployment might actually be oppositional, depending on whether leaders work from the public or the private mission of the institution. It is possible to imagine the work and risk involved for denominational leaders to realign their systems to respond to the public rather than the private mission of the church when deploying clergy.

Similarly, mainline denominations have special interest groups or caucuses that represent particular subgroups or issues that are a part of the denominational structure and have claim on the denominational resources. Each group represents a concern or an opportunity for ministry, and each, on its own, is a legitimate expression of the church. But special interest groups, by their nature, compete for attention and resources. When navigating a wilderness, denominational leaders do not face the question of whether any subgroup represents a good or a worthwhile issue or idea. Good and worthwhile are fair descriptions of each of these multiple voices. When choices need to be made, the question is whether the group represents the right idea—right being defined by alignment with the public mission and the current public goals named by the system to address the mission. Helping a system shift from the established pattern of supporting a full range of good ideas and needs to directing resources and attention to the fewer right ideas and needs that will make a critical difference is daunting work for any leader.

The difficulty of the work that now lies before our leaders, denominational and congregational, is reflected in all three of these organizational issues because the work is now at the level not of structural or programmatic change but of culture change. Schein defines *culture* as "the learned, shared, tacit assumptions on which people base their daily behavior. It results in what is popularly thought of as 'the way we do things around here.' "[39] He also notes that even the people most involved in an organization on a daily basis "cannot without help reconstruct the assumptions on which daily behavior rests." Culture change requires as much *unlearning* as it involves new learning. Consider the three-level model of transformational change that Schein offers:[40]

Stage One: unfreezing: creating the motivation to change and unlearning old ways

Stage Two: learning new concepts and new meaning for old concepts

Stage Three: internalizing new concepts and meanings

Organizational culture change is exceedingly difficult and requires a long period of time that allows for all stages of the work to be completed. We need not be surprised to discover that forty years into our particular wilderness have not yet brought us to the promised land.

CHAPTER 4
SINGING THE LORD'S SONG IN A FOREIGN LAND

The Deeper Difficulty of a Multilayered Mission Field

He was a new pastor in a rural farm community, younger than most of the members of his congregation and sure that he had a mandate to update their worship in order to attract more and younger members. He introduced drums into their worship—a drum set positioned behind the chancel rail to be used in the new, second "alternative" worship service. After only two Sundays, two of the older leaders met with him to report growing anger in the congregation about having "those drums" in sacred space. Despite a conversation about the drums being meant for a group of people other than the long-term members who attended the regular service in which the drums were not used, it was clear that a compromise was needed. The pastor scoured the area shops to find drape material closely matching the altar area's dossal cloth, and he used it to cover the drums during the traditional worship service. Two weeks went by, and he was again met by the same leaders, who reported, "Pastor, we know what's under that cloth."

Seeking a better compromise, the pastor moved the drums and the alternative worship service into new space, which was the large Sunday school auditorium where the once full Sunday school classes met to sing prior to going into their separate classes. Unfortunately, it was an old building where, according to the old Akron architectural plan, the Sunday school space and the sanctuary were side by side, separated by large sliding wooden doors that could be opened to accommodate overflow seating in worship on special Sundays. The unfortunate part was that because of age, the doors were stuck in the open position and the Sunday school space was constantly visible from the sanctuary. After two more weeks passed, the same leaders appeared to report, "Pastor, we can still see them."

Jump ahead from that local church conflict consultation to a megachurch's Good Friday worship service, which my wife and I attended with our son and his family. At the conclusion of this dramatic, yet very prayerful service, the fifteen hundred people on this special Friday evening were hit by the sound of eight large tom drums hammered at bone-shaking intensity accompanied with bright lights flashing at pyrotechnic levels. There was a hush among the people as they worked their way to the exits because we had shared something deep and it was still with us.

It is a big jump from arguments about drums hidden under a cloth to the appreciation of drums hammered at a level where the vibrations were felt in a crowd and nothing else could be heard. It is just one of a constant stream of reminders that a radically changed mission field in North America has come to surround the churches. I was born into a church where the mission field was on foreign soil. Loren Mead, founding president of the Alban Institute, called that earlier time the "Christendom Paradigm" in which the mission field was beyond the boundaries of North America where it could be assumed that the faith would encounter people who were different from us and who had not yet heard the good news.[1] The operative assumption was that everyone within U.S. national boundaries was already Christian, either actively or nominally. Mission was a far-off enterprise to be managed by professional missionaries while mainline members could stay at home comfortable in a culture shared equally by all.

The mission field did not stay "out there." Today we recognize that the mission field is all around us in a complex and diverse culture where religions, philosophies, value systems, and consumer goods compete for attention and claim to bring meaning to a person's life. Increasingly the people who come to our congregations do not have the prior Christian or congregational experience that was once easily assumed in a "Christian nation." The literature around congregational transformation over the past fifteen years has increasingly focused on the need to move the church from maintenance (caring for the institution and the members inside the congregation) to mission (focusing on the community and the people who are not yet connected to Christianity and changing the lives of the people who are in the congregation). The mainline church is increasingly aware that it has been surrounded by a new mission field and that the church must compete with other voices with its good news of the truth of Jesus Christ. The mainline church has been working to learn how to speak to the new mission field so that the good news can be heard.

Is speaking to congregations in this new mission field about drums, or for that matter about technology, architecture, or informality, important? On the one hand, the answer must be yes. To speak to the new world, the medium must be familiar to the listener (don't forget Marshall McLuhan's famous dictum that the medium is the message). Insisting on the pipe organ as the only instrument to carry sacred music is disconnecting to some in a world where the only other places organs are heard are the Phillies' game and the roller rink. Long-term members in congregations often believe that newer and younger participants are spendthrifts for wanting a new computer system in the office for the pastor and staff to e-mail members and to manage website communications and congregational records. Far from being spendthrifts, these folk simply seek ways for the faith that they found inside the church to speak to the daily world in which they live outside the sanctuary world. Paying attention to the world in which people now live is critical so that ancient truths may be heard by new ears. New parents who search the Internet for reviews of the best stroller to buy for their new baby will not drop off that baby in a church nursery with worn cribs and tattered toys.

Will changing to drums, improved technology, renovated worship space, or a much more informal clergy who no longer wear preaching robes in the pulpit fix the problems of the mainline church? If the answer in the previous paragraph was yes, the answer, on the other hand, must also be no. Such simple solutions cannot so easily be found in a time when people use a myriad of competing cultural languages according to their generational cohort or personal preference. There is no one way for congregations to worship, provide programs, upgrade their facilities, or structure and staff their ministries. Difficult conversation among leaders is necessary to determine the appropriate way for a particular congregation in a particular time and a particular place to learn to speak to its particular mission field.

A part of the hard-earned learning in the earlier years of our particular exodus was that there are no singular answers in a complex culture that experiences rapid change. We have been learning the hard lesson that it is more important for the church to be appropriate than to be right. Although denominations and congregations may view some practices as "right," it remains more critical for the church to learn how to be appropriate with the people it is called to address. "Appropriate" means being able to say what can be heard. To say more would not matter; to say less would not help. In some places young adults are seeking faith only in nontraditional congregations where the setting, structure, and music resonate with their daily experience. In other places young adults are seeking faith in very traditional congregations where the sanctuary and music speak of a world very different from what they encounter each day. Once again we are driven back to the deeper questions of identity and purpose. Who is this congregation, and with what purpose does it seek to engage a particular group of people from its own corner of God's kingdom? Worship needs to be shaped, facilities need to be offered, programs need to be developed, organizational structure needs to fit, and all must be appropriate to the people who are invited to be engaged in faith in that congregation.

Certainly the challenge is all about change. We know more and more about change—the speed of change (YouTube, which that can take an event and share it with millions of onlookers in less than a minute), the amount of change (there was no e-mail when I began congregational consulting, and now I see people sit in gatherings, texting and tweeting), the consistency of change (where once the conceptual approach to change was episodic with the assumption of calm interludes between periods of change, the approach is now "whitewater," a constant churning of change), and the immediacy of change (the twenty-four-hour uninterrupted news cycle that connects us constantly with "breaking news" even if the newscaster has to invent the importance of what is reported). The task for congregational and denominational leaders is not just in keeping up with change, however, but shaping change appropriately for the gospel to have room in people's lives. Recall John Wimmer's insight from chapter 1 in which he noted that the challenge is not just to lead change but to lead both change and continuity. We need to learn to speak to this world without conforming to the world. We need to speak freshly to the people of a changed world without losing ancient practices and teachings that shape people in faith. All of this requires that we learn how to change ourselves.

Why Is This So Hard?

Much of the difficulty in the change necessary for the mainline church comes from the depth of learning that is required of us. It is immeasurably more difficult for us to change ourselves than to participate in attempts to change others. Again, as we have seen in the fourth path of our wandering in the wilderness, leadership may be more about asking the right questions that can prompt new learning than about identifying and installing the next answer.

Much of the focus of this book is on the progress we have been making in the wilderness. Again I note that what we have tried so far, what we have learned, has moved us ahead but not offered full answers. Here I would note the same about the tools, ideas, and theories that we have developed along the way. We have benefited from a continual mining of our biblical and theological disciplines, learning how to understand ourselves and talk with others. We have benefited from organizational systems and family systems analyses that have helped us see and try new things. But we have discovered the limits of each new idea or theory to fully explain or resolve our situation. Like that of all good journeys, successful progress moves us to the beginning of the next stage of learning to be explored. Our moment is to live in a fast-changing and complex culture. To continue to live in the wilderness we will also need new ideas and new theories about our culture that can help us understand ourselves and orient us in a chaotic place. A considerable learning task is required of our established denominations and congregations that cannot be done in the immediacy of the moment or by the decision making at a board or committee meeting. In order to have more clarity about why this work of living and doing ministry in our new mission field is so difficult, our leaders must move to balcony space. Moving to the balcony is an imposing step for leaders who feel that they are beset by the problems of their organization that seem to require that the leader remain standing in the fray and produce continual action.

Ronald Heifetz and Donald Laurie of Harvard University describe balcony space as the place where leaders can look at patterns in order to understand the whole of their situation.[2] Heifetz and Laurie distinguish between the field of action, which is *reactive space* constantly framed by action, and *balcony space*, which is where learning occurs. Reactive space is where leaders spend most of their time reacting and responding to the questions and problems constantly directed to them in their place of authority. Reactive space is also where boards and committees spend most of their time solving problems, planning next steps, and looking for the next fix. Reactive space is the less thoughtful of the two spaces, however. It is in reactive space that we deal with "urgent" matters, which Stephen Covey describes as issues insisting on action: "They're often popular with others. They're usually right in front of us. And often they are pleasant, easy, fun to do. But so often they are unimportant!"[3] Where it is estimated that a highly effective governing board of an institution or corporation can make about two informed decisions per year, denominational and congregational boards feel that they are not functioning well if two or three decisions are not made at every meeting. As leaders, we have been trained primarily as reactive problem solvers who operate in the field of action and constantly make decisions, often about unimportant or ineffective issues.

To understand why it is so difficult for a denomination or congregation that has been long established in traditional practices to live in a surrounding foreign land, we must step out of the reactive space of problem solving and move to the balcony. Patterns and principles that govern institutions and that now exist in our culture make it increasingly difficult for the established mainline church to make the leap into the new mission field at both the denominational and the congregational level. The reality is that change is now, and will continue to be, a complex, interactive, and vibrant environment in which we live. To understand change completely is not possible because of its interrelatedness and constant shifting. However, key issues of change that can be viewed from the balcony help offer insight into what needs to be addressed for the mainline church to live in the changed mission field. In this chapter we will take two views from the balcony: the ten-thousand-foot view and the thirty-thousand-foot view. At ten thousand feet we will take a look at the power of generational norms, which are primary governors of institutional behavior. There is more to "we've always done it like that" than an overused and frustrating adage. At thirty thousand feet we will take a look at dominant learning paradigms that determine human behavior and have now shifted again in our lifetime. If we are asking how to make disciples and how to reform the world, we require insight into how people are formed in life and what tools the church is now using. I will argue that the established church is currently living out of the two earliest of four learning paradigms by which people's lives are shaped.

The Ten-Thousand-Foot View: The Three Steps to How "We've Always Done It This Way" Became So Powerful

In a recent interview with a lay leader in a young congregation, I was struck by the clarity of his thinking. His congregation started only a few years ago with a primary mission of reaching out to unchurched people—"seekers." In their short history they had grown quickly to an average attendance of more than five hundred people at worship and were already able to identify people who were new to Christianity but who were maturing both in their personal lives and in their leadership with others. This congregation was within a mainline denomination that could give evidence to its capacity to address the new mission field surrounding it. The question we were exploring in our interview was to what extent this congregation used the resources of the denomination and to what extent the denomination used this church as a resource for other churches and other leaders. For the most part the lay leader reported that his workshops presented to leaders of other congregations were well received. He noted that in every presentation he always acknowledged in a very intentional way that his church had the advantage of starting from scratch with no backlog of "we've always done it that way." In contrast, he reported that his congregation used very few denominational resources because his congregation and long-established congregations lived "in different worlds." Whereas his congregation was already living in the world of people's daily lives within its identified mission field, he pointed out that most of the literature and workshops from his denomination were prepared from an earlier world (where we always do it that way) or were trying to motivate and direct congregations to move beyond that earlier world, closer to the mission field where this church already was. He and his coleaders were not interested in resources to help them "do church"; they needed help to "do mission." They weren't breaking out of old ways; they were developing new paths.

But what of long-established congregations that do not enjoy the advantage of escaping the "we've always done it this way" mind-set? In order for established congregations to move into the new mission field leaders need to understand and take seriously the origin and the power of the stasis that stems from "we've always done it this way." In the case of the mainline church, I point to three key principles of rigidity that make efforts of change difficult.

1. Norms Outlive the People Who Develop Them

The first principle is that the operative norms of an organization outlive the people who developed those norms. Norms are the hidden rules, the unspoken assumptions, the learned behavior that governs how "we do things here." Norms come from making a decision or learning how to do something that, when proved by experience to be effective, becomes the unquestioned way to continue to do things in the future. Norms are important for any organization to develop because they remove the need to continually make decisions about issues already decided.

Over time, a problem arises when norms remain tacit below the conscious level and continue to be practiced beyond their usefulness without questioning. Consider the congregation that has committed itself to ministry with young families in an effort to include younger people but operates with a norm of a special Christmas Eve worship service at 11:00 P.M. in order to welcome in Christmas by midnight. The Christmas Eve service was developed at a time when most in the congregation were beyond the life stage of having young children in their homes and, as adults, appreciated the meaningfulness of the late evening service. Once settled into learned behavior, the norm of an 11:00 P.M. service served the congregation well because each approaching Christmas season did not require board agenda time or extra meetings to determine when to have the Christmas Eve service that year. However, practiced for too long without question, the norm of an 11:00 P.M. service defeats the goal of the congregation to serve young families who experience the congregation as insensitive by inviting them to an important service that they cannot attend.

If the example of an 11:00 P.M. Christmas Eve service in a church committed to young family ministry seems too obvious, then consider the norms of stewardship practiced in many long-established congregations. The dominant behavior of stewardship in most established congregations centers on the offering collected on Sunday morning as part of the worship liturgy when members are invited to ritually offer a portion of their wealth by placing money (cash or checks) into a passing collection plate. Each Sunday's offering is to be a weekly portion of an annual pledge. When stewardship is practiced in this singular way over time without question, consider the cultural distance that can build as people live more and more in a cashless (and checkless) society, so that their church is the only place where they have to shift to a less familiar way of managing their resources. Consider also the developing patterns of worship attendance: some participants, although committed to their church and to their lives of faith, attend worship less regularly; others, although deeply involved in the mission life of their church, might never or very infrequently attend worship. When the norm for stewardship education and practice is narrowly defined by previous assumptions of supporting the church budget and happening only within the context of weekly worship, it invites people into a ritual that is increasingly out of touch with the way in which they now seek to practice the daily stewardship of their personal resources.

Consider the jump to my experience in the megachurch that used thundering drums for its Good Friday service. At the appointed time for the offering on that following Easter Day, small white plastic buckets were passed with efficient speed through the rows of people to collect whatever gifts they wanted to offer and then were set on the floor by the person in the last seat of the row to be collected when the service was over. It was resonant of the experience of a large evangelical campaign like a Billy Graham crusade, where buckets were passed along the rows. However, if one glanced in the offering buckets of this megachurch while leaving worship, the lack of gifts in the drums was notable. Very little money was given in this way. Most people in this congregation who were committed to supporting their church's mission through their stewardship set up automatic withdrawals from their bank accounts as they did with so many other ongoing payments by which they directed their resources. Are white buckets better than offering plates? Not necessarily; however, the invitation to the stewardship of Christian living must be appropriate and connect with the life that the particular people lead and the way they have been culturally trained to manage their resources. Established congregations find it difficult to step away from the traditional ritual offering in worship, which is framed by ushers with offering plates formally collecting gifts while the choir sings a special anthem, because of their norms of worship and congregational life.

The power of norms is such that they outlive the people (or generation) who established them. One surprising discovery that came from reviewing the data from conflict consultations that I did over a ten-year period is that a person's tenure of membership or participation in a congregation is of greater influence on behavior in that congregation than is the person's age or the preferences of his or her generational cohort.[4] In reviewing the conflict consultations I was struck by the frequency with which younger members in a congregation were the carriers of the established way of doing things as always done. Particularly curious were the situations in which younger members were strident in defending practices in a congregation that actually were not to their advantage or that they would not practice in other settings. Consider the thirty-year-old woman who was visibly upset by other young women who did not quickly volunteer to watch children in the nursery during worship because they wanted to be in worship. The suggestion of paying a child care worker for the nursery was offensive to this woman because "mothers have always taken turns being in the nursery in our church." In terms of her cultural values and practices outside her church this young mother would no doubt choose to pay for child care or pay for her child's participation in programs that she herself would not lead. However, in her congregation, where she had participated for the full thirty years of her life, she was driven by the tacit norm that child care is always the responsibility of the mothers of the church.

2. Each Generational Cohort Develops Its Own Value System

The second principle that produces rigidness in our established congregations is found in generational cohort theory, which notes that each generational cohort develops its own value system as a corrective to the excess that its members see in the value system of the generation preceding them. One example is the continual shifting of parenting practices; one generation develops its standards of raising children as a reaction to its experience with parents who are regarded as too strict (or conversely, too permissive and attentive) in raising children. This natural compensatory shifting of values and practices from one generation to another over a host of issues and practices often devolves into arguments and opposition that ossify the life of a congregation or denomination, which I have already described as systems with deeply established and tacit norms of behavior based on earlier generations.

William Strauss and Neil Howe define a *generation* as "the aggregate of all people born over roughly the span of a phase of life who share a common location in history and, hence, a common collective persona."[5] Strauss and Howe identified a cyclical repetition of four dominant value systems that serially surface as correctors to the preceding value system. Each of the four dominant value systems comes around to take its turn to once again balance the human experience across generational shifts and experiences. They noted that every forty years or so "the persona of each phase of life becomes nearly the opposite of that established by the generation that had once passed through it."[6] Making it even more difficult for congregations and denominations in this moment of great global and cultural change is that North America has simultaneously been going through one of its forty-year moments of generational opposition. It is a "watershed moment," as described by the generational research of Jackson Carroll, director of pastoral leadership research in the Pulpit & Pew project. A watershed is that geographical ridge or boundary from which water will flow in opposite directions to the various rivers, lakes, or oceans, where it will end. A watershed speaks of movement in two opposite directions. Carroll noted that "the major generational watershed, as far as religious beliefs and practices are concerned, is between those who in our research we call Pre-boomers (born prior to 1946) and those who have come after."[7] Certainly there are differences between late boomers, Gen Xers, Millennials, and those cohorts that follow, and the marketing industry and the media highlight and exploit those differences. In terms of values and practices, however, these later generational expressions are more like one another than like those of the pre-boomers.

Writing as early as 1981, Daniel Yankelovich, a well-established voice in the market research industry, was able to identify what he called a major shift in the American giving/getting compact that helps us understand the dominant watershed divide. The established giving/getting compact for the pre-boomers was expressed by Yankelovich as follows:

> I give hard work, loyalty and steadfastness. I swallow my frustrations and suppress my impulse to do what I would enjoy, and do what is expected of me instead. I do not put myself first; I put the needs of others ahead of my own. I give a lot, but what I get in return is worth it. I receive an ever-growing standard of living, and a family life with a devoted spouse and decent kids.[8]

The list of what Yankelovich notes as the worthwhile return on sacrifice continues. However, following the pre-boomers who lived out of that previous giving/getting compact that was pushed to its extreme by the Great Depression and World War II, the subsequent generations, wary of continued sacrifices that seemed no longer warranted, sought to modify the giving/getting compact that made their predecessor generations so dour and demanding. From the boomers on through other generational cohorts there has been a continual reworking of the giving/getting compact in every one of its dimensions: work, family life, leisure, the meaning of success, and the search for meaning.

In my book on the multigenerational congregation I identified four sets of oppositional markers that live side by side in congregations and denominations as the legacy of this watershed shift in cultural variables:

Pre-boomer Values	vs.	Consumer Values
Deferring pleasure	vs.	Instant gratification
Group orientation	vs.	Individual orientation
Assumptions of sameness	vs.	Assumptions of difference
Spirituality of place	vs.	Spirituality of journey[9]

In each of these four dimensions the dominant value first named belonged to the pre-boomer side of the watershed divide while the dominant consumer value second named belonged to the various generations that followed. The second value in each case is the opposite of the first. Looking at the oppositional nature of these values that live side by side in the healthiest of our congregations and denominations offers hints to how the natural development of norms named in the first principle explaining the rigidness of many of our systems is amplified by the opposition of generational values. Because the established norms outlive the people who establish them (principle one), the oppositional nature of the established norms of subsequent generations that then seek to enter into the denomination or congregation (principle two) ratchets up the resistance expressed by "we've always done it that way" from a general resistance to change to a full-fledged battle over what is right. Let's try two examples at the congregational level.

Example One: Deferring Pleasure Versus Instant Gratification

The leaders in one congregation I worked with were planning a new addition to their church and raised the question of when it was appropriate to contact an architect to talk about developing a formal architectural plan. This small rural congregation lived close to the early giving/getting compact of the pre-boomer generations. When I asked how much of their estimated cost for the new addition they had on hand, the response was, "We only have 93 percent of the money in the bank so far." Compare that to the conversation I had with leaders of another, larger congregation that had a fair number of leaders who came from the consumer generational cohorts. The conversation in this church was about refinancing the balance of their original $1.3 million loan in order to reduce the monthly expense so that they could use the capital funds on hand from the most recent campaign to leverage an additional $4.6 million loan for the start of the next phase of their facilities development. Yes, each was a different congregation in a different circumstance. However, because of the generational divide of values around the giving/getting compact, in each of these congregations if the other strategy had been offered (deferring work in the one congregation until all money was in hand, and leveraging debt in the other congregation in order to move ahead with work), it would not have been received as a new idea. It would have been received as an offense. Values are not negotiable.[10] Values lead to people taking positions that they view as right and from which they will view other positions as wrong. Frequently "we've always done it that way" is about a lot more than how we always did it.

Example Two: Spirituality of Place Versus Spirituality of Journey

Consider one of the great differences in assumptions about where God is to be encountered in the Christian life. The earlier generational value system of the pre-boomers focused on the integrity of the group. One knew who one was because of one's group: one's family, one's profession or work group, one's social group, one's denomination or congregation. Since identity had to do with belonging to groups, the assumption in one's spiritual life was that the place in which God was most likely to be encountered was where the spiritual group was to be found—in the church building. Membership then was of great significance so that one belonged to a place and to a people where God was experienced. The church building was of great importance because that was where the group gathered to be with God. Members changed their vocabulary and even the tone and volume of their voices as they moved from parking lot to sanctuary, because they were entering sacred space. The assumption was that one would live out one's spiritual life with the same group, going to the singular congregation of one's group for all of one's spiritual needs and the marking of one's major life transitions.

Consider then the consumer cohort individual who practices not the spirituality of place but the spirituality of journey. She goes to a United Methodist church because she deeply appreciates the worship and enjoys the music. She takes her children to a local Lutheran church because it has a better youth program. She attends a Wednesday morning Bible study led by a Baptist woman who seems to know so much about Scripture. And she would never miss her yoga class on Friday afternoon because it is the one place and time in her hectic week when she feels centered and at peace. Living out of her values of individuality (where identity is established without dependence on membership in a group), she holds the assumption that God is to be encountered not just where her preferred Christian group may be but also wherever she may be, in multiple places—a spirituality of journey. The multiple places can take her from congregation to congregation and even outside her faith tradition (yoga), and she will feel no compulsion to be a member at any one place in order to participate in what she has found of value. Although deeply committed to discipleship and living a Christ-focused life, she has never formally sought membership in any one congregation because it never seemed to be an important question. This is a different attitude and different behavior based on a shift of values, of course. But seen from the perspective of those who practice the spirituality of place, those who practice a spirituality of journey are not just exercising choice; they are evidencing an offense. They are judged as "bad members" who are not faithful to the one congregation and are not disciplined in their attention to the singular group where it is assumed that all spiritual needs are to be met.

3. The Economical Response to Differences Is Regulation

The third principle to be added to this explanation of how we ended up with a rigid institution that belongs to an earlier time has to do with the regulatory nature of our mainline denominations. In their essay on the organizational structures of denominations, Craig Dykstra and James Hudnut-Beumler track how mainline denominations have moved from earlier forms of constitutional confederacies (1780s) to corporations, or at least organizations that live out of a corporate model (1830s through 1860s), to regulatory agencies (1960s).[11]

Dykstra and Hudnut-Beumler point out that beginning in the 1830s through the 1860s, mainline denominations followed the dominant cultural pattern of organizations to structure themselves as corporations. Corporations have a commitment to orderliness and structure, to predictable decision making, and to the centralization of authority. Corporations work best when norms and practices produce uniformity across the organization, a style that fits well with the pre-boomer values of group, deferred pleasure, and sameness. Beginning in the 1960s, however, the cultural uniformity surrounding the denomination began to break down. It was a change that went well beyond the borders of denominations and was experienced broadly in all organizations, corporations, and institutions in the culture at that moment. Individuality and the search for differences introduced a break from uniform assumptions that once guided corporations and denominations and that once determined the relationship between the denomination and its congregations and between the congregation and its members. Dykstra and Hudnut-Beumler note that the response beginning in the 1960s was for the mainline denominations to become more and more regulatory. It was a matter of economy. As more and more differences of preference and practice were introduced, it became increasingly "expensive" for denominations to manage the differences. Market solutions were expensive because they required competing in the marketplace for denominational loyalty by providing what was most helpful or meaningful.

Instead of market solutions or negotiation, the mainline denominations quite naturally followed a path of regulation. The simpler, economical approach was to sharpen the regulations by which congregational and denominational life was to be lived. When there are competing preferences or needs, it is much simpler and efficient to respond by saying, "Here are the rules." The dependence on regulatory responses should not come as a surprise since it is a cultural response to the messiness of deep change as experienced by an orderly and managed generation.

The preferences and experiments in congregational and denominational life were met with legislation—a plethora of new regulations blossomed in denominational books of polity as a way to manage the differences and the discomfort of change. During this same period (1960–2000), books of polity such as the Presbyterian *Book of Order* and the United Methodist *Book of Discipline* grew from pamphlet and small-book size to large complex volumes more easily managed on CD-ROM discs. The Internal

Revenue Code and health-care regulations have also grown exponentially through continuous legislation in this same period. These systems have become rigid through the imposition of accumulated rules. Yet the impulse to control through requirements does not result in clarity and tidiness but in fact creates complexity that further constrains and inhibits movement toward change. Congregational and middle judicatory leaders in mainline denominations have expressed their concern that as the need for new ideas and new structures increases within their denominations, the primary response of national offices and national denominational staff people has been to request more reports and increased compliance (that is, additional regulation). The need to control and regulate has the tendency to make change more difficult without adding any agreement or coordination to the efforts of change.

The impact of these three principles together created not just resistance to change but institutionalized the stasis of "always doing it this way." Again we can glimpse the importance of learning more about the fourth path in our particular wilderness identified in the previous chapter. Increasingly full agreement across an array of differences and preferences is not possible in our healthiest congregations and denominations. Regulation and legislation do not provide the agreement that we seek and impose further rigidity through their complexity. What does hold people together across their differences is a shared identity centered on a common purpose. Escaping the rigidity of "we've always done it that way" is not to be found by proving one way to be either right or wrong but by providing a purpose for doing it a different and an appropriate way for the specific people that the church seeks to address in any given setting.

The Thirty-Thousand-Foot View: How Four Shifts in the Way We Communicate Led to Four Shifts in How We See Ourselves

Individual and competing preferences, yes. Generational differences, yes. All of this is present in mainline congregations and denominational systems. But moving up to the thirty-thousand-foot view, we can see that the challenge of a multilayered mission field is even larger and more daunting.

From a sufficient distance it becomes clear that this new mission field surrounding the church congregations and denominations includes multiple groups of people who might live side by side in the same community, even in the same family, but who experience their lives in very different ways. The bottom line then for mainline denominations is not to help its congregations "do church" better or even to "rethink church" but to allow multiple expressions of church to exist side by side in order to do ministry with a multilayered mission field. The differences that now exist among people in North America are at the level of paradigmatic shifts driven by changes in technology that redefine life experience.

To get a sense of the depth of these differences, we will turn to a discussion of four dominant paradigms of communication theory. Through communication, we share information, we learn, and we search for wisdom; therefore, through communication, we are formed as persons. A very helpful application of communication theory comes from Rex Miller. A businessman with training in both theology and communications

70

theory, Miller offers a matrix of four paradigms of communication that humans have used to pass on information and wisdom: oral, print, broadcast, and digital. He argues the following:

- When our communication tools change, our perception changes.
- Changed perception creates a changed understanding.
- Changed understanding changes our psychological makeup.
- Changed psyches change our interaction with the world.
- Change in our interactions with our world change our relationships with one another.
- Changes in our relationships lead to changes in the institutions that facilitate those relationships.[12]

The way we communicate develops a paradigm of living—a set of assumptions and practices that are sufficiently integrated and integrating that they shape a person's experience and understanding of his or her world. In this case, Miller's argument is that the ways in which information and wisdom are received and processed by people are products of the technology available for the task and actually bring shape to the way people order their lives and relationships. The following chart summarizes the four dominant paradigms of communication that have influenced human behavior:

Paradigm	Mediating Medium	Mode
Oral: B.C. to A.D. 1500	Ear	Dominated by relationship
Print: 1500–1950	Eye	Dominated by logic
Broadcast: 1950–2010	Experience (spectator)	Breakdown of logic— chaos
Digital: 2010–	Experience (interactive)	Future perfect tense

The Oral Paradigm

Historically, the longest lasting paradigm of sharing information and wisdom began with the very first communication by humans in which one person gave information to another by telling. The oral paradigm depended on one person's passing information to another—a process mediated by the ear and dominated by relationship. In order to learn something new, a person had to be in personal relationship with the one who held the information. Learning would happen by listening. Information and wisdom were managed by the roles and responsibilities given to individuals. Teachers were the actual containers of wisdom. To learn required a relationship with the teacher who would not only share information but also practice wisdom. Storytellers memorized "text" for faithful transmission and held the responsibility of passing on the stories unchanged as an early form of historical record. They also provided interpretation, which helped shape understanding.

> When weary Anglo-Saxon warriors gathered in the mead hall to drink and heal their wounds, they often listened to the wandering poets known as *scops*. Accompanied by the harp, the *scop* recited stories of adventurers who dared to journey into unchartered territories. . . . Bearing tales of the larger world, the *scop* traveled from village to village as well as to the houses of the mighty, connecting people separated by distance and social status—connecting them as well to their literary and religious heritage.[13]

People and their understanding of the world were shaped by what they heard from their leaders, their teachers, and their interpreters.

The Print Paradigm

The dominance of the oral paradigm was broken by the subsequent stage dominated by print. The paradigm shifted at the point of the invention of the printing press by Johann Gutenberg in A.D. 1448. Writing itself was certainly not new. As early as 5000 B.C., the Sumerians invented writing as a means to stay in touch over distance with their trading partners. Although writing had been practiced for centuries, the ongoing development of written communication included the search for technologies that would increase the volume and accuracy of communications while reducing the time needed to send and receive communication. This ongoing development of communication and communication technology has, in large part, been in the service of trade.[14] It was at the point of the invention of the printing press that information and wisdom could, for the first time, be easily housed in documents to be shared broadly instead of carried by specific individuals. The medium of communication shifted from ear to eye—from depending on relationship to depending on the logic encountered in the document. The shift moved communication from the teacher to the text. Indeed, the role of teacher shifted from being the container of wisdom to being the guide who would direct the path of the learner through the documents and books where information and wisdom were now housed.

Following the initial oral paradigm, the print paradigm became dominant over recent centuries, which have been witness to the most rapid development of human civilization. It is important to note that the print paradigm has also been the dominant mode of training of the older clergy and denominational leaders of our present time. These leaders were shaped by formal and comprehensive logic-driven systematic theologies and were trained in practices of preaching that centered on explanation and persuasion as logical expressions of the conviction that faith was an issue of right understanding and correct belief. Much of the leadership training as well as the structure and practice of current denominationalism has been deeply fashioned by this print paradigm.

The Broadcast Paradigm

In the 1950s, the beginning of the broadcast paradigm, Miller points out that once again the invention and development of new technology in television and modern communication shifted our orientation. The shift this time was from eye to experience. No longer were information and wisdom housed primarily in logically regulated printed texts requiring the discipline of inquisitiveness; now they could be mediated by the individual's personal experience. The flow of information quickly became so abundant and unregulated that the individual was put into the position of spectator needing to learn how to attend to information selectively. The mode of communication at this point shifted from the initial paradigm of relationship—through logic—to chaos, which was the breakdown of logic. Individuals in search of personal wisdom needed to find their own way through an overabundance of information that was often contradictory. Miller identifies this paradigm as "broadcast," which implies a curious polarity in which one experiences communication as part of a vast group but does so individually. For example, a television viewer is part of a vast crowd of millions of viewers watching a program, but he does so individually in his own home. Similarly in this paradigm, an individual may attend a rock concert in a huge crowd of ten thousand participants, but she experiences it individually in a chaotic huddle of other individuals listening to sound too loud to permit connection even with those in the most immediate vicinity.

It can be argued that television evangelism and the megachurch are residents of the broadcast paradigm, with hundreds and thousands of people having a common experience that does not need to be shared even with the persons sitting on either side of them. Miller observes that it is congruent that this time of the broadcast paradigm was the same period of the phenomenal growth in the number of the largest churches where people could attend as part of a group of one thousand to ten thousand people in a theater setting and yet experience the communication as an individual spectator. In their research on megachurches (congregations with average worship attendance of two thousand or greater), Scott Thuma and Dave Travis note that by 1960 there were only fifty in the United States. Beginning in the 1970s, when the broadcast paradigm was at strength, that number grew exponentially until by the time of their data gathering in 2005, there were 1,210 megachurch congregations.[15] We need to keep in mind that communication in this broadcast paradigm, whether through television, rock concerts, televangelists, or megachurches, is mediated by experience, but by *passive* experience.

The Digital Paradigm

Miller points to the personal computer and subsequent digital communication through networks and Internet as introducing a new and not yet fully shaped paradigm of communication that is experience based but is now interactive rather than passive. The individual is not limited to being engaged with the tool of the communication— the computer, the e-mail, the chat room, or the video game; there is also the smaller, self-selecting community (microcommunity) that is simultaneously engaged through shared use of the tool of communication. For the people of the broadcast paradigm, playing a video game is an individual experience between the person and the game. For the people of the digital paradigm, playing a video game is a connection to a small community of people simultaneously engaged—perhaps even globally on the Internet—with the same game. In one paradigm the game isolates the person; in another it is a tool of connection to a small community. In the digital paradigm the experience is interactive and immediate—what Miller calls "the future perfect tense" in which an action is already completed at the point of intention. This paradigm is still in formation, as indicated by Miller's offering the date of 2010 as a marker for this paradigm's emergence as a dominant influence. But this newly evolving paradigm suggests the development of smaller gatherings than the megachurch offers, settings more interactive than passive, teaching done by interactive sharing rather than by trained leaders, and microcommunity relationships shaped by shared and immediate experience.

The Implication for Denominations and Congregations

Miller argues that just as the changing paradigms of communication have shifted the way in which people engage with information and wisdom, so has there been a concomitant shift in relationships between parties, both individually and organizationally. The earlier summary chart of the paradigms can be extended to note the shift in relationships and modes of learning:

Paradigm	Mediating Medium	Mode	Relationship	Learning
Oral	Ear	Relationship	*Covenant:* relational; blessings and curses	*Process-centered:* learning as a preparatory process
Print	Eye	Logic	*Vows:* contract benefits and costs (litigation)	*Content-centered:* learning as mastery of material common to all
Broadcast	Experience (spectator)	Chaos	*Promises:* no-fault agreements, mutual benefits	*Experience-centered:* the focus is on individual students and their unique needs

Digital	Experience (interactive)	Immediacy	*Agreement:* social cohesion through webbed networks; microcommunity	*Context-centered:* collective experience takes precedence over individual and private needs

In the earliest oral paradigm the relationship between the congregation and its members or between the denomination and its congregations was understood covenantally—a deep pledge of being connected, much as the idea of covenant in the Old Testament frames the relationship between God and Israel. It is a deep commitment in which the people pledge to be faithful to Yahweh as their only God and God pledges that Israel will be God's people. The relationship is managed by blessings and curses. When Israel honors the relationship, the people are blessed; when the relationship is broken, they experience being cursed.

The language most used currently by established denominations to describe their intended relationship with congregations is still covenantal (or "connectional" in its more organizational form). Such covenantal constructs assume a belonging: Israel belongs to God and God to Israel; the congregation belongs to the denomination and the denomination to the congregation; the member belongs to the congregation and the congregation to the member. Faithfulness in the relationship is measured. God blesses and curses people depending on their actions and attitudes, and at their bravest, the prophets blessed and cursed God in return. Continuing the covenantal paradigm, blessings and curses are modified as sanctions by denominations as they evaluate congregations as either "good" or "not good," depending on their levels of support, participation, and compliance with denominational positions. Congregations that use denominational literature and pay their missional support of the denomination give evidence of their covenant relationship and are blessed as good congregations. Members who don't attend worship regularly or don't support the church budget with their pledge and gifts are cursed as bad members.

In the oral paradigm, forming a person in faith was highly relational between the individual and the leader. Clergy, in an earlier time, inquired directly about an individual's experience in living out a Christian life either one-on-one or in small covenant groups. Over time the inquiring relationship moved beyond the clergy to other leaders, but in many of our small and midsize highly relational congregations, faith formation continues to be expressed through relationships.

As the paradigm shifted from oral to print, the foundation of relationships shifted from personal contact to contracts. Contracts are logically defined agreements based on benefits and costs. When trade was beginning to develop beyond regional limits, the merchants in Portugal who financed the trading ships that traveled to the East Indies for spices could not hope to manage the agreement with the ship's captain face-to-face over such great distance, so they set out clear expectations in writing that stated who was to bear what costs and who would reap what portion of the benefits. The medium of print quickly introduced such logical frameworks to all relationships. Indeed, one founding purpose of the legal profession was the management of property rights: who owns, who benefits, who pays costs, and what consequences are levied if agreements are not met. These are logically and methodically managed relationships.

If Christian community was originally framed covenantally because it was embedded in the oral paradigm, the creation, development, and maturation of both congregations and denominations over the past several centuries happened while embedded in the print paradigm. It is not surprising, then, that relationships between denominations and congregations are still described covenantally but are overlaid with contractual agreements and limits as found in books of polity. Especially in the last century, as the print paradigm reached its zenith, books of polity, which began as founding documents and descriptions of basic governance, blossomed into the large volumes of legislated agreements, rules, and procedures described earlier.

Faith formation, similarly, went through a movement from relationships to information and dependence on curriculum to carry the necessary information. The printing press made Scripture available to all without dependence on clergy. The sharing and shaping of the information common to all and needed for faithful living continued over time into full-blown systematic theologies for adults and age-level appropriate materials for children.

In the final two paradigms, broadcast and digital, Miller points to relationships less clearly formed, less dependable, and less predictable. In the broadcast paradigm the deep pledges of covenant have morphed into more malleable promises to stay in relationship as long as both parties continue to find mutual benefit. Walking through a parallel interpretation of the marriage relationship using these paradigms, one can see the earliest stage of marriage as a covenant (recognized sacramentally in some traditions) modulated to a more contractual agreement with costs levied if the contract is broken in divorce, to a promise that endures as long as the partners find mutual benefit but can be broken or ended without claim—no fault. One of the frustrations of denominations is the "weakening" of the relationship between the congregation and the denomination, much like the weakening of the bond between husband and wife in the marriage covenant. A measure of that frustration is seen as denominational offices worry over the covenanted or connectional financial support of the denominations through the congregations' missional giving while the members in the congregation increasingly ask about what services they receive for their annual "franchise fee." As noted above, a measure of that frustration in the congregation is the evaluation levied by long-term members of the congregation on those people who participate fully and faithfully but see no need to join. In these final two paradigms there is also a commensurate shift in faith formation. Once managed by relationship and a standardized content, the end result was a church "member," a person added to the covenant group. Faith formation focuses no longer on membership but on discipleship—a changed life for the individual. But movement into these two newest paradigms is raising difficult and confusing questions about how the life of a disciple is formed: whether formation can be taught or must be more simply learned; whether formation needs a leader or is shaped by the theological interpretation of the experience and driving questions of the individual or group.

In the long line of human history there have been only four communication paradigms, two of which have dominated all of human history until the most recent generations. And certainly development of human experience over centuries is not so neat and tidy that as a new paradigm develops, others drop away. More accurately, we shift from paradigm to paradigm as the situation warrants, and we operate out of all four paradigms (with more or less comfort depending on our age and generational cohort) through which we understand ourselves and our world even as one paradigm becomes dominant. However, it is helpful to remember that within the past fifty years the culture has shifted from using two paradigms to four paradigms. It can be argued that while four paradigms are operating in the culture, the Christian church remains most dependent on the first two. For example, Christian denominations and congregations are organizational constructions of a biblical people, so it is fitting and important that covenantal pledges of faithfulness are used to inform the relationships of community. Nonetheless, the argument here is not that this covenantal/connectional model is inappropriate, but employed as the only model it may not serve denominations or congregations well in effectively managing the variety of relational assumptions now operative in the present culture. Although framing faith-based relationships as covenantal may be foundational for the church's theology, Miller's overview of paradigms suggests that a single model may produce ongoing and growing disappointment. Before 1950, there were only two paradigms operative: the oral and the print. While the print paradigm was dominant, the people of congregations and denominations easily understood the covenant relationship because of its biblical origin and its similarity to contractual costs and benefits. With the speed of technological development, we now live in a new swirl of assumptions about relational connections that introduces a messiness and unpredictability undermining the singular assumption of covenant. A similar argument can be offered about how we remain tethered to relationships and right content as the most important tools of formation. The new mission field that surrounds the church is complex and interactive and requires the church to develop leaders who can engage the culture in multiple ways.

Conclusion: Why It Is So Hard, along with Thoughts Concerning What to Do

Steady in purpose but flexible in strategy. Living now amid competing generational preferences and living now amid multiple paradigms of human learning through which people order their world, the church can no longer be wed to a "right way." God, community, and meaning are now sought after in multiple ways. The multiplicity of our current culture makes our efforts at change so much more difficult. It seems then that the appropriate response of leaders is first to accept the fact of this multiplicity. A helpful way to summarize the impact of the changes that have developed in the mission field now surrounding the mainline church is to note that we have moved from a convergent to a divergent environment, a distinction drawn by British organizational expert Charles Handy.[16] A convergent environment is one in which the question is the same for everyone and the answer is the same for everyone. For any group of people seated in the same room a convergent question would be, how far is it to the nearest airport? The question would be the same for everyone, and the answer would be the same for everyone. A divergent environment is one in which the question is the same for everyone, but the answers are different. A divergent question for that same group of people seated in the same room would be, why do you want to go to the airport? The question is the same for everyone, but the answers will be multiple and different. The old environment that surrounded the mainline church at its strength was a convergent world that prompted and prospered in a convergent denominational structure. The new mission field is divergent. Old questions that were once convergent (such as, What is meaningful worship? How do you live a faithful life? or How do you build community?) are now divergent and dividing in the new mission field, prompting new and divergent strategies even within the same denomination.

There is no identifiable form for the new church in the wilderness yet. Some would point to the contemporary church, while others want to point to the postmodern church. The large church and the megachurch have their advocates. The emerging church, the emergent church, and the practicing congregation are being watched closely to measure their connection to the culture. The appropriate question is not, Which of these is the new wineskin that will hold the new wine? The church will not find and does not need a uniform voice in which to speak to a diverse and divided culture. There cannot be one form or a dominant model of church in a future in which the learning paradigms are now more realistically changing every fifty years or less with technological advances, as opposed to our earlier histories where a paradigm might last five hundred years. The learning in the journey through our particular wilderness is that multiple expressions of the church will be needed to speak to the multiple people living side by side in the new mission field. Once again our path in the wilderness is driving us back to getting clear about identity and purpose not only as a denomination but also congregation by congregation, agency by agency, office by office. The new mission field has so many voices that those who would do ministry must be clear about their purpose and hold their strategies very loosely.

The challenge for mainline denominations will be to discover ways to hold a much wider array of congregational forms together around a shared story of identity and purpose. The corporate vestige that remains within denominational structures on both the national and the regional level will be severely tested because it is no longer time for uniformity and control. Among other prices to be paid will be the disassembly of "fairness"—equal treatment of all who share in a common community. Emergent churches built around microcommunities are intense and unique and cannot be branded. Very large churches and megachurches are the exceptions to the congregational rule and require forms of leadership not practiced or needed in other forms of congregation. Small family churches are resilient and have an important continuing role to play for some in our new mission field but will increasingly be unable to pay for professional clergy leadership and will learn to live by another standard. If denominations are to house within their community such a disparate group of forms of congregations that are now developing, a new model of denomination will begin to emerge that is less about regulations and uniformity and more about a shared story of purpose and identity that holds a network of unmatched congregations, leaders, and people in a whole. In order for multiple expressions of the church to live as needed in an increasingly complex culture, the challenge to denominational connection will need to grow even more complex and difficult even as we search for simpler, and as the sciences say, more "elegant" solutions.

The challenge will also extend into the way that we train our leaders. We no longer will be able to depend on experts in theology or congregational leadership. Experts are those who are steeped so deeply within their own discipline that they become exceptional at the practice of that discipline. Such expertise serves well when there is a uniform mission field and questions can be divided into their disciplinary components. Instead the new mission field will increasingly demand what Jagdish Sheth and Andrew Sobel call "deep generalists"—people who are so deeply grounded in their central way of understanding the world that they are able to look widely around them to bring meaning in multiple situations.[17] Whereas the expert is deep, the deep generalist is both deep and broad. Whenever I consider the deep generalist, I think of a conversation with my friend and teacher Harrell Beck, who was professor of Old Testament Wisdom literature at the Boston University School of Theology, where I studied. Harrell began each class with a prayer. And even though the maximum number of people who could register for the course was around twenty-five, there might be an additional twenty-five or more people in the room for the opening prayer. Harrell prayed for the school, for the city, for the world, and for the moment. When he finished, those not registered for the course quietly left and the teaching began. I once asked Harrell how he did it. How could he understand so much about the city and the world that his prayers could make sense of it all? He responded by saying that he didn't know any more about the city and the world than I did and he didn't read any more newspapers than I did. But he did know, he continued to explain, Old Testament Wisdom literature. And when looking through that lens, he was able to see things otherwise hidden, and he was able to find meaning otherwise missing.

Harrell was a deep generalist. Deeply grounded in his discipline, which was also his passion, he could see beyond his specialty to work broadly across many people, many cultures, and a mass of issues to speak the word of faith. The new preparation of leaders will require more attention to deep generalists. The new mission field will need clergy who are so deeply grounded in theology and faith practices that they develop not only a profession but a personal passion and way of life for themselves. From that deep grounding they will be able to speak broadly using multiple strategies to present the central purpose of faith, teaching a vocabulary of faith not as a specialized language but as an interpretation of the experience of life that people are already having—in their multiple forms. This may be close to what Craig Dykstra calls "the pastoral imagination," a practical wisdom that includes theological knowledge but also the skill to interpret contexts and situations in appropriate forms of leadership.[18]

The purpose of the church is to change people's lives through an encounter with the truth of Christ, an awareness of the immanent incarnation of God, and a sense of grace that sustains life. To bring such change to the disparate people who live in the new mission field, the church in all of its forms will need to hold its strategies loosely enough to allow the mission field to change the church.

CHAPTER 5

THIS IS NOT YOUR FATHER'S WILDERNESS
The New Leadership

The message that I got clearly when I entered my first church as a twenty-four-year-old pastor was now that I had arrived, young adults were expected to follow. A number of the church leaders felt that their problem was solved. With a new young pastor in place, other young adults and married couples with young families (like the pastor and his family) would not be far behind. But the other message that I discerned more slowly was that these new young people were to arrive and be part of the congregation without those already there making any adjustments to their way of doing things, as discussed in the previous chapter. Changes in worship were suspect. New members elected to the administrative board were welcomed only if they didn't suggest new ways to do things. New community groups were not to be invited into the church building because they might break windows or scratch the walls of the fellowship hall, which wasn't fully paid for yet. Some changes moved ahead by crisis, such as the time my wife and her friend Joanne announced that they were boycotting worship and would not leave their children in the nursery until the nursery was habitable and safe. But the dominant message was that I was expected to bring new life and new people into this congregation as their pastoral leader as long as I didn't change anything in the process.

Of course, that was quite a few years ago when I stepped into that first church as their new pastor, and it can be argued that much has been learned since then and that conditions are different now. In fact, that is part of my argument in the first chapters of this book that the first three paths in the wilderness have already brought us far. But something quite a bit deeper was also going on in that congregation in those earlier days that continues at the heart of the mainline dilemma today. The deeper something had to do with assumptions about leadership. I was being asked for leadership and simultaneously being constrained from using it

Congregational lay and clergy leaders and denominational executives and staff are being asked today to provide new direction for the mainline denominations that wish to steer away from trends that have dominated past decades and that are believed to have weakened the denominations. These leaders, however, are being asked for leadership in a managerial system. It is a task for which the denominations have not trained their leaders. It is a task that, if well done, will not be met with full appreciation but will be challenged by resistance in many quarters—not least of which will be the national church itself because of its most recent form as a regulatory agency.

The United Methodist Church as a Managerial System

The United Methodist Church and the central role of the bishop in this denominational system can be easily used as a prime example of the dilemma that has plagued us. The United Methodist denomination was identified as a "managerial episcopacy" by Edward Leroy Long in his 2001 study of the polities of a range of denominations and expressions of the Christian faith. Long looks at three denominations with episcopal heritage in which the biblical principle of oversight *episkopē* is located in leadership persons and is a means of system organization. Long distinguishes United Methodism as a managerial episcopacy as distinct from the Roman Catholic "monarchical episcopacy" and the Episcopal "pastoral episcopacy." Each of these episcopal systems defines different roles and responsibilities for leaders. When describing The United Methodist Church, Long states that "a managerial episcopacy is concerned primarily with making the church function effectively. It views the office of bishop in functional terms, as involving managerial skills, rather than giving it theological dimensions or sacerdotal significance."[1] Similar statements can be made about staff of other denominations and local church clergy who have for decades now been given the function of institutional management as their primary role.

This does not imply that the role of the United Methodist bishop (or the role of other managerial leaders) does not have theological or sacerdotal functions and responsibilities. Indeed The United Methodist Church looks to bishops within the United Methodist denomination to assume teaching and priestly roles. Nonetheless, Long argues that the governance pattern of The United Methodist Church was heavily developed "in an era in which efficiency was becoming a desired goal in the culture as a whole, when the business world was developing complex logistical systems, and when decisions, more than heritage, were seen as influential in human affairs."[2] He argues that the defining role of the United Methodist bishop and of denominational leadership is managerial, as symbolized by the location of United Methodist episcopal offices in office centers rather than in congregations or cathedrals and by the United Methodist episcopal attire, which is more commonly of the same order as ministers in full connection than defined by symbols of the office.

Like all managerial systems, a managerial episcopacy has checks and balances on authority to establish boundaries and limits on the use of the authority given to leaders. Such checks and balances within United Methodism include the following:

- The primary role of bishop as limited to the interpreter of polity (*Book of Discipline*)

- A limited tenure of eight years as the episcopal leader of an annual conference, giving only tenuous authority
- Nonmembership in the annual conference that allows the bishop to preside but without vote
- A council of bishops that gathers all bishops, active and retired, but does not designate a "head" of the council who is allowed to speak for the entire church or even for the entire council
- A system for setting fundamental denominational policy through the legislative powers of a representational body (general conference nationally or annual conference regionally) rather than in the singular or collective authority of a leader or key leadership group. The general conference speaks only once every four years, and the annual conference speaks only once every year with no clear authority located in other groups for making decisions in between
- A judicial council that serves as a "watchdog" tool receiving appeals that can be lodged by anyone questioning episcopal or conference decision making or action
- Bishops' subjection (in practice, if not intent) to conference and jurisdictional points of professional and spiritual evaluation (that is, conference and jurisdictional episcopacy committees), much like the constraints offered to local church clergy by personnel, mutual ministry, or staff parish relations committees

Boundaries and accountability, of course, are healthy in community and protect against an inappropriate or excessive use of power. It is important, nonetheless, to recognize the limits that a denomination places on the very leadership it seeks, particularly when practiced within a managerial system.

Management and Leadership

The primary point is that the present United Methodist Church has inherited and developed a managerial system from which it now asks for clear leadership. Management and leadership are not disconnected, and no organization can live with one of these functions to the exclusion of the other. Indeed, all living systems need management and leadership in a continuous and complementary relationship in order to maintain balance and health while also negotiating change and development. While complementary, management and leadership address distinctly different needs of an organization. One manages the present; the other defines the future. One provides stability; the other, change. One provides smoothness and efficiency; the other, disruption. One provides comfort; the other, anxiety.

A classic distinction made between management and leadership is that each seeks to answer a different question.[3] Management seeks to answer the question, Are we doing things right? This is a question of appropriateness and efficiency; pursuing this question provides security and stability for the organization. In the local church, a clearly managerial question is, Did anyone order enough candles for the Christmas Eve candlelight service? If the candles were ordered, the service goes smoothly. If not, there are disruptive consequences. This does not infer that managerial questions are trivial. Indeed management is commonly based on experience—good management practices avoid many problems while providing stability and security. Management systems also provide standards of practice for workers and participants to follow. Note, however, that managerial questions and managerial leadership assume that there is a "right" way for something to be done and that the appropriate strategy is to replicate what was done and what was seen to be right in the past. Management is heavily guided by the norms reflected in "we've always done it that way."

Leadership seeks to answer a very different question: are we doing the right things? This question of purpose and meaning is often experienced as disruptive. A well-formed leadership question does not increase efficiency but creates disruptive challenges that cause the system discomfort by requiring inquiry, learning, and making choices. In doing strategic planning work with congregations while on staff with the Alban Institute, I commonly used three leadership questions (when appropriate), which can be identified as "formation questions."[4]

1. Who are we? (the identity question)
2. What has God called us to do or to be? (the purpose question)
3. Who is our neighbor? (the context question)

Such questions are disruptive and difficult to pursue because they raise to a conscious level the investigation of what has usually been assumed as known. Such questions require active learning to make faithful choices about the future. For example, What is the purpose of a middle judicatory such as an annual conference, synod, or presbytery? and What is the purpose of our congregation? are leadership questions that cause disruption and require active decision making about the future goals and uses of the conference's resources. People frequently assume that there are clear answers to such questions, only to discover that any serious pursuit of such questions can be disruptive and divisive.

The Paradox of an Established Management System

It is common, if not axiomatic, for established organizations to request leadership (which prompts disruption and anxiety), only to resist it and reward management (which maintains stability and security) instead. I was asked to bring new young members into my first church, but I was rewarded only when there were no complaints about what those new young members were doing. Bishops are asked to deploy clergy in missional ways for the future of the church but are rewarded only when all feel that they have received the appointment that they deserve by their tenure and loyalty. Rewards themselves are tools of constraint in managerial systems since they are withheld when there are complaints in the system. However, complaints are the natural and healthy accompaniment to leadership. This natural paradox is further complicated in highly relational systems like denominations and congregations where rewards often take the form of friendliness, inclusion in conversations or activities, shared information, or appreciation and can easily be withheld.

Leadership

The tension between the interrelated functions of management and leadership is heightened in a time of great change when old practices do not serve well and when new directions are not solidified. In such a time what constitutes appropriate leadership is questioned and contested. Does the leader focus the attention of the group on answers or on questions?

Living without clear answers and expectations (such as what it means to be a *good* pastor, a *vital* congregation, or an *effective* judicatory) creates anxiety and discomfort in which people turn to the leader with the expectation that he or she will reduce the anxiety by providing clear answers. This is the assigned role of the singular leader who is expected to be able to provide answers and calm fears. A leader with a clear vision is expected to galvanize followers to action—if not for great purpose, at least for reduced anxiety. We are familiar with the idea of the "lone-ranger" leader, the person who single-handedly seems to come up with needed answers and clear directions. It has long been an expectation that clergy are to perform as lone-ranger leaders. We are, however, also coming to terms with the reality that such leadership is rare and perhaps even inappropriate, if not impossible, in a complex time of deep change. Nonetheless, people seek the solitary leader who can thus calm fears, and they are willing to rotate through a quick succession of leaders in their search for such calm. The temptation to want to play such a role as leader is constantly present for those given leadership responsibilities.

What we are less familiar with—or sensitive to—is the way in which leaders in complex organizations such as large congregations or denominational offices are pulled into the singular leader role despite being surrounded by others who form a leadership team or administrative structure. Deferral to the singular or highest status leader in this setting is identified by Jim Collins as leadership understood as a "genius with a thousand helpers."[5] The system may be more complex, the number of people involved may be larger, but the wish for someone to "make it right" does not subside, even in the heart of the singular leader who would like to be able to bring order and calm to a chaotic time. The temptation of the singular leader, either as the lone ranger or as the genius with a thousand helpers, limits the creativity and the inventiveness of the organization by creating dependence on the limits of one individual to originate or sign off on all ideas about moving into the future.

The search or desire for a singular leader is commonly centered on the need for clear answers in an anxious time. In arenas where there are clear problems and clear answers, this is a fully appropriate role for leaders to play. In places and times when clear answers are not available, however, something else is needed. In times of deep change the "something else" is particularly needed.

The Constraints of a Managerial System

In the current tension between management and leadership, becoming familiar with the assumptions and demands of management is important in order to understand the natural resistance that makes leadership difficult. Among the foundational assumptions of management are the following:

- A commitment to orderliness—everyone and everything in its appointed place doing appointed tasks in unison.
- Replication and sameness. Local congregations are assumed to be the smaller replication of the structure and the goals of the regional office. The regional office is assumed to be the smaller replication of the structure and the goals of the national denomination. In a managerial system all regional offices are assumed to be the same; all congregations are assumed to be the same (or at least similar) in structure, goals, and even passions.
- Checks and balances. The long history of Protestant clergy in America is the repeated story of authority assigned to individuals, simultaneously accompanied by structure and processes put in place to guarantee that leaders cannot use their authority freely.[6] The 1784 founding Christmas Conference for Methodism in America called out particular clergy to serve as presiding elders and immediately began a prolonged argument over the conditions under which the new presiding elders could use their authority. The previous discussion of checks and balances placed on bishops of The United Methodist Church is an example of a wider and historic practice.
- Centralization. Authority is located in the primary governing body, and any other person or part of the organization is not readily given authority to act on local issues. (For example, denominational decision making about clergy and local congregations is commonly located in the regional denominational offices, and a great deal of time and energy is given to the wide sharing of information and to including all members of the central body in debate and decision making without concern for their involvement or investment in the issue.) While practices of centralization provide a good deal of alignment within the organization, they also constrain and slow the amount of work the organization can do, and they produce rigidity rather than agility in the organization's ability to respond to change.[7]

Managerial systems turn to regulatory practices in times of great change as a means of fulfilling the assumptions noted above. The growth of mainline denominations into regulatory systems was an economic response to dealing with the diversity of needs and preferences that began to build in those denominational systems. The dependence on regulatory responses should not come as a surprise since it is a cultural response to the messiness of deep change as experienced by an older, orderly, and managed generation. The impulse to control through the requirements of growing rules and legislation, rather than provide clarity and tidiness, creates a complexity that further constrains and inhibits the movement toward change without adding any agreement or coordination to the efforts of change.

Technical Versus Adaptive Work

In his study of leadership, Ron Heifetz offers new insights and tools to the present generation of leaders who are faced by a changed environment and a new mix of challenges. In particular, he differentiates between *technical* and *adaptive* work, each of which must be addressed by the leader.[8]

Technical work is the application of known solutions to known problems. This is clearly managerial work and depends on one of the most highly developed skills of managers—problem solving. In problem solving the manager (1) identifies the problem (and by building consensus on the very identity of the problem has already moved the system toward solution and change); (2) identifies the alternate options available to address the problem (brainstorming); (3) chooses the most likely alternative (decision making); and (4) moves to implementation (action). The appropriate response to a known problem with a known solution in technical work is *action*. Technical work, problem solving, is effective and works well. It works well, however, *only if there is a problem*. The dilemma in the current moment in the wilderness is that leaders are often confronted with new questions and situations that do not lend themselves to old assumptions and practices. They cannot appropriately be addressed as known problems. Instead of being problems, these questions and situations without easy answers are conditions under which the system now lives. They require new learning.

Because technical work and problem solving have been the primary tools of management for the past several generations, it is difficult for bishops and district superintendents in the current situation to resist searching for answers and enter into the more complex realm of learning. A well-proved adage of systems is that whenever a system does not know what to do, it does what it knows. Anxiety creates a need for action, whether the action provides a helpful solution or not. And so leaders overuse their problem-solving skills even when confronted with a changed situation that cannot be defined as a problem.

Heifetz offers a second way for leadership, which he calls *adaptive* work. Adaptive work is quite different from the problem-solving activity of technical, managerial situations. Adaptive work "consists of the learning required to address conflicts in values people hold, or to diminish the gap between the values people stand for and the reality they face."[9] In this arena Heifetz offers an alternative definition of leadership as "influencing the community to face its problems." The appropriate response to adaptive work is not *action* (problem solving); it is *learning*. In order to address an adaptive situation, someone must learn something. In fully adaptive situations of deep cultural change, everyone, including the designated leader, needs to learn together.

When a bishop provides faithful leadership to move a conference to address particular goals but leaders pull the bishop aside out of concern for those who feel left out or are displeased with the process, it is an adaptive situation in which there are conflicts between the values that people hold and the behaviors that they practice. When there is a widely shared call for excellence in pastoral leadership but the poorest performing or poorest motivated clergy still receive an appointment or call, it is an adaptive situation in which there are conflicts between the values that people express and the actions that they take. When, in a time of concern over church growth, large congregations in demographically supportive environments grow naturally yet the majority of denominational resources remain focused on the redevelopment of recalcitrant churches, it is an adaptive situation—a conflict between the values that people hold and the actions that they take. When the denomination claims the making of disciples (a focus on the change within the *individual*) is the driving mission but asks only for reports on the state of the congregation (a focus on the change within the *institution*), it is an adaptive situation. When lay leaders, clergy, and denominational staff are challenged to provide leadership (complete with messiness and anxiety) but are rewarded only for management (orderliness and institutional harmony), it is an adaptive situation in which there are conflicts between the values that people hold and the actions that they take.

The real task of the leader in the wilderness is not to pick up the daunting challenge of somehow finding the right answer that will resolve these conflicts between values and actions. The task of the leader is to help the people face into the tension of the adaptive situation and learn. As in all difficult moments, the starting point of change is finally to name the tension or conflict between expressed values and actual behavior. Not to name the tension is to remain trapped in a double bind.

Much more than a clichéd expression, a double bind is a debilitating trap for leadership. In his provocative work on the nature of order, anthropologist Gregory Bateson identified three essential elements of a double bind that must be present if the person is to be trapped and remain incapacitated:[10]

1. The situation or message must be important and cannot be ignored.
2. There have to be at least two competing and contradictory meanings in the situation or message that cannot be held simultaneously in agreement.
3. The leader is not allowed to comment on the contradiction that is present and does not allow resolution.

For the leader to be faced with all three elements is for him or her to be constrained and to remain ineffective as long as the double bind remains unspoken. To be asked to lead in ways that require change and be rewarded for management that provides stability is a clear double bind if the leader is not free to talk about the contradiction. Bateson is perhaps best remembered for his development of the double-bind theory of schizophrenia, a specific application of his study of paradox in communication. To be asked to provide leadership in a managerial system is a schizophrenic experience unless the competing values and behaviors are named and the people are helped to face the adaptive situation in search of new learnings.

Adaptive work is not tidy. In his theory of change from a systems perspective that takes into consideration the insights of chaos theory, organizational consultant John Scherer notes that in order for change to be birthed, two "parents" must be present—pain and possibility.[11] There must be a discomfort sufficiently strong to make the people want to be different and a possibility that is promising enough to support the people through change. Walter Brueggemann once commented that the central task of leadership is to manage the hopes and the fears of the people. Indeed, managing hopes and fears—possibility and pain—in a congregation, a conference, or a corporation is a spiritual task of great faithfulness. Scherer demonstrates that if the leader can surface the appropriate pain, hold clearly the possibility of what can be, and help people let go of old assumptions, then the people will enter a stage of chaos—the truly creative environment where change happens. It is a change that the leader can neither anticipate nor control.

Chaos is, in fact, necessary. Turning first to contemporary literature, the creative place of chaos is well described in Michael Crichton's novel *The Lost World*, part of his Jurassic Park literature. The character of Malcolm is the voice of systems theory in this novel of prehistoric dinosaurs that are reclaimed and cloned from ancient DNA to live in a contemporary jungle. Malcolm explains:

> Complex systems tend to locate themselves at a place we call "the edge of chaos." We imagine the edge of chaos as a place where there is enough innovation to keep a living system vibrant, and enough stability to keep it from collapsing into anarchy. It is a zone of conflict and upheaval, where the old and the new are constantly at war. Finding the balance point must be a delicate matter—if a living system drifts too close, it risks falling over into incoherence and dissolution; but if the system moves too far away from the edge, it becomes rigid, frozen, totalitarian. Both conditions lead to extinction. Too much change is as destructive as too little. Only at the edge of chaos can complex systems flourish.[12]

This is a rather elegant description of a scientific principle embedded in a novel. But along with being both a scientific and a literate people, we are a biblical people, so it is not difficult to turn to our sources to realize this same truth. The biblical word commonly used to express chaos is *wilderness*, which is the creative place where people are changed. This is where the Israelites wandered with Moses for forty years, during which time they were transformed from slaves into a nation. Without the wilderness, without the wandering, without the chaos that made them trust in God, they would have arrived in the promised land as unchanged slaves with no purpose other than to escape their oppressors and no identity other than as an oppressed people. John the Baptist appeared in the wilderness with the promise that there could be a straight path. Jesus was sent to the wilderness to put away his role of carpenter in order to begin his public ministry as Son of God. It may be helpful to recall that the wilderness is required. In Mark's Gospel, as soon as John baptized Jesus in the Jordan and the voice from heaven proclaimed Jesus as God's Son, we are told that the Spirit immediately *drove* Jesus into the wilderness (Mark 1:12). Wilderness, chaos, change is neither tidy nor comfortable, which underscores the true difficulty of adaptive leadership in a system designed for problem solving and neat, tidy, complaint-free management.

The New Leadership for Our Particular Exodus

"Imagine the difference in behavior when people operate with the idea that 'leadership means influencing the community to follow the leaders' vision' versus 'leadership means influencing the community to face its problems,' " writes Heifetz.[13] Perhaps one of the critical skills needed by our leaders in our particular exodus is the ability to lead from questions instead of from answers. It is, if you will, a 180-degree shift in our assumptions and skills of leadership. We are now at a point where the workable answers that we have discovered are already being employed. Reconsider the inheritance of the first three paths that we explored in chapter 2. There is a limit to what we have figured out so far, however, and we are still not out of the wilderness. It does not help to simply work harder at the answers that we already have when additional learning is needed. New learning comes from leaders being able to ask and sustain conversation around appropriate questions that will help us link our values and our behaviors in much more direct ways.

Beyond the double bind of the constraints of our managerial systems, there remains the issue that the dominant way in which North American leaders have been trained and rewarded is as problem solvers. We have been trained to format every situation as a problem in order to focus attention and resources on what we want changed. We have been trained to be persuasive, to talk people into following our solutions. Heifetz refers to this as the assumed task of the leader to influence the community to follow the leader's vision. Leadership is understood as the action of talking. Leaders talk and persuade. I appreciate Stephen Covey's observation that we have been trained to listen only long enough to figure out what to say next.[14] The real dilemma comes when old answers don't produce the intended change and when new answers are not apparent. In such situations even the best of our leaders are tempted to announce their answers and evaluations even more slowly and loudly with the hope that increased clarity, attention, or motivation will make the difference. When results are not achieved, leaders begin to try to "fix" what is broken, working harder at what has proved not to work.

A well-known adage attributed to Edwards Deming, the industrial consultant credited with turning around and rebuilding Japanese manufacturing following World War II, is that a system produces what it is designed to produce. If you want something different, working harder at old answers does not produce wanted results; you must change the system. Deming's significant contribution was to develop principles for the needed change in a system.[15] In part he pointed out that the natural temptation and the more common response when there is stress in a system is simply to work harder with the hope that it will make the wanted difference. He also is clear about the failure of leaders trying to make change by persuasion and fixing. He points to the futility of setting goals as a way of motivating people (that is, setting a goal of a 10 percent increase in average attendance at worship in the next year) because without changing the system any increase or decrease related to the goal is simply the product of random variation within the limits allowed by the way the system is designed. He points to the limits of mandatory training—"fixing people"—(that is, increased standards for ordination, legislated training for clergy and laity, redevelopment training for all congregations) because the newly trained, "fixed" people still work within the designed limitations of the unchanged system. He discourages the use of performance evaluations because of the arbitrariness of measuring performance within a system over which the person has little or no control. Until changes are designed into the system itself, what is produced continues to remain unchanged—except for the random positive and negative results that already are designed into the upper and lower control limits of change that any system accommodates but cannot control. Working harder, training people in order to "fix" their inability to be different, holding people accountable for what a system produces without changing the system—all are typical "answers" that have disappointed us. The new leadership in the wilderness needs to find a different way. For that different way to live, our leaders will need to find new roles; our people will need to learn how to live in the anxiety of not being sure. The question "How can one feed these people with bread here in the desert?" (Mark 8:4) that the disciples asked Jesus when they faced the four thousand was one of those anxious questions without apparent answers. As do leaders today, Moses had his share of those unanswerable questions also.

Heifetz suggested the alternative that leadership influences the community to face into its problems. Facing into the problems is not solving them but shaping the questions that will bring learning, which will free us from the problems. Learning, and thus change, is directed by asking the right questions. This is the province of the new leadership because the leader has both the authority of position and the power of agenda. The leader has the position and authority to direct what people will attend to. When people arrive at the board meeting concerned about the number of candles for the Christmas Eve service (a managerial concern that, if addressed, will make people less anxious although not produce any change), the leader can respond yes, let's ask the custodian to count the candles and check with the secretary about how many we typically use each year. Then the leader can suggest a much better question for the people to work with, a question that will require learning and that will increase rather than relieve the anxiety the group is feeling. The task of leaders in the wilderness is to give the people something better to talk about, even if the leader has no resolution to the conversation and even if the conversation makes the people more uncomfortable rather than more satisfied.

Two worries live with leaders in this new form of leadership that rests on questions. The lesser worry is, what if the question proposed by the leader is the wrong question? The more worrisome issue for the leader is, what if the question is the right question?

What if the question proposed by the leader is the wrong question? This is the lesser concern because good questions, even when they are not quite the right questions, prompt learning if managed well. Remember that the mainline church is not the only institution and those in the Christian community are not the only people facing problems that defy fixing. Consider the list that Heifetz offers as examples of problems for which no adequate response has yet been developed: "poverty at home and abroad, industrial competitiveness, failing schools, drug abuse, the national debt, racial prejudice, ethnic strife, AIDS, environmental pollution."[16] The ability of established institutions such as the mainline church to offer hope and change lives in a deeply changed mission field is just one of a host of questions, and perhaps not the most immediately dangerous, that plague us in the wilderness.

The wilderness is a place of learning, not a place of right and wrong solutions. One requirement of the wilderness is the ability to embrace disappointment and failure. The appropriate response to disappointment and failure in the wilderness is not to ask what we did wrong, but what we learned so far. Stumbling over the "wrong" question can lead to a better question and new learning. By definition, adaptive questions in adaptive situations where technical fixes are not available are not clearly defined and require learning to clarify the question, let alone find answers.[17] If the first three paths in our particular exodus have brought us partial learnings that led to the better adaptive questions of the fourth path, then the issue before us is not whether the fourth path of exploring identity and purpose will resolve all our ills but what the fourth path will teach us about faithfulness and effective ministry.

The larger danger for leaders in the wilderness is not in framing the wrong questions but in framing the right questions. As discussed already, helping people steer into the adaptive questions that face them increases the discomfort that the people have with their leaders. On the fifteenth day of the second month the people began to grumble against Moses (Exod 16:1-2). It wasn't that they felt Moses was wrong about God's people being called out of slavery. They just wished that he had left well enough alone since their new situation in the wilderness seemed even more tenuous than what they had known in Egypt. Disturbingly Moses didn't seem to have all the answers to keep them going and to feel secure in the process. Adaptive questions and adaptive times prompt an environment of fear, which produces an even greater dependence on leaders, a dependence that even as early as the 1950s was recognized by W. R. Bion as debilitating.[18] How do we in our local congregation shift our attention from satisfying the preferences of the people who already come to our church and learn to speak to the changed neighborhood and culture that surround us so that we can, through Christ, change people's lives in a way that makes a difference in the world? This is a very large and very adaptive question for congregations used to being membership organizations in which the primary agenda is making more members and satisfying them. It is a question that is not sought out by many people who already come to the church and are satisfied by what they find there. It is a question for which the answers are multiple and competing when viewed by the larger group in the now highly diverse community and culture. It is a question that requires both leaders and people to learn together.

The real risk is that the right adaptive questions in wilderness environments threaten leaders with a misplaced dependence placed on them by others. No system ever calls a leader to make it uncomfortable. In other words, people do not expect their leaders to ask questions for which the leaders do not already have answers. The reality then is that leaders have authority in their system only to the point where they make people uncomfortable to an unacceptable level. It doesn't matter what the book of polity says about the authority or role of the denominational executive, the local church clergy, or the lay leader of the congregation. Authority can be exercised freely without challenge only to the point of unacceptable discomfort. As Heifetz and Marty Linsky observe in their study of sabotage, "You appear dangerous to people when you question their values, beliefs, or habits of a lifetime."[19] People want their leaders to comfort them, protect them, and provide satisfaction to their system. The problem is that change does not happen under those conditions. Recall Scherer's observation that in order for change to take place, the two parents—pain and possibility—must be present. Pain, or discomfort about the current state of things, provides motivation. It gives a reason for people to want something different. Writing about our life stories, Donald Miller notes that it is a general rule in creating stories "that characters don't want to change, they must be forced to change."[20] It does not help for leaders to work doubly hard at coming up with good answers and making sure that everyone is satisfied. Leaders pursuing necessary change must work to make people, including themselves, appropriately uncomfortable in order to give reason, energy, and direction to change.

Obviously making people appropriately uncomfortable invites resistance, even sabotage. For the moment it is sufficient to understand that in order for change to happen, the leader must exceed the level of authority that the system is willing to give—a goal directly achieved by helping the people face into a good, a "right," adaptive question that will prompt them to question their current values, behaviors, and habits that block the future. Leaders need to accept the reality that substantive and healthy change cannot happen if they operate only within the rules established to provide managerial constraints. Robert Quinn underscores this point with his recounting of the effort of a state government to find transformational leaders in their system in order to use those stories as examples to prompt transformational change, which was felt to be sorely needed. Quite a few examples of transformational leadership were found in the state: "One person took over an office renowned for long lines and offended citizens. A year later, it was the best office in the system. Another person took over a hospital where conditions had long been scandalous. Two years later it was a nationwide model."[21] Finding such leaders, the state officials commissioned videographers to go out and tell the story of these people so that other leaders could follow suit. The interviewers returned, saying that the video could not be made because in every case the transformational leader had broken at least one state law in order to get the results of excellence wanted. Quinn points out that organization and change are not complementary ideas. "To organize is to systematize, to make behavior predictable," he notes. Change requires something much less comfortable, and the leader who is able to frame a good adaptive question that will prompt all of the people in the system, including the leader, to question established values, behaviors, and habits will find his or her leadership challenged and perhaps sabotaged.

Adaptive leadership in a time of cultural change obviously is not an exercise for the faint of heart. Nonetheless, it must be taken on if the mainline church is to change sufficiently to live in the new mission field. It must be taken on wisely if the leader is to survive. Exceeding one's authority cannot be taken on lightly or with a sense of self-righteousness. Such leadership requires both bravery and thoughtfulness. "See, I am sending you out like sheep into the midst of wolves; so be wise as serpents and innocent as doves" (Matt 10:16). On the one hand, such leadership requires the development of support for the leader from outside the congregational or the denominational system in order to sustain this new exercise of leadership when management is requested. Leaders in adaptive situations cannot be nurtured by the system they are asked to lead. Since rewards in a managerial system such as congregations and denominations are highly relational and therefore easily withheld, the leader must find relationships and support for herself or himself from outside the system in order to be sustained. On the other hand, such adaptive leadership of asking questions instead of providing answers requires a skill set different from the problem-solving skills that have been so thoroughly taught and learned by managerial leaders. We now turn our attention to this different skill set.

What Does the New Leadership Look Like?

Problem solvers frame a problem, brainstorm options to deal with the problem, make a decision about which option seems best, and then move directly to action. It is the well-known path of managerial leadership in which known solutions are applied to known problems. It is technical work. Heifetz states that "the single most common source of leadership failure we've been able to identify—in politics, community life, business or the nonprofit sector—is that people, especially those in positions of authority, treat adaptive challenges like technical problems."[22] Adaptive challenges require a different set of behaviors from leaders that involve different personal and organizational skills. Below is a discussion of seven forms of leadership that I find helpful when thinking about adaptive leadership. Beyond the basic problem-solving skills, these are behaviors that adaptive leaders must employ in order to help create and protect the learning conversations that a wilderness people need when seeking new paths of faithfulness.

1. Frame the Adaptive Question

Framing a good, a "right," adaptive question for the congregation or denomination to address is a way of giving people a better conversation to have. It is a way to help people discover new learning rather than practice old answers that have been proved no longer workable. Heifetz suggests key differentiating criteria that leaders can use to figure out if they have a good adaptive question to work with: "Does making progress on this problem require changes in people's values, attitudes, or habits of behavior?"[23] The something better to talk about requires us to rethink how we work rather than motivate us to work harder at what we already know. Adaptive questions give us a need to learn rather than a problem to solve.

Currently within the United Methodist denomination one of the most widely used resources by leaders and governing boards in congregations is a book by Bishop Robert Schnase titled *Five Practices of Fruitful Congregations*.[24] The five practices identified by Schnase are radical hospitality, passionate worship, intentional faith development, risk-taking mission and service, and extravagant generosity. One of the ways in which this resource has captured the attention of denominational and congregational leaders is its emphasis given to the descriptive adjectives: *radical, passionate, intentional, risk-taking,* and *extravagant.* The practices of hospitality, worship, faith development, mission, and generosity are not unknown to the mainline church and can easily be seen as fundamental and can also be seen by some as old ground to plow since much has been learned about these issues in the earlier three paths that the mainline church explored in our particular exodus. However, as discussed in an earlier chapter, over time the forms by which established congregations address these practices are set by norms developed in an earlier cultural moment and are maintained by managerial leaders seeking to satisfy the people already attending established congregations. Questions about these practices of fruitfulness can easily be framed as technical problems to be solved. Hospitality: how can we invite more people to join us? Worship: how can we increase our attendance at worship? Faith development: how can we increase our attendance at Sunday school? Mission: how will we direct our missional giving this year? Generosity: how will we increase our pledges this year? These are all technical questions meant to solve the problem of how we can care for institutional needs of getting more people to do what we already do. These questions do not ask how the leaders and members of the congregation must learn how to change their values, attitudes, or habits of behavior. Instead they ask how to solve the problem of getting more people to practice with us the values, attitudes, and behaviors that we have already established for ourselves. While solutions can be sought, such technical questions do not prompt new learning. At best they prompt increased activity around solutions already known and already proved to be inadequate to the changed mission field.

Attention to the adjectives allows the leader to frame adaptive questions requiring learning. Radical hospitality: not, Are we friendly enough? (a technical question) but, Is our hospitality radical enough to provide space for people to do what they need to do in their own way in order to deepen their faith and relationships even if we don't do it that way? (an adaptive question requiring learning and changes in values, attitudes, and behaviors of the people wishing to practice radical hospitality). Passionate worship: not, How do we increase our attendance at worship? (technical) but, Are we passionate about worship so that we, and those who join us in worship, feel connected to God and to one another by being here? (adaptive). And so it would go through all five practices. The task of the adaptive leader is to frame important questions in ways that require thoughtfulness, exploration, and learning.

The primary tool that leaders use in framing an adaptive question is the power of agenda, a basic responsibility of all leaders. The power of agenda—to build the agenda that groups will use in their meetings and conversations—gives the leader the authority to direct attention. It is the leader's opportunity to give the group a better conversation to have.

Framing adaptive questions also requires that leaders be selective and judicious about the better conversations into which they invite their people. Adaptive questions can overwhelm a system because they challenge old norms and practices without providing clear answers about new norms and practices. These are leadership questions that slow the denomination or congregation down and produce discomfort rather than management questions that move things ahead and satisfy people. Few organizations can sustain attention to multiple adaptive questions at any one time. This is especially true of voluntary association network organizations like congregations. Smaller congregations cannot manage more than one adaptive question at a time; larger congregations may be able to hold two or three questions at a time. Nonetheless, it is the responsibility of the leader to identify the question by assessing which question will, at this moment, be most important for us to address. This is difficult leadership work because the helpful question needs to be found, it needs to be asked in an adaptive form, and it has to be the "right size." Because the church deals with ultimate things, eschatological matters, and issues of meaning, it is easy to ask questions that are too large. Clergy and denominational leaders seem to be good at framing the largest of questions: How do we address sinfulness? How do we provide salvation? How do we make disciples of Jesus Christ for the transformation of the world? These are good questions. They are the right questions. But they are much too large to be helpful adaptive questions for denominations and congregations that need to ask, What do we need to make a difference in the next three to five years in order to be more faithful? Asking the good adaptive question, the "right" question, seems to be both a gift and a skill of the new form of leadership needed. The ability to ask the good, right, question is a skill to be developed by leaders who also need to trust that asking the best good question they can find may lead them to an even better adaptive question while in search of a path to faithful living in this new mission field.

95

2. Move to the Balcony

Earlier I referenced the difference between balcony space and the field of action or reactive space, a distinction made by Heifetz and Donald Laurie. Balcony space is described as the place where leaders can look at patterns in order to understand the whole of their situation.[25] It is quite different from reactive space where leaders spend so much time with problem solving. I often ask groups of people how many use a "to do" list to identify the things they hope to accomplish in a given day. Multiple hands go up to say yes. I then ask how many people have had the experience of making their daily "to do" list only to realize that twenty minutes after they arrive at work they might as well throw their list away because of what is now facing them. People laugh with recognition and even more hands go up. The reframing of the day's work caused by waiting problems is the product of reactive space, and the problems in reactive space claim the majority of time, energy, and attention of our leaders, our governing boards, and our decision-making groups.

Leaders need to be able to move personally from reactive to balcony space in order to keep perspective on daily work and frame the bigger picture of the future. Leaders also need to take others in the system with them when they go to the balcony. The balcony is that time and space where leaders take people in order to have a learning conversation, which is a different order of work from problem solving. Balcony space often requires a literal shift in the space in which the conversation happens as well as a change in the question to be addressed. If the leader offers a good adaptive question but invites others to address the question in the same physical space in which they have their board or committee meetings, then the others will treat the question with the behaviors of a board or a committee and will seek to "solve" the question. The boardroom is where leaders make decisions; it is where they expect to make decisions. A good adaptive question that becomes another item on the board agenda will prompt a search for the next decision. What is needed is not a decision but a conversation that allows us to see the larger issues and prompts us for creative discernment.

Intuitively in my second church where I served as pastor, I framed balcony work before I understood what and why I was doing it. One evening at a board meeting I asked if anyone on the board would be interested in talking with me about what keeps me awake in the middle of the night. I explained that the church seemed to be doing well, attendance was strong, programs were going well, mission outreach was engaging more and more people all the time, and the building was filled to overflowing with people at least five to six days each week. But I pointed out that in another fifteen years or less, we would deplete our facilities, our reserves, and the energy of our leaders at the rate we were going. What we were doing was not sustainable, and we needed to ask if we were about the right things for which we had the right gifts. The simple invitation to conversation led to a series of lunch gatherings with a small subset of leaders over the next several months in a little corner restaurant up the street from the church; there we reshaped the questions that the church needed to face into. As pastor, I was able to return to the board and to committees with new questions to address that would require new values and behaviors. More important, I was able to ask the new questions with the full support of other leaders who understood the importance of the new questions because they had helped me find and frame them.

Balcony work requires a good adaptive question. It requires the right environment that will invite people to talk, discuss, and discern without feeling that they need to make quick decisions. It also requires safety that invites people to say what is on their minds or hearts that would go unspoken in other settings. The leader himself or herself needs to provide the safety or find a third-party facilitator who can allow the group to talk about difficult things without being personally involved. Balcony work requires conversation that is not guarded, so there may need to be agreements of confidentiality so that one person's comments are not repeated outside the conversation and attributed to that person. Balcony work may require agreements to read books or to share learning trips to another church or ministry that will allow the group to talk about themselves in a new way shaped by the shared reading or visit. Balcony work takes time, and the leader will often need to "protect" those in the balcony group by not allowing others to rush them to judgments and decisions about the future.

3. Use Your Locus of Control

One of the central lessons learned on the first three paths in the wilderness is that leaders can control or change others only to a given limit. Leaders do not have direct control over other people. Trying to change another person has a limited return, and at a certain point the other can choose not to move further or choose not to accept change. Much of the earlier work on church growth, congregational transformation, and leadership development consisted of efforts by leaders to get other people to "do church" in a different way, to accept new ideas and accept new people, which would require people to learn and live a different role or accept a different responsibility. Although some people have been eager to engage such change, others have demonstrated their limits. Still others have been fully resistant, behaving as if they had been given an answer to a question they were not asking.

In times of deep change leaders need to go to their "locus of control," the place where they have their greatest control, in order to work with issues of change. The primary locus of control for a leader is over himself or herself. We can't control others, but we can make decisions that will have much more direct control over ourselves. The critical insight that allows control over ourselves to be a central leverage point of change in our congregation or denomination comes from the understanding of living systems as interconnected and interrelated parts in which each part has influence on all other parts of the system. In an interrelated system, changing any part of the system creates change throughout the whole system.

A familiar example of an interconnected system is the art form of a mobile. A mobile is a sculpture or decorative arrangement made of items hanging from a frame of rods so that they can move independently from one another. While all of the elements can move freely, the whole sculpture seeks to move to the place of equilibrium, that is, the comfortable point at which all parts of the system are in balance and at which the mobile can come to rest. Although it is a mobile (capable of movement), the art form naturally seeks its point of rest—the place of equilibrium and comfort. Without some external force such as a push from someone's hand or moving air, the mobile will remain at rest. Yet as an interrelated system, a mobile can easily undergo great change by someone's altering or removing only one part from the frame. Add more weight to one part, or remove one part, and the whole system shifts dramatically, not into chaos or confusion but in search of the new point of equilibrium where comfort can be reclaimed and rest is found.

Change one part, any part, of the system, and the rest of the system will shift to accommodate the changed part. A leader's point of greatest control is within herself or himself. The leader is an integral part of the interrelated system, and by changing oneself, the leader can effect deeper change within the whole system. By changing one's values, beliefs, and behaviors, the rest of the interconnected system will naturally shift to accommodate the change in the leader. It matters what a leader gives himself or herself to. Another way of saying the same thing is that it matters what a leader pays attention to. By shifting his or her attention to some issue, the leader is also shifting the focus of the system to that issue. If the leader gives full attention to complaints within the system, then the system will produce more complaints. A system produces whatever is rewarded. Rewarding complaints by giving them full attention makes the system very sensitive to complaints, and any discomfort that will surface as a complaint will have the power to shut the system down. If the leader, however, gives his or her attention to purpose and mission, the system will redirect itself in that way.

A favorite example comes from a consultation with a very large congregation that was in the midst of deep and significant change that involved a capital fund campaign, the building of a new facility requiring relocation of programs, and the retirement of the senior pastor all at the same time. Some of the staff reported arguments and complaints among staff members to the senior pastor, expecting that the senior pastor would intervene and set things right. The senior pastor called a staff meeting at which the other staff members thought that she would want them to talk about what was making them so unhappy. Instead the senior pastor noted that she had been hearing of the complaints and arguments between staff. She talked about the deep change that the church was going through and how it was natural for people to be uncomfortable. She then went on to talk about how important the changes were and how much hope the changes would bring to the future of the church, and she concluded, "Of course, you know that." Instead of trying to mediate complaints, the senior pastor gave her attention and focus to the purpose behind the discomfiture and the hope for the future. The message that she gave her professional staff concerning their discomfort was simply, "You're better than all this complaining." The end result of the meeting was that staff left feeling affirmed for what they were trying to do, they did see themselves as better than complainers, and they set out to work more collaboratively on what needed to be done. A system gets what it measures. Instead of measuring the worth and size of complaints, the senior pastor helped her staff take a new measure on the importance of their goals and the hope that the goals brought to the future ministry of the church. Did all complaints disappear? Of course not. Staff continued to bump into one another's boundaries and expectations. But instead of using complaints to stop change, the staff used complaints to indicate what they had to negotiate with one another. As leader, the senior pastor used her locus of control within herself to focus on purpose, future, and hope, which, in turn, aligned the staff members in the same direction.

4. Focus on Outcomes

If a system produces what it measures, then nonprofit, voluntary association organizations like congregations and denominations are faced by an even greater challenge because they routinely do not know what they are trying to produce. Don't forget the earlier discussion in chapter 3 about the two pillars of purpose and relationship in which we noted that religious systems are inherently more relational than purposeful. Congregations have historically been built and guided by managing the relationships rather than shaping purpose and outcomes. Even our leaders of regional and national denominational offices, where purpose is expected to live most clearly, tend to be persons who demonstrated their excellence in congregations where their training and attention focused on resources and relationships. The end result is that our leaders are much more focused on the resources that go into our congregational and denominational systems and on the internal harmony within the system than on the purpose or the outcome the system is intended to produce. We know what we put into our congregations and denominations in terms of people, money, and effort, and we are careful about how we manage and negotiate what is in the system. But we are unsure of what we are trying to make different because of the congregation or denomination. This lack of clarity on what is to be produced is a fundamental weakness and challenge of nonprofit, or "social sector," organizations. Jim Collins, author of *Good to Great*, gives special attention to this challenge to nonprofits in a follow-up monograph to that book in which he states, "The confusion between inputs and outputs stems from one of the primary differences between business and the social sectors. In business, money is both an input (a resource for achieving greatness) and an output (a measure of greatness). In the social sectors, money is only an input, and not a measure of greatness."[26] Without a clear, measurable output such as money, social sector organizations like congregations and denominations have the much harder task of defining what they produce.

Knowing what we are trying to make different is one of the greatest challenges for the contemporary mainline denomination and its leaders. A critical leadership skill in this new arena that takes us beyond problem solving is a clear description of what the congregation or denomination is trying to make different. Leaders need to help their system describe clearly what will be different in the near future because of their ministry and work. The leader, as noted above in the discussion on locus of control, then needs to keep his or her attention on the outcome so that the full system will begin to align itself with the discerned purpose. A congregation in Florida set itself the task of building a new community and family life center because it felt called to do direct ministry with the very large number of youth and young adults in the immediate community who had no contact with the church. Building a new facility is an all-encompassing task that takes energy, resources, and the full attention of the congregation's leaders and members. Because of the size of the task, building a new facility can consume the leaders and members, and the completion of the building can seem like an outcome—an end to itself. However, the new facility of the community and family life center was not an outcome. The new building was a resource needed to address the actual outcome, which was the involvement and changed lives of the youth and young adults in the neighborhood. The pastor and key leaders of this congregation had to intentionally focus themselves and continuously ask questions about the outcome—the changed lives of young people—in order to align the system to the goals of ministry. In the design phase the pastor and key leaders kept asking not about what would be most pleasing to the members of the church but about what would be most welcoming and least intimidating to the young people who had not yet stepped into their facilities and ministry. In the program stage the pastor and key leaders had to keep asking staff and committees not about what programs the members of the church wanted in the new facility but about what programs would be most inviting to the youth of the community and how the programs would be both welcoming and invitational to open paths for new people to encounter faith and a supportive faith community.

Continued focus on outcomes is a skill and a discipline for leaders to learn. But systems produce what they pay attention to, what they measure. A critical new skill that moves us beyond problem solving is the ability to describe outcomes and to measure the steps we take toward the described outcome.

5. Protect the Voices of Creative Deviants

"Creative deviants" is a name given to the original voices brought by people new to the system.[27] It seems to fit well. These voices are creative because they represent new insights and understandings that come from fresh eyes, which can see beyond the norms and practices developed by "we've always done it this way." These voices are also perceived as being deviant because they offend. Not knowing how "we've always done it," these new voices are free to ask questions that can tread on the paths of sacred cows. Creative deviants tend to be the newest, and often the youngest, participants in the congregation or the newest, youngest leaders in the denomination. Not normed into old behaviors, they are free to ask why things can't be different, and in asking, they offend. It is the offense—the suggestion that seems insensitive to what we have worked long and hard to accomplish, the question that makes us uncomfortable because we are not sure we know how or are able to live out the answer—for which the rest of the system seeks to shut the voice down. The voice of the new board member who asks why, if the church talks about doing ministry for the community, the church facilities can't be rented to the AA group or the new Buddhist congregation that is without its own facility, can be heard as an offense to tenured leaders who have always protected their buildings for use by members, and if not members, certainly by Christians. The voice on the denominational finance committee that asks why, when the denomination claims to want to include and change the lives of so many new people, so much money is being directed to support congregations that have not received new members or participants over the past five years, can easily be heard as an offense by other leaders who feel a responsibility to care for all congregations, no matter how effective they have been in fulfilling claimed mission. Yet without the voice of the creative deviant, the balcony conversation that may be so needed will not have life because all of the conversation partners will be able to see and agree only to what is already established.

We need help to appreciate the potentially uncomfortable insights of the one whose experience is different from ours. Early on in my pastoral ministry in Philadelphia, several of us went to hear Eli Wiesel, noted survivor of the Holocaust of WWII, speak in a nearby congregation about his experiences as a survivor of the Holocaust. One very memorable observation from that evening was the distinction he drew between the three words for "stranger" that his Polish community used to identify people. One word, he explained, was for the Jew who came to visit from another village. That stranger was to be treated as a guest because he or she knew of information and events from beyond one's own village that could be helpful in understanding one's life. The second word for "stranger" was for the Gentile who came from beyond one's own village. Not only did this person know of information and events from beyond one's village, but as a non-Jew, he or she could see this information through very different eyes not available to the Jew. This person was to be treated as an honored guest because he or she carried a gift that a Jew could not bring. The third word for "stranger," he concluded, was for the person who lived next door or down the street for years on end but was someone whom you still felt you didn't know or understand. This third stranger was the only one who was dangerous because he or she could not be trusted, and the appropriate response to this stranger was to kill him or her if the community was being attacked.

Of course, the response of killing the neighbor who still remains a stranger feels dramatic and harsh to we who live in communities that have not been threatened with pogroms meant to destroy and eliminate us. But more to the point, we are not accustomed to treating people from other perspectives, who give voice to what we can't see, as honored guests in our midst. Quite naturally those who break the norms of the system are shut down as a defense against discomfort and loss. However, the voice of the stranger is fundamentally needed in a time of deep change, and the voice needs to be protected.

The new skill for leaders in this adaptive moment is to protect those voices, to keep them safely engaged without trying to speak for them. If the voice of the creative deviant is heard as an offense and if the others in the system hear the leader try to speak for the creative deviant, it is not a difficult step for the people to claim that the leader has "taken the side" of the creative deviant and also needs to be shut down as a threat. Once in a very highly charged consultation, the leader called a congregational meeting to help people learn more about the differences in worship and music over which their congregation was splitting. At that meeting a young man who was a new but very active participant in the new contemporary worship service stood up out of frustration, shook his finger in the air, and proclaimed, "What these people [meaning the folks in the traditional worship service] don't understand is that their music sucks!" It would be hard for a creative deviant to be more offensive. It took only seconds for long-tenured members to begin to shut him down. Yet as consultant and third-party convener of the meeting working with this congregation through its conflict, I could see that he held information that the members needed. Despite his inappropriate and offensive way of expressing himself, what lay behind his frustration were messages of how important this church and its contemporary worship had been to him over the past year, how for the first time in his life he had stepped into a church and felt that there was a place for him, and how he wanted to protect the contemporary worship service because he wanted to share his discovery of faith and his new church home with his friends and others like him. Because of my work with him, it was clear that his voice needed to be protected and heard because this congregation was already demonstrating its effectiveness in reaching out to new people and making a difference in people's lives. Why else would this young man stay at the church and attend such a meeting if what he discovered there was not making a difference in his life? If, however, I had stepped in at that moment to interpret for this young man ("Wait now. . . . Let me tell you what this fellow is trying to say to you"), I would, as consultant, be clearly identified as taking his side and could no longer offer my leadership during a difficult time. Instead I needed to protect him and keep his voice involved. I worked with those offended to begin to differentiate between what they heard in his message and what positive things he was trying to say by being there and participating in the meeting. I worked with the young man to ask what he was actually trying to say and how he might say it in more acceptable ways.

Creative deviants and their messages are not always as offensive and divisive as the young man in the example. Nonetheless, the leader(s) need to develop the sensitivity and the skills to keep the voice protected and involved. Without the voice all we can do is what we already know.

6. Align Resources and Attention to Where Outcomes Are Wanted

Highly relational systems such as congregations and denominations can easily become decisionphobic. Making a decision has the potential of impeding or breaking a relationship because in situations of limited resources the act to decide in favor of one thing is to decide against another. However, as noted above, a system produces what it measures, and you get what you pay attention to. When we put those principles of systems together, it becomes clearer that if a change is wanted, leaders must give focused attention to what goes into the system (input) and what is to be measured on the other side (outcome). Leaders need to direct resources to produce wanted outcomes. Resources include the well-known triumvirate of time, money, and people. But resources also include the attention of the system, the learning agenda of the system, the prayers and discernment of the system, and the focus of leaders. Systems align to attend to the place where the leader(s) focus attention. Leaders can direct resources by where they give their time and attention, by what questions they ask, and by what they talk about. Resources follow the attention of leaders. It is a principle of systems alignment.

A favorite example of systems aligning with the leader comes from the 1983 movie *Blue Thunder*, starring Roy Scheider. The main "character" in the film is a high-tech urban assault helicopter that has the capacity to fly into very dense urban territory in the midst of riot and chaos and choose its targets carefully, shooting the bad people and not shooting the good people. One of the frightening thoughts of such equipment, which the closing credits of the movie assure us certainly exists, is that a pilot positioned above chaos would be able to pick out the bad people from the good people and shoot. But more to the point, the helicopter is seen as effective because it is so highly responsive in the midst of riot and chaos. The pilot does not have to take time to aim the guns in order to shoot. The key is the pilot's helmet. The helmet's visor, which drops down in front of the pilot's eyes, has a target scope built into it, and the guns of the helicopter are tied into the pilot's helmet. Wherever the pilot looks, the guns automatically follow. When he or she looks to the right, the guns travel to the right. When the pilot looks to the left, the guns travel to the left. The pilot does not have to aim the guns, only look and make a decision about what he or she sees. It is an example of a fully aligned system. The whole helicopter is tied into and aligned with the movements and the attention of the pilot. It is a helpful example of how a system focuses on whatever the leader gives attention to.

A primary skill of leadership in change that goes well beyond problem solving is the ability to choose what to give primary attention to and then focus oneself (locus of control) on that target. It makes a difference in working with staff whether the leader asks the staff person if everyone in the program is satisfied with the program or asks the staff person if people are evidencing change in their lives through the program. One is a managerial question because it focuses on satisfaction; the other, a leadership question because it focuses on a wanted change. When deploying clergy who evidence high performance or potential, it makes a difference if the denominational executive asks which congregations have the capacity to pay a good salary that will satisfy such clergy "moving up in the system" or instead asks which congregations evidence the highest levels of performance or potential for ministry in the changed mission field and whose performance or potential would grow with the right leadership. One is a managerial question since it keeps a clergy advancement system neat and tidy, making sure people can "move up" in the system; the other is a leadership question since it looks for ways to put resources where ministry and mission have the highest potential of happening.

Along with aligning oneself with the intended outcome of the system, the leader needs to align other resources, putting the best people where the change is needed, directing limited dollars to priority goals, and giving the most time on both the learning and the action agenda to the desired results. To make such choices over limited resources is to satisfy some within the system and to dissatisfy others who may feel equal claim on the resources. To have to make such choices is difficult in a highly relational system where great value is placed on satisfying everyone. Making such choices requires letting go of old standards of operation—old norms of behavior—which will be the subject of our next chapter. For the moment it is sufficient to note that being able to focus on aligning resources with outcomes is a new skill and a challenge for leadership in change. Leaders must be very intentional about not allowing problems and anxiety to consume valuable resources on fixing everything that people think is wrong and on making people feel secure and comfortable.

7. Practice Poise

The distinction between management and leadership offered in this chapter has been used to make the point that management offers satisfaction to the system and leadership introduces discontent. Scherer's hypothesis is that in order for change to be birthed, both pain and possibility must be present. From any perspective discomfort can be seen not as a by-product of leadership and change but as an integral part of change needed to adapt to living in a wilderness. Discomfort, like resources, must be managed. Too much discomfort and the system breaks down. Too little discomfort and there is no felt need to change and nothing new happens. Leaders must learn how to manage levels of anxiety and discomfort in their system in order to protect and support change.

Anxious systems become very sensitive to their leaders. Heifetz notes that people look to their leaders to resolve their anxiety and problems, and so in times of organizational discomfort the people look more closely to their leaders, giving them an even higher profile: "They search for indications of how worried *they* should be about the situation. If *he* [the leader] appears alarmed, then their fears will rise."[28] Some level of anxiety is required, but leaders can keep the level at a manageable point by indicating their ability to function with hope and purpose in an anxious environment. In order to modify and manage the anxiety that permeates a system in times of change Edwin Friedman introduced leaders to the idea of the "non-anxious presence," the capacity to contain their anxiety regarding organizational matters.[29]

The leader must bear an outward appearance of calm and behave with clarity and focus, despite the internal feelings that may be quite different. In the managerial systems of an earlier day, which were geared to making everything go smoothly and satisfying people, the leader could live fully within the system and expect to be cared for. A norm for clergy in that earlier managerial time was for them to live fully within the congregation where they could expect to find their calling and their employment but also have their full circle of friends, find outlets for their interests, and spend their leisure time. To lead in such a managerial time, the clergy could expect to be nurtured by the congregation or denomination that they were called to nurture. In a leadership time, however, the leader cannot live fully within the system because while leadership is required, management is rewarded. Another way of saying the same thing is that leadership tends to be "negatively rewarded." In order for the leader to provide what is required in the wilderness he or she needs to expect negative rewards, which in a highly relational system will mean dealing with people's personal dissatisfaction, losing personal support, and having friendships and nurture withheld.

In order to maintain the poise needed in such a situation the leader must learn to live with "one foot outside the system" at all times. There must be a support system that comes from someplace other than within the system. Moses had his moments when he walked away from the Israelites to be with God, and from those encounters he returned with a shining face, clear once again about the purpose of the journey and the next steps to take. Leaders in anxious systems need also to go where the encounter will provide clarity of purpose and progress. Clergy and denominational leaders are coming to a new sense of the importance of being spiritually and theologically grounded in order to be clear and to feel support for their work in times when leadership is demanded. Personal retreat days and renewal leaves have new importance. An ongoing practice of spiritual disciplines undergirds the leaders. Spiritual directors and therapists step in to help leaders be grounded and connect with God's purpose. Professional peer groups function to provide support and nurture. Self-care practiced through attention to diet, exercise, recreation, and sleep is a tool of managing self as well as a healthy practice.

Hobbies and avocations are not seen as distractions but as undergirding a fuller sense of self that is not bound by or limited to the congregation or denomination where the leadership role is played out.

We Should Not Be Surprised

As a twenty-four-year-old newly appointed pastor to my first church in Philadelphia, I needed some time to finally figure out that I was being asked to bring change to the church in a way in which the people already there would not need to do things differently. I was asked for leadership, but I was rewarded for management. I was given authority and then constrained from using it. We should not be surprised. Leadership creates change, and change challenges the normative way of doing things—requiring more work, slowing people down to learn new things, and requiring people to give up control where they once had it. We should not be surprised and we should not assume that this tension between management and leadership, between authority and constraints, is missing within church structures. Rather this tension is widespread, with multiple examples easily found not only in church systems but broadly across all organizations. Consider the example from a June 2009 deadly crash on the subway system in Washington, D.C., known as the "Metro." Several people were killed because of a mechanical failure with the signals and switches. The fact is that to avoid such tragedies, all public transportation systems are subject to a safety review and inspection process overseen by an agency external to the service provider. The reason for the safety review and inspection by an outside agency is that it may not be in the company's interest to make changes that would certainly be in the public's interest. Someone or some group is given authority to provide oversight requiring necessary changes for public safety. In the case of the D.C. Metro system that group is the Tri-State Oversight Committee, which was given clear authority over issues of safety. In other words, leadership on the issue of public safety was given to a committee. However, the Tri-State Oversight Committee was then highly constrained so as not to impede the Metro system from moving ahead in making its own decisions. The committee had no direct regulatory authority and could not order Metro to make changes, was provided with no employees of its own, had no dedicated office or phone or website, and needed to borrow space for its public meetings.[30] The deadly subway crash was a tragic but simple example of change being designed in ways in which nothing would have to be different; leadership was assigned but then constrained from being used. If nothing else, this tension between what needs to be done and what we are willing to do demonstrates the power of our assumption that if we just keep doing what we already do, everything will be all right. The wilderness challenges the assumptions that we can continue down our current paths, whether we are talking about mainline denominational systems, public transportation, banking and financial institutions, or anywhere else that our gaze may take us within the established order of things during a time of great change. The wilderness is much more interesting than that. An exodus through the wilderness requires much more than that.

CHAPTER 6

THE JEREMIAH MOMENT

Moving Ahead Means Letting Go

The very large middle judicatory body was in the midst of strategic planning. A central concern that surfaced continuously as a complaint was the bureaucratic complexity of its 130 boards, agencies, commissions, and committees (someone counted!). They were rigid when they wanted to be agile. They were stuck when they wanted to be creative. The strategic planning team brought back a proposal to drop from 130 to a new structure of 35 boards and committees. Everyone asked for it, yet the proposal was almost turned down, much to the frustration of the planning team. In follow-up informal interviews it became clear that some people who fully supported the new structure voted against it—it seemed they were afraid that a much smaller structure might not have room for them on one of the committees. They were not against the plan; they were against losing a place at the table. "People do not resist change, per se," write Ronald Heifetz and Marty Linsky. "People resist loss."[1] Resistance and loss. The focus of the present chapter is loss.

In the happiest of moments when a young couple bring their newborn baby home from the hospital, their joy is mixed with their loss of privacy, loss of sleep, and loss of time to give attention to themselves and their marriage. In the most difficult of moments when the doctor announces to an ailing man that the bewildering symptoms have a diagnosis, the relief of finally knowing that it can be dealt with is tempered by the prospect of the loss of control over life that will come with the treatment regime. Somewhere in the back of the young couple's minds is a weighing of the cost that the new child brings into the home. In the back of the man's mind is a curious weighing of scales that asks whether the treatment is better or worse than the illness. Pleased with the change, we still weigh the loss. At times the deep sense of loss and the reluctance to let go of what we know defeat the hope and possibility of the change.

The difficulty of exploring behaviors and assumptions that must be left behind is that we must necessarily talk about ourselves. Resistance to loss is not an issue that leaders need to cajole others to move through. Rather, it is a common and shared reaction of both leaders and followers that is part of the hard work of deep change and must be identified in all of our behaviors and assumptions. Indeed, the effort to change others can be a way in which we resist or try to avoid having to change ourselves. What I hope to describe in this chapter is what I see in myself as well—my own assumptions and behaviors. It is easier to talk to others about what they must let go of while remaining blinded or confounded, when I hold tightly to those very things. Letting go of old behaviors and assumptions is first the work of leaders with themselves and then with others who are invited to understand and follow.

As with us, so with the Israelites. Shifting our metaphor for the moment from the Exodus to the Exile, it is easier to see that in order to claim the new, people must let go of the old. Theologian Walter Brueggemann points to the year 587 B.C.E. as the pivotal point in the Old Testament, marking the shift between what God did of old and what God was doing new in the present: "The year 587 is the occasion when the temple in Jerusalem was burned, the holy city was destroyed, the Davidic dynasty was terminated, the leading citizens deported. Public life in Judah came to an end."[2] Brueggemann talks of this decisive moment as an experience of ending and dismantling the known and the subsequent requirement that the people receive the new acts of God: "Judah had two tasks in this crisis of life and faith. It had to let go of the old world of king and temple that God had now taken from it. It had to receive from God's hand a new world which it did not believe was possible and which it would not have preferred or chosen."[3] Brueggemann identifies the time of the Exile and the writings of Jeremiah, Ezekiel, and Second Isaiah as similar to our own and offering instruction in a faithful trust in God. Only when we are able to let go of what is lost can we claim and hold on to what is being offered. Jeremiah stood with others and watched the hordes descending from the north to destroy Judah. But Jeremiah announced to the people that this hand that descended to destroy Judah was not just Babylonian greed and aggression; it was also the hand of God come to change the people. Able to let go of what once was, able to see the possibility and hope of what was ahead, Jeremiah played the role of prophet by announcing what he could see. Concluding that the future had hope, he bought new property. If the Exodus tested the hope of Israel, the Exile tested their trust.

Letting go is more than passively accepting a loss. It is no longer clinging to the hope that the old will, or should, return. It is a full and active letting go, which is difficult since the old is rooted so deeply. Consider the end of the story of the Exile when the Israelites were able to return to Jerusalem to rebuild the Temple. Ezra tells of the laying of the foundation of the new Temple two years after the arrival of the people back in Jerusalem. It was a historic and deeply important moment because only when the foundation was completed could the people return to the cultic practices of worship and renew their relationship with God. The text tells us that when the foundation was complete, there was great celebration with the priests in full vestment, there were cymbals clanging and people singing, and all praised and gave thanks to God. But then comes the curious passage that reflects what we know so well about ourselves, the pain of loss that holds us back from joy:

> All the people responded with a great shout when they praised the LORD. . . . But many
> of the priests and Levites and heads of families, old people who had seen the first house

on its foundations, wept with a loud voice when they saw this house, though many shouted aloud for joy, so that the people could not distinguish the sound of the joyful shout from the sound of the people's weeping. (Ezra 3:11-13)

But many who had seen the first house wept. Joy cannot be full until the weeping is let go. It is all part of the stages of transition, each of which must be honored, each of which must be cared for. It is often the stage of letting go that proves to be most difficult and can be the downfall of hope.

The Three Stages of Transition

Perhaps the best-known voice describing the various stages of transitions in life is William Bridges, consultant and lecturer who turned his attention to transition management in the mid-1970s. He identifies three stages of transition: endings, the neutral zone, and making a beginning.[4] His second rule about transitions makes the point: "Every transition begins with an ending. We have to let go of the old thing before we can pick up the new one—not just outwardly, but inwardly, where we keep our connections to people and places that act as definitions of who we are."[5] Note that letting go means letting go not only of what we do but of definitions of who we are—who we understand ourselves to be. Letting go in the stage of endings is so difficult that people routinely avoid the work. It is painful to bring both relationships and personal identity to an end. If it is painful to bring things to an end and we avoid this work, it is also difficult to live in the neutral zone, which can be described as that place of confusion and chaos where the old no longer works and the new is not yet discovered (the wilderness). If we *avoid* the difficult work of letting go, we *deny* the need to live in a neutral zone where questions live without answers. We revert to the solution of colluding with ourselves to try to begin our transitions in stage 3, making a beginning. Skipping over stages 1 and 2, we start with new beginnings. The belief that hope lives here allows us to avoid pain and deny confusion.

My first pastorate out of seminary lasted nine years, which is a long tenure for a first assignment. From a difficult start in which I needed to sort out encouragements to lead from the constraints I experienced while doing so, the years proved to be remarkably rich for my family and me, for the growth of the church, and for the people who still mark those years as a turning point in their faith and in their families. And then came the time when I was appointed to my next assignment a few cities away. This church that I was leaving was precious to me, and I was passing on a jewel to the next person who would serve as pastor. Following the instructions of my denomination, I gathered all the information that would be needed by my successor, which in my concern for this place turned out to be reams of paper, notebook after notebook, and a long list of details that my successor surely would not want to miss. We set the time of our meeting, and I was quite thorough in making sure that this poor fellow had everything that he would need. Not once, not twice, and probably more than three times, I assured him that if he had any questions—any questions at all—he should give me a call. We said good-bye, and I heard nothing for some time. Finally about three weeks later, I received a call with the one and only question that he had for me: "Gil, where's a good place there to get a haircut?" To say that I was upset is an understatement as I thought about how he was treating his new appointment to "my church" so lightly that his only question was about haircuts. It took me a while to get over the offense, but I finally realized that what I was hearing from this fellow, who was quite a good pastor, was stage 3 thinking. Facing the anxiety of his transition, he was already behaving as if he were in stage 3. In his mind he was already living in my parsonage, already preaching from my pulpit, and already working on his "to do list," which included finding a doctor and a barber in his new home. He was skipping over the pain of letting go, and he was clearly in denial about having to live through the confusion of the in-between time in which he would need to figure out what he didn't know.

The dynamic of letting go is fairly well understood. If one does not let go of the issues in a first relationship, then the issues revisit the next relationship, re-formed in some way perhaps, but a revisit by the same issues nonetheless. Divorce counseling is an example in which the task of letting go is addressed rather directly so that the divorced person does not take old issues into the new relationship. In the church much of the letting go has to do with relationships. Roy Oswald, former senior consultant with the Alban Institute, has helped generations of clergy in his boundary research to come to terms with the necessity of the difficult work of saying good-bye.[6] It is painful to rehearse both the good and the bad with people as the pastor leaves, but without letting go, the issues hang on and arrive in the new place. Without the hard work of letting their former pastor go emotionally, the people in the church leave no emotional room to receive the next pastor.

The Even Harder Work

Congregations and denominations are highly relational organizations, a fact that leads many people to think that if relationships are cared for, then all is well. So we have learned much about saying good-bye to people and releasing roles and relationships. Yet the even harder work in the time of much larger transitions, such as an exodus through the wilderness, is the letting go of and saying good-bye to the old, established norms that have much less to do with people and relationships. Recall that norms are the established ideas, values, and behaviors that are rooted in an organization and determine how the organization works or does not work. Norms are the informal, usually unwritten, agreements and rules of the organization, and they are exceptionally powerful even when invisible.

David Valera, director of Connectional Ministries in the Pacific Northwest Conference of The United Methodist Church, shared with a group of colleagues a YouTube video that offered a stunning metaphor for such invisible but powerful norms. The video was a PlayStation 2 commercial in which a person dressed in a white lab coat was shown placing a large number of fleas into a glass jar and screwing the lid on top.[7] The fleas started hopping around inside the glass jar. The narrator explained that the fleas were left in the jar for three days, during which time the limits of their behavior were set by their glass-encased environment. When the lid was removed after three days, no fleas escaped the jar. The norm of space was set, and despite the opportunity, no flea jumped higher than the limit imposed by where the lid had been. The narrator explained that the next two generations of fleas born to that group would also pick up the established norm of limited space and never escape the jar. Remarkably the commercial showed the jar completely removed from around the fleas, yet their living space remained unchanged. The fleas continued to jump and fly but remained within the shape and the constraints of the jar that no longer surrounded them. Whether the commercial was reporting actual science or using advertising license, the image serves as a powerful reminder for the norms that still trap us in the established behaviors of the congregations and denominations that we are trying to change. Like glass walls, norms are tacit and difficult to see. They operate below our conscious attention. Nonetheless, they form exceptionally powerful limits and boundaries along with efficiency and stability.

Because they are tacit, norms become deeply embedded in our ideas, values, and behaviors and are difficult to change, producing rigidity and resistance to change. I have already named several tacit norms that need to be changed in order for the mainline church to move into the future:

- Problem solving as the dominant mode of leadership, which values answers over questions
- The use of polity to constrain leadership
- Denominational offices behaving like regulatory agencies

What follow are an additional six norms that the mainline church and its people will need to release in order to move ahead into the changed mission field. Tacit and hidden from view, these norms operate on an assumptive level, providing unseen limits like the glass jar around the fleas. Since they are assumptions—unquestioned truths—they are exceptionally difficult to ferret out and address. They guide *normative* behavior. In a time of deep change, however, normative behavior represents limits and boundaries rather than efficiency. To pick up new work, we need to let go of old ways.

1. The Assumption of Egalitarianism: "The Tyranny of the All"

Egalitarianism is the political doctrine that all people in a society shall have equal rights from birth. The expression of egalitarianism within mainline denominations over past decades has developed norms of equality and inclusiveness. All clergy must receive equal and standard treatment. All congregations must be resourced and given equal attention. All issues must be given equal attention.

In a covenantal community there is real purpose in practices of equality and inclusiveness. If we are all in this together and have covenanted to be community, then egalitarianism serves us by underscoring the importance of each individually and of all together. The dilemma is that in a deeply changed mission field, we are not all functionally and missionally equal. If the mission is to make disciples with the intent of changing people who will then, in their changed lives, transform the world, some congregations are more effective at this than others, and some clergy are more effective and invested in this new work than others.

111

Consider a quite important functional difference among congregations. The current North American culture has five generations living side by side, from children all the way up to great-great-grandparents. The most effective of our congregations is able to span all five of these generations with their ministry. The potential of such congregations to speak to the present generationally complex mission field and therefore make disciples is considerable. Look then at the congregation that has within its members and participants only the oldest two of the five possible generations. Such a congregation has a clear ministry to people who already attend and participate. Given the differences in values and behaviors between generational cohorts, however, the stretch that would allow the great- and great-great grandparents in the two-generation congregation to be radically hospitable to children and their parents from their community is relatively unlikely. These congregations are cut off not only from their community but also from their future. Many of our oldest congregations are our smallest. The central issue here is not size. The smallest of our congregations may be vital and effective at disciple-making ministries in intimate and personal ways impossible for the larger church. But what is at heart here is that many of these small congregations, because of the age disparity and generational distance from the youngest generations, will not be able to make the leap into the new mission field. In fact, many of these congregations will not live into the next two decades. In these congregations new disciples will not be made, but current members will be nurtured and cared for.

Consider then the report from the Study of Ministry Commission that was given to the 2008 General Conference of The United Methodist Church gathering in Fort Worth, Texas. This study, which was to bring clarity to the orders of ordained ministry, noted that The United Methodist Church has congregations in all but 138 of the 3,141 counties in the United States. The report then stated:

> Because of this range, The United Methodist Church is reluctant to leave any preaching post without a preacher. More than 10,000 of our 35,000 local churches have 35 or fewer people present for worship on a typical Sunday. The vast majority of these churches were built to serve the population as it was 100 years ago when 40 percent of Americans made their living by farming.[8]

In this report the norm of egalitarianism determines that the denomination must resource each and every one of these congregations, even though, as the report noted, more than 40 percent of United Methodist local churches have had no new members join by "profession of faith"—people entering the Christian life by decision as opposed to joining one local congregation by transfer from another. The report is equally inclusive of clergy as of congregations. Later in a section on preparing and supporting clergy for the work to be done, the commission suggests that "*every* deacon or elder" be part of a learning group; that "*every* pastor" moving to a new appointment of a different size be given training; that "*all* full-time clergy under appointment" be assigned a mentor.[9] This report from the Study of Ministry Commission is not singled out as a rare instance of the dominance of this norm of egalitarianism. It is simply one example of a widely shared assumption that influences our strategies, our practices, and our attitudes.

All congregations must be given equal attention in receiving an appointment of a pastor. All clergy must participate in learning groups and be mentored. All members must be satisfied before we can agree on a change in our worship or programs. Yet not all congregations will be effective in making disciples, not all clergy are interested in or capable of learning new skills that will lead to disciple making, and not all members are willing to change their worship to make it hospitable to new participants. This is another of the conflicts between our values (what we claim to be important as our missional goal) and our behavior (how we distribute the resources of the church without regard to effectiveness in addressing mission). Egalitarianism practiced in this way leads to "the tyranny of the all." We cannot move ahead until all churches have the pastor they desire. We cannot move ahead until all clergy have received proper continuing education and are willing to go. Not moving until all are ready is a commitment not to move. "No church left behind" is a commitment not to move ahead.

Sometime at the beginning of the twentieth century, Italian sociologist and economist Vilfredo Pareto offered the concept of the Pareto principle, alternately known as the 80/20 rule, the law of the vital few, or the principle of factor sparsity. This principle pointed out that 80 percent of the effects in most situations come from 20 percent of the causes. It is a principle that seems to live out in many forms across all of our organizations and institutions: 80 percent of sales come from 20 percent of the salespeople; 80 percent of the giving to a local church comes from 20 percent of the givers; 80 percent of the problems experienced in an organization come from 20 percent of the people. The Pareto principle is a more helpful guideline in our mainline wilderness than is an indiscriminant norm of egalitarianism. If the mission is to make disciples, we can expect 80 percent of the disciples to be made by 20 percent of the congregations. If the goal is ministerial excellence, we can expect that 20 percent of the clergy will commit to new learning and deeper disciplines to effect 80 percent of the increase in excellence.

In their research based on in-depth interviews with eighty thousand managers in four hundred companies, Marcus Buckingham and Curt Coffman of the Gallup Organization identify a number of norms that need to change, rules that need to be broken in order to move a company toward excellence. One rule that must be broken, they contend, is equal attention to all employees, and they give reasons why the best managers "spend the most time with the best people."[10] A fundamental insight to support the shift from assuming that the leader's task is to change and improve everyone to supporting the gifts that people already have is an "insight we heard echoed by tens of thousands of great managers: people don't change that much. Don't waste time trying to put in what was left out. Try to draw out what was left in. That is hard enough."[11]

The deeply changed mission field requires a continued learning curve that remains steep and demanding and requires the innovation of new ideas and behaviors. If Pareto is helpful in recognizing that most of the change will come from a smaller section of the system, Everett Rogers's work on the "diffusion of innovations" is further evidence that the old norm of egalitarianism no longer serves mission. Diffusion of innovations is the process by which a new learning or a changed practice is communicated and picked up by members of an organization over time. New learning and changed behavior are critical in traveling a wilderness and being surrounded by a changed mission field. Diffusion research began by rural sociologists investigating how agricultural innovations spread through groups of farmers and by educational researchers studying how new teaching ideas spread among school personnel. To the point of our discussion here, Rogers identifies categories of adopters of any innovation that range from innovators, early adopters, early majority, late majority, to laggards (which he estimates at 16 percent, which is fairly close to the Pareto principle expectation).[12] Using the Bass model for forecasting the rate of adoption of a new product, the curve for the acceptance of an innovation appears as follows with the X-axis (horizontal) indicating the time over which an innovation is accepted and the Y-axis (vertical) indicating the percentage of the group that accepts the innovation.[13]

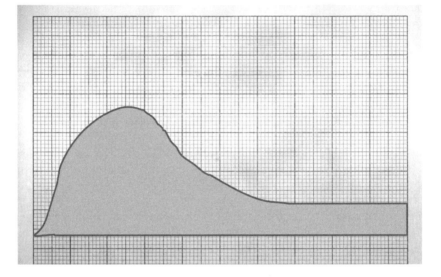

Note that the acceptance of an innovation is steep at the beginning. Some persons (members, congregations, clergy, denominational executives, and staff) quickly see the need for a new way and are eager to put new ways to the test and adopt what works best. Following them is the large part of the group that is willing to follow after the innovators once results can be demonstrated. The right-end tail of the curve needs our attention—the 20 percent of the congregations that cannot or will not make the jump to use innovations that will allow them to live in the new mission field, the 20 percent of the people (members, clergy, executives) who cannot or will not retool for new forms of ministry.

The practice of egalitarianism in which all must be treated equally and no one moves ahead until all are on board directs missional resources and attention toward weakness rather than strength. If 80 percent of the missional effectiveness will be accomplished by 20 percent of the system that is willing to learn new ways in the wilderness, *egalitarianism paradoxically requires leaders to focus 80 percent of their time, attention, and resources on the 20 percent of the system that demonstrates recalcitrance, weakness, inability, and disinterest.* Asked for leadership that will produce the innovations and change that will allow the church to live in the new mission field, leaders are still most positively rewarded for caring for and directing resources to the 20 percent of the people and congregations who complain most about the changes needed or are unwilling or unable themselves to take the trip into the new wilderness. Holding to old assumptions of not moving ahead until all are ready to take the trip precludes living into the new world.

2. The Assumption of Representative Democracy

The second norm that must be let go is the assumption of representative democracy. The commitment to a democratic process through representation undergirds the denominational and congregational norm of constructing committees and conversations in which all interested voices must be physically present at the table and in which all can assume that they have an equal share in the decision making. Such commitment to representative decision making is an inheritance from our North American culture and history to be sure. In the mainline church, however, this practice also served as a legitimate tool of social justice to address the need of inclusion and diversity so that there was shared access to power. The changed mission field has introduced new limits to this well-established assumption of organizational behavior so that it now does not serve well our need to be able to make decisions or our need to find ways to share power. Representative democracy as now practiced in our denominations and congregations invites and assures the presence of all differences as well as all competing issues and preferences to be at the table in ways that hamper discernment and decision making needed to live in the new mission field surrounding us. In a time of cultural divergence in which all preferences are given equal weight, representative democracy as practiced within the church is severely strained.

A primary dilemma of representative democracies is that they encourage people to represent. If I am told that I am to sit with a governing board as a representative of the women's guild, I will surely pay attention to whether the interests of the women's guild are getting attention. If I am the Latino ministries representative on a denominational committee, I will push for the interests and the needs of the Latino church. Representative groups represent, which takes us back to Robert Quinn's observation in chapter 3 that long-established organizations are, in fact, constituencies of constituencies in which the private mission of the group becomes the satisfaction of the strongest constituent voice. Representative democracies, over time, become a contest to see which voice at the table can become the strongest constituent voice and command the most attention and resources.

What is missing is the need to have a leadership group attending to the need of the whole organization, attending to the claimed mission of the group. The idea of governance is helpful here. It is widely recognized that the governing board of an organization has a fiduciary responsibility. The fiduciary responsibility is most commonly thought of as being sure that the resources of the organization are safe and deployed properly. More to the point, a fiduciary responsibility is the fulfillment of a trust (from the Latin *fiduciarius*, held in trust, or one who holds a thing in trust for another). It can be argued that in a for-profit organization, the board holds responsibility for the proper use of assets of the organization in trust for the investors and stockholders. But in the nonprofit organization such as a denomination or congregation, the board holds the organization in trust not for other individuals or for constituent parts of the organization, *but for the mission of the organization*. The role of the governing board is to hold the organization responsible for behaving in the most strategic way to accomplish the stated goal or mission of the organization. The work cannot be done by a representative group since the people at the table represent the interests of the parts of the organization and not the interests of the mission of the organization, which is the whole to which the parts are to align. In their work exploring the responsibilities of nonprofit boards, Richard Chait, William Ryan, and Barbara Taylor point to the need for boards to shift their attention away from problems of performance (Are we doing things right? Are our resources fairly shared? Did our staff do what we told them?) to problems of purpose (What are we to be about?).[14]

Attending to the need of the whole, holding the organization in trust for the mission, requires making decisions, making choices. All interests cannot be served, no matter how good or how important, since the mission has stated outcomes that are claimed to have priority over other needs. The mission of making disciples cannot also legitimately hold and address the needs of some congregations for survival or the desire of some clergy to have their preferences of appointment or call met. Given limited resources, divergent preferences, and the problems facing and threatening some congregations and organizational parts of our denominations, choices will need to be made so that the claimed mission will be central to the purpose of the church rather than another in a long list of priorities that will get attention when time and money allow. The dilemma is that representational groups tend to be decisionphobic. To make a decision is to make a choice in favor of one issue or group and to choose against another. But at a table of representative leaders, each of whom represents a need or a preference of their group, to make a choice means to choose against others at the table. In highly relational systems such as denominations and congregations, the need to choose against someone else at the table is unacceptable. The decisionphobic nature of such representational groups has two consequences.

The first consequence is that representational groups, even if chartered or tasked with decision making, will revert to a reporting agenda. If a group is to meet regularly and decision making feels inappropriate because of the requirement to make choices, then the agenda will revert to a reporting function as a way of trying to be responsible. The fallback position is for the representatives at the table to report the work that they are doing so that others will be informed. The sharing of information feels as if it supports the mission of the organization by assuring that the "right hand" knows what the "left hand" is doing. Reporting and other forms of communication are often considered sufficient ways of aligning the staff, program, and other resources of the organization to missional ends.

The second consequence of representational groups that are unable to make decisions about the mission or stated outcomes of the group is that they focus on problem solving—addressing the most pressing or urgent issue that is brought to the table in the reporting. Without clear goals for what is to be accomplished and the ability to make decisions, leaders cannot know what is important. Attention then turns to pressing needs and problems to be solved. Continued focus on problem solving and meeting the most urgent needs as the only measure of priority leads organizations to serve the weakest parts of the system, those parts experiencing the most problems and therefore those parts least able to engage the staged public mission (see the norm of egalitarianism above). Focusing on the weakest parts of the system may feel just and satisfy relational preferences, but it also impedes change and the effective addressing of missional goals.

Let me be clear here that I do not advocate leadership and decision making that are deaf to the voices and issues that live within the organization. Nor can we turn away from issues of social justice and the need to share power. I commonly work with groups on issues of board training in which much smaller, nonrepresentational boards develop necessary and formal ways to listen to and be informed by the voices of all in the organization. However, the smaller boards do not bring everyone to the decision-making table but work to replace representation with trust and transparency. The smaller board has members who are elected or appointed because they have the requisite skills and aptitudes for balcony work (learning on behalf of the whole organization), for missional clarity, and for decision making, not because of any other organizational role or representation of any other group or voice within the organization. The smaller board listens widely and frequently across the organization so that it is well informed about what others are facing. The smaller board also listens widely and closely to the changing mission field surrounding it where disciples are to be made. And then, being clear about mission, the smaller board shares its learning, its work, and its decisions in a very transparent manner so that others can both see and be invited to understand and support the choices made.

3. The Assumption of Scarcity

A third assumption that must be released is the assumption that we don't have enough to do what needs to be done. If the challenge of the new mission field has grown, if the needs of our suffering clergy and congregations require additional attention and resources, if the needs of the least and disenfranchised people of the world are even more apparent to us, then we don't have enough money, people, or energy to do all that is required of us. Measuring the size of the challenge against the assumption of limited resources can be incapacitating if resources and our dependence on God are not rethought.

At a time when our mainline denominations and congregations must be much more agile and decisive about using resources, the reality is that most denominations and congregations are tightly bound by inherited budgets and commitments that already direct the use of any and all available resources. Budgets, quite naturally, are constrained by fixed costs. There is no, or very limited, control over how much money is required to pay for medical insurance, heat, electricity, and a whole array of costs that the congregation or denomination must cover. But beyond those fixed costs are the costs fixed organizationally by legislation, resolutions, and commitments made at an earlier time in response to a missional or ministry need. The earlier commitment and direction of resources then continue into the current day.

The feeling within the church is that it is unfaithful or unjust to choose against historic commitments, set-asides, and practices. Compounded with the current economic situation, which in the earliest years of the twenty-first century has brought an end to a continually expanding economy, the growing list of mandated expenses is being met by a reduction in the flow of income, which in turn leads to a feeling of crisis.

One impact of this perfect storm of increased fixed costs and a declining economy is that almost no new needs or efforts to address the new mission field can be easily accomplished by garnering new money or redirecting budgets. Consider just one example in the deployment of our denominational leadership. Within most denominations there is insufficient continuing education or professional development money or time budgeted for persons elected or appointed to the highest leadership positions such as bishop, presbyter, district superintendent, canon, or regional director. At a time when we need our most influential leaders to be able to provide actual leadership (rather than management), which requires new thinking, new knowledge, and new courage, most denominational systems provide no resources to allow it to happen. We have long assumed that our leaders come fully formed, and there is no room in budgets and calendars already overcommitted by previous decisions to allow for what is needed by the wilderness. We can't send our leaders to the balcony because they are too caught up in the action of reactive space.

A second impact of this perfect storm is that the competition for attention and importance among competing interests, groups, or issues is heightened. Talking about the myth that there is "not enough," Lynne Twist, author, global activist, and international fund-raiser, points out that the assumption that there is not enough "generates a fear that drives us to make sure we're not the person, or our loved ones are the people, who get crushed, marginalized, or left out."[15]

Twist challenges the assumption of scarcity by pointing out that we live in a culture of "not enough." We wake in the morning saying that we didn't get enough sleep, and we look at our calendars with a complaint that we don't have enough time. "What begins as a simple expression of the hurried life, or even the challenging life," she writes, "grows into the great justification for an unfulfilled life."[16] Our sense that there is never enough burdens us and traps us from behaving in new ways. She also points out that the alternative of wanting to assume a culture of abundance rather than a culture of scarcity can be a corresponding trap. The assumption of abundance when framed as "more is always better" traps us because abundance has no limits. Whatever we have, when seen through the lens of abundance, can always be bested by the more that we can see. Our needs go unmet because our wants grow exponentially. Scarcity deprives us of energy and ingenuity to be different; abundance drives us to accumulate. Instead Twist invites us to consider the surprising truth of sufficiency. Sufficiency is the knowledge that there is enough. When we are not limited by what is not given, or driven to seek more, sufficiency allows us to steward and shepherd what we already have with the assumption that, if directed appropriately, it is enough. Directing our resources appropriately means making decisions, choices, that are missional rather than relational. Nonetheless, what if we operated with the assumption that we have enough—not enough to do what we have been doing organizationally and histori-cally—but enough to do what we are called to do missionally?

The reality is that the assumption of sufficiency is a test of faith. Talking with Moses, God explained how bread from heaven would be provided each morning. "In that way I will test them, whether they will follow my instruction or not," said God (Exod 16:4). Taking pity on the crowd that followed him for three days, Jesus instructed the disci-ples to feed them. "His disciples replied, 'How can one feed these people with bread here in the desert?' " (Mark 8:4). Four thousand were fed, and seven baskets of broken pieces were left over from the seven loaves with which they started. We do not natu-rally start from a position of thinking that our resources are adequate to the task. Our culture of "not enough" and our search for "more" compound our dilemma. Yet as the Israelites struggled to let go of their memory of full meals that suddenly seemed like a benefit of slavery, and as the disciples struggled to let go of skepticism and futility as they picked up seven loaves to feed the crowd, the assumption of scarcity reflects not a truth but a need to trust. To not let go of scarcity is to be limited in possibilities of doing mission in other ways and instead to be captured by the search for abundance, even if abundance can't be shared by others.

4. The Assumption of Control

There is a difference between exercising leadership and exercising power. In his work on nonprofit leadership, Jim Collins distinguishes between executive and legisla-tive leadership.[17] Executive leadership is able to be exercised when the leader has power. He or she, as leader, can simply make the right decision and expect that people will follow. Legislative power is the alternate form in which the leader has not been given full structural power to make important decisions himself or herself and must rely on persuasion and shared interests to help the organization make the right decisions. True leadership, writes Collins, "exists only if people follow when they have the free-dom not to."[18]

Nonetheless, the executive form of leadership, with its attendant power, is the com-mon notion of what should be expected from leaders. We expect leaders who can see what others can't, come up with the right answer, and make other people follow. When the right way is pointed out, we expect that all will move in that direction in neat order. Such expectations worked rather well in an earlier managerial time in a con-gruent culture. Because the group sets the standard of expectations, and because in a convergent situation the answer to any question is expected to be the same for every-one, the leader needs simply to announce the right decision and the whole group will move together in a neat and orderly way. Egalitarianism works well in such moments, and all are expected to be treated the same and all are expected to move together in unison toward the goal set by the leader. The values of neatness and uniformity lie within assumptions of control.

There are, however, different forms of leadership, and the appropriate strategy of leadership must fit the situation, the cultural moment, and the organization. Executive leadership that announces right answers and exercises power to control the response does not live well in the wilderness, which, for us in our particular wilderness, is a divergent environment with multiple and competing expectations, managerial constraints on leadership, and leaders with legislative rather than executive authority.

One of the most helpful constructs identifying different forms of leadership that I have found in my work with issues of denominational change comes from Calvin Pava of the Harvard Business School and his work on new strategies of systems change.[19] Pava identifies four different leadership situations requiring four different strategies of change. The four situations can be placed in a quadrant (see below) using the two variables of *complexity* (the messiness of the situation and the number of intertwining or unstable conditions that exist in the situation) and *conflict* (the level of interdependence and divergence that people feel with one another about the situation or issue). While the two variables of complexity and conflict may be intuitive measures, they offer a way to describe different approaches to leadership with different levels of control, neatness, and uniformity.

	Low Task Complexity	*High Task Complexity*
Low Conflict	**Straightforward Linear Planning** • defines the problem and the preferred solution • moves to action plans	**Normative Systems Redesign** • reformulates the problem • involves widespread participation • seeks ownership of the process • redesigns the system
High Conflict	**Incremental Nonplanning** • bargains • negotiates • votes action • adjudicates	**Disorderly ("Nonsynoptic") Planning** (an indirect approach to systemwide change) • uses unclear objectives • uses imprecise methods • encourages disorder • uses tacit emphasis on changing the system

In the first quadrant, "Straightforward Linear Planning," the level of complexity and the level of conflict are low. An example in a local church is a broken heating system in the month of February. The task is not complex; repairs are needed, and someone must make the call to get action. There is a very low level of conflict. Everyone wants the same thing—heat by Sunday. The appropriate leadership strategy is straightforward linear planning, which is another name for problem solving. The leader identifies the problem, figures out whom to call, and moves directly to action. This is strictly technical work, and the leader moves quickly to solve the problem in order to get on with more important things.

In the second quadrant, "Incremental Nonplanning," the task is still not complex, but there is a high level of conflict—different expectations. A simple congregational example is picking the color of the new carpet for the renovated sanctuary. There may be multiple and conflicting preferences at work as people consider the color of the new carpet, but the task remains simple since one color must be chosen. The appropriate leadership responses are bargaining, negotiating, voting, or adjudicating.

The third quadrant is the "Normative Systems Redesign" situation in which the task is highly complex, but there is low conflict. People basically agree that they want to see an identified change or further development of what they have. Normative systems redesign, which can also be identified as strategic planning, is a familiar model of leadership for introducing change. Consider the steps that Pava names. The leader identifies the need for doing strategic planning by pointing out problems that are mounting up or opportunities that are being missed. The leader then involves as many people in the system as possible in the conversations about the present and the future (small-group meetings, focus groups, surveys and data collection, and personal interviews) so that everyone is listened to and invested in the outcome. New directions are then set, commonly based on what the majority of the people are willing to take on in terms of change.

Less familiar and more foreign is the fourth quadrant, "Disorderly ('Nonsynoptic') Planning," that Pava offers to serve in a highly complex situation of high conflict in which there is a great mix of hopes and expectations. It is an arena of ill-defined and complex problems that will not respond to the previous three modes of leadership. It is, if you will, much more descriptive of the wilderness where questions are more available and more functional than answers, where learning precedes action. Pava identifies this quadrant as "nonsynoptic." It is nonsynoptic in the same way as John's Gospel, which doesn't see (optic) things in the same way as the other three Gospels. In non-synoptic settings people see things quite differently, and agreement, neatness, and order are not possible while control—the exercise of authority to make people comply to one right answer—is not an option. Pava claims that the appropriate way for leaders to function is with unclear objectives, imprecise methods, and disorderly action, using a tacit emphasis on changing the system. That certainly sounds like the wilderness and is an appropriately creative strategy in such a setting of deep change. Leadership in this quadrant does not seek to require uniformity and does not move neatly ahead. Rather, leadership in this quadrant identifies a measurable or describable goal or outcome. The leader aligns his or her attention and resources on that identified outcome and then invites others to move toward that outcome with the promise that those moving toward the goal will receive the leader's attention and a share in the resources that can be brought to hand.

Disorderly, nonsynoptic planning is not neat, is not tidy, and is not uniform, but it requires and depends on new learning, it begins to align the system with the outcomes to which the leader gives his or her attention, and it moves ahead into change in ways not allowed if all must agree and move together. It is a wilderness strategy that will lead to as many disappointing paths as to new insights about how to be more faithful. And it can thrive only if old assumptions of control—of leaders coming up with the right answer and then compelling others to follow in neat uniformity—are let go. Asking leaders to help us move into ill-defined and complex new problems cannot live if we continue to impose the old standard rewards for the control, neatness, and uniformity of a managerial time and a managerial church.

5. The Assumption of Harmony

The GI generational norms of group that still dominate so many of our congregations (egalitarianism, the highly relational nature of denominations and congregations, and the practice of representative democracy that brings all voices and therefore all competing preferences to the table) are part of a rather powerful matrix that makes anything less than full agreement in congregations and denominations highly suspect. The earlier generational assumption of harmony as practiced in many places confuses harmony with agreement. We seem to believe that everyone must be in agreement before the group can move ahead. We feel that no one can disagree or else we are not really "community" or "church family"—favorite descriptors to refer to congregations and denominations. Such earlier assumptions of harmony now function effectively as norms to dampen needed new ideas and experimentation with new practices in the wilderness. Harmony, treated in such a way, must be let go of if we are to live in the wilderness with any creativity.

A favorite observation comes from the creative writing of Wally Armbruster, who loved to play with words and ideas back in the 1960s and early 1970s. Reflecting on harmony, Armbruster wrote, "If everybody's singing the same note that ain't harmony. That, baby, is monotony. Harmony happens when people sing different notes . . . and even some which sound (at first) like discord suddenly start to sound great . . . once your ear gets used to the idea."[20] Harmony begins with dissonance, with disagreement, with different people in different places singing and saying what they see and then working to bring their differences into play with one another until there is resonance. Harmony depends not on one idea that everyone agrees with but on multiple ideas that people work with.

When teaching leaders about conflict management, I always point out that my operational definition of healthy conflict is simply two or more ideas in the same place at the same time. Two or more ideas interacting is not a problem; it is a necessity. If a congregation or a denominational office can hold only one idea at a time, it can do only what it has already done. In a consultation with a small congregation a number of years ago, we were working on the issue of the Christian formation of children as a part of the church's ministry with children and families. The question was, how could the church offer faith to the neighborhood children in a time when family structure had changed and families either ignored the church or used the church programs for child care? We were meeting in April, and during the meeting, I asked if they were planning to have a vacation Bible school that year. The energy of the group suddenly went up, and they explained that yes, they would have a VBS during the third week of June, they would have sixty-five to seventy children, they would have ten to twelve volunteers, they would have a special opening event and a closing ceremony, and they would have special refreshments each day. At that April meeting I asked if they had already had their planning meeting for the upcoming June VBS, and the answer was no, not yet. How did they know, then, what they were going to do in June except that it was what they had done the year before and the year before that? Although it was asking questions about how the church needed to change to serve children and their changed families, this congregation already had its one answer and expected everyone to agree with it and volunteer to help. The congregation desperately needed a second idea beyond VBS that it could allow to live, be taken seriously, and try something new.

From a systems perspective, having only one idea and being able to do only what has already been done in the past may feel like harmony, but it is actually a precursor to death. Any organism that separates itself from its environment will die. Living, healthy organisms and organizations must have permeable boundaries in which people, ideas, and energy can pass back and forth. The effect of not having interaction with the environment is easily seen when an organism such as a flower is separated from its environment of light, water, and soil. Nurtured by what passes back and forth across the plant's boundary from the environment, the flower dies without it. Surrounding our denominations and their congregations is a fast-changing environment with shifting values, diverse lifestyles, growth of technology, competing generational practices, and a growing litany of fears—real and perceived. To separate from such a fast-changing environment is an act of death for any denomination or congregation. The environment of change nurtures the future ministry of the church and allows us to keep living.

The high regard for relationship over purpose that is lived out in established religious organizations—and was installed as a norm requiring agreement by all labeled as harmony—is not a measure of Christian community but a dangerous practice that can lead to stagnation in a fast-changing world. Psychiatrist and founder of the Foundation for Community Encouragement, Scott Peck identified four stages of community making that would lead to mature and healthy communities.[21] The first stage of community making is "pseudocommunity," where the essential dynamic is conflict avoidance. Conflict (multiple ideas in competition with one another that lead to exploring meaning, purpose, and identity) is the lifeblood of vibrant and healthy communities. Without such conflict we live only in false community. The conflict, of course, must be managed well, and relationships must be valued during the discomfort of the trip toward full community, which moves from pseudocommunity through chaos and emptiness before beginning to live in real community. Once again we have confirmation of the hard work of transition that Bridges framed in the correlating stages of endings (letting go of old comforts), the neutral zone (with its chaos and emptiness), and making a beginning (authentic community with identity and purpose).

Without a willingness to reframe harmony as dissonance and to reframe dissonance as healthy conflict the assumed norm of harmony as continual agreement actually gives power to any voice within the system that is able to say no. In a recent consultation with a middle judicatory I asked the people how they would go about proposing a new idea in their system. The picture that emerged was of a path leading to various persons or groups, each with the power of saying no, because the norm in the system was full agreement of any and all parts. The new idea would be taken to the judicatory executive to see whether he would support it. Then the idea would go to the other executives on staff. The next step was the program staff. Step number four was to check the idea against polity to see whether it was allowed, and then, step five, the idea would be checked against the structure committee of the judicatory to see whether it was allowed by judicatory policy. Finally the idea would go before the judicatory board, a large and representational committee, to see whether it could garner support to be taken to the churches. If you count the churches at the end that also would need to accept the idea and support it, that amounts to seven stops along the way, each one having the power to end forward movement with a simple statement of disagreement. Like the language of so many congregations and regional and national agencies, the language used in this system was of community and family. But interpreted as dependent on agreement, it was a system that could not live in a wilderness because it was stuck in what I refer to as the "happiness trap."[22] Overattention to complaints or to nos is a predisposition to stability and to the status quo.

In part the recent interest in models and methods of consensus among church bodies has had its attraction because consensus, properly practiced, allows disagreement without requiring problem solving and full agreement. We are most commonly taught to frame ideas as propositions: "I think that we should . . ." Propositions of action are commonly needed in order to bring an idea to a decision. Framing an idea in this familiar way, however, seems to lead too quickly to making a decision. With norms of agreement and pseudocommunity, people either avoid decisions altogether or use known tools such as *Robert's Rules of Order* to quickly measure where the majority stands and then impose agreement by expecting minority voices to shift and stand with the majority. The price paid for such harmony is the absence of new learning and a denial of change. The real potential in new and competing ideas is not the final decision that is made as much as the conversation that will lead to a decision. Writing of consensual decision making within the Quaker community, Michael Sheeran points to this difference: "The goals of Quaker decision making are basically different from those of majority rule, a process to which most Americans are conditioned. The proposals made at the beginning of a discussion are thus usually seen by participants as starting points, not as finished products unsusceptible to modification."[23] Change comes not from having the right idea, not from having the most powerful data, and not from making right decisions. Change comes from conversation about the different ideas, the different data presented, and the different decisions to be made until something new is learned or tried. "Human conversation is the most ancient and easiest way to cultivate the conditions for change—personal change, community and organizational change, planetary change," writes Margaret Wheatley, cofounder of the Berkana Institute.[24] Conversations can be messy. They can be uncomfortable as people talk from their different hopes and different perspectives. They can be confusing because they don't lead quickly to action until enough time is allowed and enough room is granted for discernment. Nonetheless, the conversation in the wilderness respects different ideas that offer the hope of new directions. And that conversation cannot live until false norms of harmony are let go.

6. *The Assumption That Ministry Can't Be Measured*

"So those who welcomed his message were baptized, and that day about three thousand persons were added" (Acts 2:41). "And day by day the Lord added to their number those who were being saved" (Acts 2:47). According to the scriptural text, the apostles were careful to count the results of their ministry and the change that was being brought by God. We come from a people who, early on, were comfortable with counting and with expecting results that changed people. The word *number* is used twenty-six times in the book of Acts alone. Yet we assume that ministry cannot be measured. We argue that the end "product" of the church is the changed life of a person, which is a "product" that is hardly measurable. Measuring effectiveness by how many changed lives or how deeply a life is changed is even more difficult since the ability to change a person is not actually under control of the church or its leaders. The changed person, the changed heart, the rebirth of an individual into a new wholeness is not the province of another person. This is not something that we can do to one another; this is the work of the hand of God. At best the church can provide the opportunity, the environment, the resources, and the practices that will allow space for God to move in the person's life. So, the change is hard to measure. And the change we want is not under our control.

Further, when it comes to the counting—the number of members, attendance, baptisms, or dollars—we often feel vulnerable because community demographics have even more of an influence on results than our efforts. If community demographics and cultural changes are forces that deeply influence how and how many people will be touched by the church, these are hardly forces that respond to either the hard work or the wishes of congregational and denominational leaders. The result is that we fear counting. Surely counting, some arbitrary quantitative measure of something over which we have little control, cannot be a reliable measure of the effectiveness and impact of our work.

Compounding this even further are the negative experiences of how measures seem to be used against leaders. Counting can be a punitive activity when persons are held accountable for things over which they do not have direct control. Many leaders in the church, clergy and lay, congregational and denominational, have experienced evaluation in its *summative* form based on the results of counting members, attendance, participation, or changes in categories of membership or relationship to the denomination. In his very helpful book on evaluation written in the mid-1990s, Jeff Woods draws the distinction between *summative* and *formative* evaluation: "Summative evaluation involves discovering how well someone is doing, while formative evaluation tries to help the person improve."[25] Summative evaluation brings an evaluation to a conclusion: How good or bad is the person? Should the person be rewarded or warned, continued or discontinued in the position? Leaders in the church routinely fear summative evaluation because so much of what they deal with is beyond their direct control, and also because the persons doing the evaluation commonly have little awareness or understanding of the scope of the work being evaluated. Friend and consultant colleague Ed White would often say that 90 percent of the people in a church don't know more than 10 percent of what a pastor does. Summative evaluation can be rather dangerous in such a setting.

The church has not been good at formative evaluation—of gathering information and data to "measure" where we are at the moment so that we can have *conversations together* about what we have learned so far, and based on what we have learned, what we have tried, the results to date, and what might be done next to move us closer to our goal. Formative evaluation measures where we are, what we've done, and what we've learned so that we can then go further. A participant in a seminar I was leading brought a new focus to this difference between summative and formative evaluation by saying that what the cook does with a bowl of soup is formative when she tastes the soup to see what is needed to make it better, and what the customer does with that bowl of soup is summative when she tastes it and pronounces it good or terrible. We would like to talk with the cook but fear that we will end up with an unpleasant conversation with the customer.

Regarding measures, a system gets what it pays attention to. Another way to say the same thing is that a system produces what it measures. If the system measures nothing, that is what it gets. Without measures we cannot focus on what we are called to produce. "What if your outputs are inherently *not* measurable?" asks Jim Collins in his monograph on social sector organizations, which include churches and denominations. "The basic idea is still the same," he writes, "Separate inputs from outputs and hold yourself accountable for progress in outputs, *even if those outputs defy measurements.*"[26] In other words, if the result of ministry cannot be measured quantitatively, it must be *described* so that conversation can continue about whether we are approaching the description.

We have a good bit of learning to do about measuring the results of congregations and denominations. As a culture driven by a scientific worldview, we respect numbers, and so we hope to be able to "count" the product of our ministry. The default measures used by the church are "how much, how often, and how many."[27] The result is that we are currently counting some things about ministry because they can be counted, not necessarily because they are the best measures of ministry. Membership, average attendance at worship, and dollars are easily counted but may well be faulty measures. Counting membership at a cultural time when people participate in organizations without feeling the need to officially join as members misrepresents the actual ministry happening by undercounting, as does average attendance at worship at a cultural time when people choose a relationship with a church that may or may not include worship. Such measures as membership, average attendance, dollars, and other things easily counted are flawed because they don't tell us what we really need to know about the impact or outcome of ministry. Nonetheless, we need to measure. Without measuring we cannot learn how to be more effective. Without measuring we cannot hold ourselves accountable to the mission that we claim or that claims us. However, we have much more to learn about measuring ministry. Reggie McNeal, seeking to go beyond the limits of "how much, how often, and how many," suggests a wide array of other measures that would be more helpful.[28] Unfortunately the capacity to measure the critical differences of ministry is not present in most denominations or congregations at this time. For the moment what needs to be said is that in order to move ahead, we will need to let go of our protectivism, our fear of counting, and our assumptions that ministry cannot or should not be measured. This is new learning in the wilderness, and there is still much to do.

Letting go means moving ahead, as paradoxical as it may at first seem. As noted, the longer one is in the wilderness, the more difficult the work seems to become. Certainly changing the tacit norms that have silently guided our lives in the past may be some of the most difficult work. We need always to remind ourselves that progress is being made in the wilderness, changes are on the horizon. We have evidence of new life in a growing number of congregations, and evidence of increased courage and risk in a growing number of leaders.

CHAPTER 7

PICTURES OF THE PROMISED LAND

Past, present, and future: no one lives in the wilderness without engaging all three time frames. Sitting at the campfire in the evening, we rehearse the past as we talk about what it was like back in Egypt, how far we have already come, and what the travel was like in the heat of the past day. Sitting at the campfire in the evening, we measure the present—how tired we are, what aches and pains we feel, what enjoyment is found in the company as quiet, rest, and food are shared. But the conversation also turns to the future—what it will be like, what can be expected not just for tomorrow's travel but when the promised land is reached.

It would not be fair in this book to rehearse the past lessons learned and the present challenges faced without reference to what can be seen ahead. Here we come to the futurist's dilemma. People want to know the future, but how can one tell?

A number of years ago I was invited to Rhode Island to work with a national group of Lutheran executives. The invitation was to share presentation time with a professional futurist. Not knowing what to expect, I was intrigued. The futurist and I met to prepare for our time with the executives, and I was instructed in futuring. I learned that the future cannot be forecast or foretold. One can measure and describe only what is and what has been happening and extrapolate from both to describe what might be, if all trends continue uninterrupted. Any conclusions about the future are necessarily suspect because they are subject to unknown and uncontrollable conditions and variables. Conclusions are not the stuff of futuring, but projections (extrapolated trends) can be. Based on what we have experienced, based on what we see at the moment, it is possible to project what might happen— as long as we are willing to be wrong! It is all right to look through a glass darkly in the present moment as long as we are willing to see clearly later when things are different than we expected.

Of the many things that we could discuss for future projections of our wandering in our particular wilderness I would limit this conversation to four interrelated themes: the large church, the small church, the denominational connection with clergy and congregations, and denominational size and structure. Each of these four areas offers a lens into the way in which denominations and congregations are shifting as we learn to live into the new mission field. While conclusions must be held very lightly, we can say some things.

Large churches, very large churches, and megachurches will continue to carry denominations in terms of members, dollars, and access to the culture.

Large churches (average attendance more than five hundred at worship), very large churches (average attendance more than eight hundred), and megachurches (average attendance more than two thousand) will continue to be our most comfortable forms of congregations in the present culture and speak most easily to a large and growing percentage of the North American population. The great explosion of the number of large churches began in the 1970s and has continued through the first decade of the twenty-first century. As noted in chapter 2, the 2003 statistical report of The United Methodist Church indicated that the largest two hundred churches (by membership) represented only 0.5 percent of all United Methodist churches but held 9.5 percent of the national membership of the denomination. A very few very large churches hold a disproportionate number of people who are members and participants in denominations. This pattern is well established across denominations. These largest congregations are also the sources of a disproportionate amount of money that is directed to the regional and national levels of the denomination.

One projection for these large and very large churches is related to the expansion of the number of such congregations and their locations. Two strategic variables are attached to the future development of new numbers of these largest congregations: one is generational and the other is geographical. In our look at the mission field in chapter 4 we used the work of Rex Miller and the perspective of his four communication paradigms. The fourth paradigm of digital communication is heavily driven by generational values. Younger generations of people who were born into a highly technological world have learned to manage their experience and form communities in small formats, which Miller calls microcommunities. Earlier generations, particularly the late boomers, were the inheritors of the broadcast age when information and entertainment were shared in very broad and large brushstrokes through TV, concerts, news broadcasts, and standardized education. These earlier generations learned to participate in very large settings. They learned to be comfortable in very large institutions in which they would form smaller subgroups. It is not surprising that the large church not only engaged large numbers of people but also led the way to understand the multicelled congregation in which the whole was made up of the aggregate of multiple small replications. In the very large organization or institution the participant is able to be a part of something very large, rich, and diverse, but at the same time hold personal control over how deep to venture into the organization and how involved to be in the activities. Such large organizations were both a product of and built for the baby-boomer generation.

Younger generations of leaders and participants of the digital paradigm, however, seem to be seeking smaller microcommunities from the start. While the evidence that I have is anecdotal, a growing number of persons entering ordained ministry are less interested in leading large and very large congregations as a professional or personal goal for their ministry. Inheriting someone else's congregation and making it grow are not attractive for many new leaders entering ministry and for many new generations of participants. At a time when so many mainline denominations are becoming increasingly aware of the large glut of clergy retirees looming on the horizon in the next five to seven years as the first wave of babyboomer clergy move into retirement, the diminished interest in large congregations by entering clergy is a concern. Middle judicatory executives in a number of denominations are becoming increasingly intentional to identify young clergy in their early years of preparation for ministry who have the potential to develop both the interest in and the tools for leading large congregations. Because of the distinct skill set needed to lead such churches, the leaders of these large and largest congregations cannot be fully prepared through usual channels. Because of the small number of these large and largest congregations and the proportionally small group of clergy needed for future leadership in these congregations, developing formal paths of preparation for clergy is a challenge. The small stream of people intentionally preparing for these churches presents an economic challenge to institutions (seminaries, denominational or middle judicatory units, or parachurch organizations) where preparation could take place. Because of generational values and preferences, it is reasonable to project that while the current very large churches and megachurches will continue with vitality, it is less likely that we will continue to see explosive growth in the number of these congregations.

Location is the other variable that will offer constraints on the addition of numbers of new large, very large, and megacongregations. As conversant as these congregations are with the culture, and as effective as they are in addressing the changed mission field, the largest congregations can live easily only in an ecology large enough to sustain them. A number of years ago my wife and I, along with our oldest son and his wife, took our grandchildren on a field trip to the Tennessee Aquarium in downtown Chattanooga, which, unique for many aquariums, has a very large display of freshwater fish. I used to do quite a bit of fishing in my high school years and thought that I was pretty familiar with freshwater fish. Another way of talking about my familiarity with fish is that the length of the fish I used to catch could easily be described using my hands without stretching my arms. Once a fish could be described in pounds, it was clearly a *big* fish for me in those years. I was not prepared to see displays in the aquarium of freshwater fish five, six, and seven feet long! The signs in the aquarium noted that fish of such size could be found only in rivers of commensurate size, like the Amazon. It takes a river of such immense size to sustain fish of such immense size. There is a direct relationship between the size of any organism and the size of its environment, organizations included. For this reason the largest of our Christian congregations, denominational and independent, are found in the southern half of the United States, particularly in the south central region and in Southern California where booming populations and open space can accommodate such institutions.

In a 2007 Brookings Institution publication, Robert Lang and Jennifer Lefurgy take a close look at *boomburbs*, which they call "accidental cities."[1] Boomburbs are overgrown suburbs outside older metropolitan centers. These large and rapidly growing incorporated communities of more than one hundred thousand residents, though incorporated municipalities, do not have downtown centers despite having the full range of housing, employment, and services of formal cities. Curiously these boomburbs are growing to such size that while not recognized as traditional cities, they are larger than many older cities. For example, the boomburb of Mesa, Arizona, is larger than more traditionally recognized big cities such as Minneapolis and Miami. These boomburbs are environments that hold most of our largest churches and megachurches. Recognizing the natural connection between size of environment and size of congregation, we should note that the current and future strength of our denominations as defined by participants and resources will continue to be in the South. The Northeast, Midwest, and Northwest are older and more developed, with fewer large concentrations of people and no space for expansive growth. Yet in understanding trends for the future, we also should note the conclusions of the Brookings Institution research, which can project the limit on both time and size of the continued expansion of boomburbs and the kinds of environments that support the largest congregations. The end of the continued expansion of boomburbs can be calculated by measuring the limits of space and resources available to them, which suggests that the continual increase in the number of the largest congregations also has a limit. While our large, larger, and largest congregations are a dominant presence on our current congregational landscape, simply "getting good" at planting, growing, and leading the largest congregations is not a denominational long-term strategy for engaging the mission field with the good news of the gospel. The largest congregations will continue to be a vital presence. However, more and more of a good thing is not the way of a changing wilderness. We will necessarily find ourselves trying to accommodate newer generations and the shifting demography of the North American population with a broader choice of congregational forms than we currently have.

In the meantime there is a good bit of work for denominations to do, learning how to hold our largest congregations in the denominational connection. Our largest congregations provide the larger portion of resources to denominations but are highly underrepresented in missional and organizational decision making since the large congregation of fifteen hundred members often has the same number of votes as the small congregation of fifty members in most denominational polities. Similarly, the largest congregations and their clergy often live somewhat on the boundaries of the denomination as the clergy and leaders of denominations experience discomfort with the leaders of the largest churches. Highly relational clergy of smaller congregations often find the more purposeful manner of the clergy of large congregations somewhat off-putting and can be jealous of the resources available to clergy in very large congregations. A fear of the tail wagging the dog makes it uncomfortable for regional denominational systems to invite the leaders of the largest congregations into meaningful participation. A common example was the senior pastor of a very large Presbyterian church whose membership represented 20 percent of all of the Presbyterians in the presbytery to which this church belonged and whose missional support represented 18 percent of the total presbytery budget. The senior pastor was nationally known for his leadership, but he was offered no positions of leadership in his presbytery despite his interest in serving.

Our national denominational policies and our regional practices were designed in the time of small congregations, and we have not learned to accommodate our congregations of largest size. Learning to live with and include our largest congregations is a challenge for the present moment and for the future as our denominations will also quickly need to learn how to live with and include new forms of small congregations. Indeed, the real challenge will be for our denominations to learn how to include multiple sizes and forms of congregations and their leaders. We will turn our attention to the shifting future of the small congregation next. But let us note that our inherited denominational (and our most regulatory) practices are based on conformity in which clergy, laity, and congregations are assumed to accommodate the needs of the denomination rather than the denomination developing a wider practice of relationships to accommodate the growing differences in congregations.

The small church as we know it will diminish and be reduced in numbers while a new form of small church will emerge and seek a different relationship to other congregations and denominations.

Several times in reviewing what we have learned in our present wilderness, I have noted the dominance of the number of small congregations in North America. Earlier I reported Mark Chaves's study of American congregations in which the average attendance over all congregations in the United States is seventy-five people. In my United Methodist denomination about a third of our more than thirty-five thousand congregations have average attendance at worship of fewer than thirty-five people. The number of small congregations in our denominations and associations drives our history as well as our current experience of congregations.

There are essentially three threats to the population of the smallest churches: location, economics, and a generation gap. Location is a product of history. The location of mainline churches historically followed the places where people gathered and lived. As people settled into villages and towns, congregations followed. Shifting demographics and migrating populations now mean that we have congregations in places where populations that once supported the congregation have diminished or changed. Many of the oldest and smallest of the mainline congregations are unable to replenish themselves as people move out of regions en masse, which happened in the Northeast when the manufacturing industry moved in both southern and global directions and in the Midwest as the farming and automobile industries struggled under the weight of global competition. Small towns in the West and Southwest have withered from population shifts in which younger generations of people left for education, military service, and employment and did not return home, as had previous generations. The depletion of populations capable of sustaining the once active and viable small congregations is widespread and can be encountered in urban, suburban, and rural geographies. In many cases the absence of a population able to sustain a congregation may not be defined simply by the aggregate number of people in the community but by issues of diversity as well. In some communities where small congregations are not thriving, the issue is not the number of people in the community but the turnover of population. The people whom the congregation best knew how to serve and include in its ministry left the area to be replaced by a people sufficiently different in race, ethnicity, religious background, or socioeconomic identity so that the congregation no longer has the capacity to connect to its new neighbors.

The threat of economics to these smallest congregations is related to the way these faith communities are wedded to their definition of *church*, which requires located, residential clergy (preferably full time) and dedicated facilities. The picture of the New England white clapboard church located on the village green with the pastor's residence next door is still a dominant image of what it means to be church, even when the image needs to be adapted to fit brick buildings among row houses in urban centers or adobe buildings at country crossroads in the Southwest. The idea of a congregation needing, by definition, *our* pastor and *our* building is strong in North American congregations shaped on the values of earlier generations. It is a definition of church that can no longer be supported by an increasing number of communities. The presumed need for a church to have its own located clergy and the escalation of clergy compensation packages, often driven by pension and health-care benefit provisions, can easily shift the purpose of a small congregation from fulfilling mission to supporting the pastor. The care and maintenance of facilities that were built to serve earlier generations, including the accumulation of deferred maintenance costs, can push the expense of congregational life beyond the capacity of the now small and dwindling numbers of supporting members and participants in small congregations.

Perhaps the greatest threat, however, is the gap of generational differences that exists in many—not all—of these smallest congregations. Longevity of life now allows five generations to live side by side in the same family; an infant child can be born into a family where parents, grandparents, great-grandparents, and even great-great grandparents still live. Many people alive today easily remember an earlier time when only three generations lived side by side with commonly shared values and similar lifestyles. In a now highly mobile and highly technological culture of individualism the current five generations do not so easily live together, may not share the same values, and certainly have differences in lifestyles. The most vibrant congregations are able to engage the wider swath of these five generations where differences create a dissonance that keeps the practice of the faith always questioned and therefore always growing. The generational threat to small congregations is the frequency with which so many of them now hold only the oldest two of the five generations in their fold, thereby losing their ability to speak to or include the youngest generations that might carry the congregation into the future. When the gap between generations becomes so great that there are multiple missing younger generations in the congregation, the congregation has likely slipped beneath the threshold of change. While this generational gap can be found and is equally devastating in larger congregations, it is most commonly found in congregations with average worship attendance below one hundred persons.

Size is neither a determinant of nor a deterrent to mission. Our smallest congregations can be highly effective and faithful in mission, often excellent at nurture and care, and frequently sensitive to and focused on mission to others. But the effect of the multiple threats of location, economics, and the generation gap suggests that a noticeable percentage of these congregations will close over the next two decades, leaving denominations significantly smaller in number of congregations and less visible with less impact in many communities.

Much denominational work needs to be done to manage this shrinking segment of congregations. But the needed work will be challenged by current practices. In denominations where there is an oversupply of clergy or where there are agreements that "require" the denomination to locate active (nonretired) clergy in a congregation, a percentage of these struggling congregations is kept on "life support" not because of the viability of ministry but because clergypersons who must be placed by the denomination need congregational homes. Rather than congregations that use clergy to support ministry, these become congregations whose purpose is to support clergy. When denominations extend extra measures to subsidize such settings with extra dollars, time, or attention from denominational resources in order to meet the minimal requirements of clergy support, then the resources are, in fact, directed to the weakest part of the denominational system, not the places of greatest potential or productivity to accomplish what the denomination claims as its mission.

The smallest congregations will also present denominations with one of their greatest challenges in the next decades as newer generations of leaders and participants form new congregations. As noted above, small institutions and organizations are attractive to many of our youngest adults as they think about faith communities. The closing of so many current small congregations is not a prelude to the disappearance of all small congregations. There is within younger adult populations a great interest in forming congregations that are microcommunities, using Rex Miller's description from chapter 4. At issue is the fact that these new small congregations, usually forming under the flag of "emergent" or "missional" congregations, are greatly different from the congregations with which our denominations are familiar. These new congregations often form less as products of denominational new church starts than as emergent new communities with leaders in place. The role of leader in these new forms of congregations does not conform to old models of clergy either in terms of preparation, certification, or prominence in the congregation. Seminary training, ordination, denominational certification beyond baptism, and a sense of call are not necessarily seen as criteria for leadership in these congregations. Separately owned facilities are not necessarily required or desired; regular Sunday corporate worship may or may not be a major component of the congregation's life. Because they are still new on the horizon, it is difficult to tell how much of a pattern these new forms of congregation represent and how interested they will be in denominational connection. What is sure is that they are of a different breed from the congregations built by the generations that preceded this newer movement, and denominations will need to adapt their practices significantly to allow these new congregations to replace the ones that will disappear. Consider the differences that can be drawn using the following descriptors:

Denominational Congregations	Emerging/Missional Congregations[2]
Internal focus	External focus
Inherited denomination	Independent network
Monocultural	Multicultural
Theologically conservative	Theologically liberal
Attractional	Missional
High-profile celebrity leader	Low-profile situational leader
Negative toward popular culture	Engaging popular culture

Like the large and very large congregations, the forms of the newly developing congregations are sufficiently different that denominations will be challenged to relate to them. Learning how to relate to and include the new large congregations and the new small congregations will be difficult work requiring redefinition of the relationship. This is the next issue that we consider in describing our future.

The relationship between denominations and their clergy and congregations will be reformed.

Earlier in this book I described denominations and their middle judicatory offices as regulatory agencies. Using the historical overview of denominations by Craig Dykstra and James Hudnut-Beumler, we saw that the regulatory stage was an economic response to an increasingly differentiating ecology of clergy, congregations, and religious service providers. For the denomination to meet the explosion of different preferences for goods, services, and theological perspectives, and the growing array of social justice movements was both too difficult and too costly. The more efficient response was regulation—the expectation that all clergy and congregations in the denominational covenant or connection behave according to polity and established practice. Those congregations and clergy who obeyed and fulfilled the expectations of the covenant/connection were identified as "good congregations," while those who veered from the regulations were "bad congregations." Such sanctions that encouraged congregations and their leaders to denominational conformity remained effective during the period when the generational values of belonging and membership remained strong in the leaders and congregations. As those values shifted from group to individual, from belonging to participating, the effectiveness of regulations and sanction slipped. It is no longer a badge of honor to be a "good" denominational church or pastor. In my tradition the language of connection has shifted. In the generation of United Methodist clergy that immediately preceded me, conversation about making congregations "United Methodist" was strong. In the cohorts of United Methodist leaders that followed me, it is now more common for me to hear people talk about having their congregations connected to their Wesleyan heritage—a theological perspective able to be practiced in multiple forms and not held exclusively by the United Methodist denomination.

A denominational practice based on regulations produces a system of conformity that is a value increasingly difficult to sustain in a diverse, multicultural, multivalue, and global environment. We are now in a position where denominations routinely want more of a connection with congregations and clergy than congregations and clergy want with their denomination. Such a situation suggests that in our denominational futures, we will need to face into at least three issues: a reframed purpose and identity of our denominations, a new claim on entrepreneurial leadership, and an ability to engage discomfort and inequality in relationships.

The first issue, the reframing of purpose and identity, has been a major theme of this book in a postestablishment era for mainline denominations and congregations. As earlier described, the previous connections that once lived at the center of denominations were the strong bonds of history, theology, race or ethnicity, and geographic location. These bonds have more recently been replaced by much more institutional and therefore much less powerful connections, such as clergy deployment practices, pensions, health insurance, and denominational polity. Hammering out a new identity in a diverse environment is difficult work because the goals cannot include conformity and the agreement of all involved. Instead the center needs to be a story sufficiently strong to make others want to tell it, a purpose sufficiently important and difficult to make others want to pursue it, and an identity clear enough to make others want to live it.

A new and clear connection between the denomination and its congregations and clergy that rests on purpose and identity will make a new demand on leaders at all levels of the denomination, from the congregational to the national level. If uniformity cannot be the goal, if conformity cannot be the expectation, then leaders will necessarily need to negotiate their differences and willingly break old norms of compliance, equality, and egalitarianism to live together in connection. How else, for example, could a leader responsible for certification of ordained leaders in a denomination require seminary training for the clergy of established congregations, accept other paths of preparation for leaders of ethnic congregations, and also make room for new generational forms of congregations, which may or may not depend on ordained leadership? Leaders will need to enter into more difficult conversations in which certification becomes a process of more than signing off on the legislated experiences and content of preparation and focus equally on character formation and the needs of the specific congregation. If we are about to enter a time when the mainline church has the clear opportunity to hold multiple forms of congregations connected by a clear identity and purpose, then different forms of congregations will require different paths of leadership preparation, different expectations of missional performance, and different levels of accountability to the norms and practices of denominations. The wilderness is about to become even messier.

Emerging from a time of regulations and conformity, the new leaders in the wilderness will need to continue and extend the practice of breaking old rules. Finding new paths is not congruent with following old rules since old rules restrict movement and options. Increasingly I am aware of watching a small but growing cohort of denominational and congregational leaders push the boundaries of old practices. For example, some denominational leaders responsible for clergy deployment no longer give priority to clergy tenure or the clergy career ladder in assigning clergy. Some clergy are breaking old rules of representational nominations and elections of church officers in order to get to smaller groups of gifted leaders who can make missional decisions. Some laity are insisting on accountability for their congregation's use and direction of resources to assure that the resources are aligned with missional outcomes. In fact, conformity is now more routinely questioned when purpose is at risk.

The new mode of leadership that is emerging and will continue to swell is a form of entrepreneurialism, the second of the issues necessary to the reforming of denominational connections. We do not yet have a clear name for this new leadership. *Entrepreneurialism*, while accurate, is not sufficient since this term has a changing history and a wide variety of interpretations. Where entrepreneurialism once spoke more of the independent maverick leader who risked going his or her own way for gain, the new entrepreneurialism has a different and more mature character. These leaders actively look for opportunity that goes beyond standard practice of their organization. They willingly risk as all entrepreneurial leaders do, but they accept having to live in the tension between purposeful risk and obedience to the history and the heritage that belong to their institution. Rather than find their own path as rugged individualists, these new leaders seek to join a movement with others who are also looking for new paths in the wilderness. These are rule breakers and practice benders still faithful and wanting to live within their institutions. These new leaders now make up a growing cadre of people. In order for the mainline church to thrive in the wilderness their number will have to continue to grow.

We are then brought to the third issue that faces the newly formed connection between the mainline denomination and its congregations and clergy. The wilderness is messy. As described above, our more entrepreneurial leaders will necessarily lead us into a growing inequality among people and congregations that are connected at the center through a denominational identity but widely different in their specific practice of ministry. As congregations get better at proclaiming Christ in clear and understandable ways to their specific corner of the highly fluid and diverse mission field, the congregations may be connected together denominationally but confuse and offend one another individually with their practice. The urban congregation that is surrounded by a community with a concentration of gay, lesbian, and transsexual adults will relate as carriers of the good news of faith to these people and include them into the faith community with full access to the sacraments and practices of the faith, including the ritual of marriage. This will deeply offend sister congregations that live in suburban or rural sections of God's kingdom where the absence of homosexual communities allows them to be comfortably distant from such difficult questions. The young upstart congregation that seeks to own no building, nominates and elects no leaders, and replaces Sunday morning worship of Word and Sacrament with a Sunday morning activity of community service as a missional form of worship will baffle and offend the neighboring established congregations that follow normative practices of worship. However, each of these connected but highly different congregations may be vibrant and vital, connected in authentic ways to the specific mission field of groups or individuals to which it has been called to serve. Each can be equally faithful and effective at doing what the denomination asks of its congregations, yet still be sufficiently different from other congregations to create a deep dissonance and discomfort.

Our mainline denominations have started down a path where conformity among leaders and congregations is being replaced by shared purpose and identity. Further movement down this path will be rocky since a connection through purpose and identity does not require conformity. Some in our mainline denominations want to resolve their discomfort among congregations and leaders with censure of or schism from those who are too different from themselves. But the multiple mission fields facing our denominations call for a bolder response. In part the response will require a theological wrestling with the change that is being prompted by the deeply different mission fields. The work of our theologians and our historians will become increasingly important as we seek to build a base from which our leaders and congregations can work faithfully but also effectively and appropriately among very different people. The work of our growing cohort of entrepreneurial leaders will become increasingly important as these will be the people most willing to risk changes in order to live into this next part of the journey.

Denominations will reduce in size and structure.

What does one take along for a prolonged journey? It seems as if one lesson of a sustained time in the wilderness is that too much baggage can be both burdensome and draining. Mainline denominational and congregational structures grew in line with other North American institutions in a period of organizational expansion dominated by management that included multiple layers of decision making and middle management to follow directives that came from the top. Such organizations provided consistency and orderliness while also creating overhead and rigidity that eventually became costly for the wilderness. A shrinking membership base, a growing competition for people's discretionary and charitable spending, an inflationary economy, and a need for agility over orderliness have combined to increasingly strain large and rigid organizations, including denominational and congregational structures.

We are now in a sustained pattern of questioning the structure and organization of our institutions—a pattern that will continue in a search for a more simplified and less expensive structure for doing mission and ministry. At its least thoughtful expression this search for simplicity and reduced costs is a response to budget constraints.

At its best, however, the downsizing that is being prompted by the wilderness has been an opportunity for a growing number of leaders to ask more missional questions of purpose. The inability to sustain the cost of our congregational and denominational systems and the cumbersomeness of the systems have prompted leaders to ask, what actually needs to be accomplished? What is to be different because of these systems? A growing cohort of leaders is learning how to shape their systems and align their resources to try to make the differences they have identified as necessary.

In all of this we have been observing a downsizing of control structures in our congregations and denominational offices. Smaller decision-making groups that are actually authorized (or that are willing to claim authority) to make decisions are more prevalent. There is less of a programmatic emphasis trying to meet the needs of "all" members, the "whole" community, or "all" congregations. Instead leaders are searching for the most productive leverage points and investing their prayers, attention, staff, and dollars where the differences need to be made. There is also an increasingly creative use of technology to connect people, communicate information, and manage data. For example, one very creative experiment to watch comes from a middle judicatory office of a denomination that has gone *virtual*—no office, no residential staff, no common meeting place, no physical resource center, and no file cabinets except for a few in a rented storage unit to house historic documents. Technology is being used creatively, new roles for staff and leaders are being developed, and a new understanding of the purpose of a middle judicatory is being invented in the process.

Experiment is a good and appropriate term to describe this virtual effort. It is also an appropriate way to think of a large and growing number of other initiatives now dotting the landscape as leaders seek new ways in the changed cultural wilderness. Experiments are appropriate to the wilderness as people try to find new ways to live in a changed environment. Much of the trend within the experiments now being observed includes a search for a simplification of staff, structure, and decision making at the center of our institutions and organizations.

Epilogue

So many years in our particular wilderness, so much gained, so much learned. The biblical lesson is that people are changed in the wilderness. The same can be said of faith communities. When living in the wilderness, people discover that old ways don't always work, old rules don't always help. People have to find new ways to form community and be faithful. How will we now be with one another and with God? The response in the original Exodus to that question was the Ten Commandments, which defined the relationship with God, and a new communal hierarchy of leaders that defined the way in which the Israelites would live with one another and be governed. The response to that question in the Exile was the Holiness Code, which provided answers to the same question appropriate to the people in that moment. The response to that question in our particular wilderness is still being formed. There is more to do.

I began this book with reflections on my first appointment as pastor to a church in Philadelphia in 1972. It was a healthy, eager congregation that had suffered some recent bumps before I arrived but was rebounding strongly and wanting to move ahead. As time went on, however, it became clearer that people wanted most to move on with life as usual. Like so many congregations at that time, it was living with questions of ministry much too small to sustain it through the wilderness changes that were on the horizon. While Philadelphia was struggling with a racist city administration and while generational changes were swirling all about it, that first congregation kept measuring its faithfulness by the participation of its already active members and their worry about any who might become inactive. It evaluated its performance by its conformity to denominational standards and community practices. It demonstrated hospitality by including others who were most like its members, and it shied away from people too different to "fit in."

This is not an indictment of that congregation. I remember it with love as a formative place where my early ministry was shaped, where my children were born, and where our family was nurtured. I also remember those years as some of the most frustrating times I had as a pastor. Was this what I had felt called to—managing an organization, satisfying members, and following denominational rules?

The years since that first appointment were immeasurably more confusing and messy as I and many others were constantly challenged to know what was right to do and what was worth doing. Living in the wilderness requires developing an acquaintance with insecurity. But the wilderness is full of energy. It prompts new thinking, new behavior, and new trials to accomplish old ends of faithfulness. Learning to live in the wilderness provides, above all else, a new introduction to hope.

One of the joys of the wilderness is to be reacquainted with hope that is connected to God but to realize that it is a different form of hope. Over the years I have learned that hope is an active, not a passive, verb. In common conversation we often make statements such as, "I hope you have a good day," or, "I hope you have a nice trip." These are essentially passive thoughts that we share with others. Quite honestly it is probably OK with me if your day is not so good or your trip not so nice. And quite frankly I don't usually see myself getting involved too deeply in assuring you a good day or nice trip. In common parlance hope can be very passive. It is a wish without risk or responsibility.

In the wilderness, hope is an active verb. Saint Augustine said that hope had two beautiful daughters—anger and courage. Hope depended on anger over what could be but is not, and on courage to make it different. The North American mainline churches, including my United Methodist denomination, are filling with hope. Anger and frustration have grown over what could be but is not, and a growing cohort of denominational and congregational leaders with courage is seeking ways to make it otherwise. Part of the next stage of our work is to help this growing cohort of courageous leaders identify one another and talk with one another. We are trying to learn what no one can teach us, and it takes conversation with one another and awareness of the multiple experiments that are being mounted for us to find our way ahead together. There is no guarantee that what we see and do next will be enough, especially as the mission field around us continues to be reshaped kaleidoscopically by technology, globalization, and generational differences. We have, however, learned enough so far in the wilderness to see new things to do. And since God is in them, they are worthy of our next steps.

Notes

Introduction: Welcome to the Wilderness

1. Karen Armstrong, *The Case for God* (New York: Alfred Knopf, 2009), 268–78.

1. Our Particular Exodus

1. Etienne Wenger, *Communities of Practice: Learning Meaning and Identity* (Cambridge: Cambridge University Press, 1998), 4. One of the four central premises held by Etienne Wenger, who has examined communities of practice, is, "Knowing is a matter of participating in the pursuit of an enterprise." We learn by doing.

2. Walter Brueggemann, "Preaching Among the Exiles," *Circuit Rider* 22, no. 4 (July-August 1999): 22.

3. Father Thomas Tifft, presentation (Regional Forum for Pastoral Leadership, Roman Catholic Dioceses of Michigan and Ohio, Ann Arbor, Mich., January 3, 2006).

4. Robert William Fogel, *The Fourth Great Awakening and the Future of Egalitarianism* (Chicago: University of Chicago Press, 2000). Fogel is the winner of the 1993 Nobel Prize in Economics and as an economist offers a compelling connection between American Protestant religious movements and the state of the national economy.

5. Phyllis Tickle, *The Great Emergence: How Christianity Is Changing and Why* (Grand Rapids: Baker Books, 2008).

6. Ibid., 27. Kindle #303–8.

7. Linda J. Vogel, *Teaching and Learning in Communities of Faith* (San Francisco: Jossey-Bass, 1991), 7.

8. John Wimmer, "Edge Organizations, Entrepreneurial People and God's Dreams" (Texas Methodist Foundation, Austin, Tex., May 20, 2009).

9. L. Gregory Jones and Kevin R. Armstrong, *Resurrecting Excellence: Shaping Faithful Christian Ministry* (Grand Rapids: Eerdmans, 2006), 5.

10. Richard Lischer, *Open Secrets: A Spiritual Journey through a Country Church* (New York: Doubleday, 2001), 95–101.

11. Ibid., 95.

12. Thomas Kuhn, *The Structure of Scientific Revolutions* (Chicago: University of Chicago Press, 1970), 84–85. In his now famous study of scientific revolutions Thomas Kuhn, a theoretical physicist, offered clear insight into how knowledge does not progress developmentally at all times and that at some points must leap ahead with disconnected insight, a "paradigm shift." Writing about the progression of science, Kuhn stated, "The transition from a paradigm in crisis to a new one from which a new tradition of normal science can emerge is far from a cumulative process, one achieved by an articulation or extension of an old paradigm. Rather it is a reconstruction of the field from new fundamentals."

13. Randy Maddox, "The United Methodist Way: Living the Christian Life in Covenant with Christ and One Another" (paper, The United Methodist Way: A Convocation of Extended Cabinets, Lake Junaluska, N.C., November 9–11, 2007).

14. Robert Quinn, *Deep Change: Discovering the Leader Within* (San Francisco: Jossey-Bass, 1996), 3ff.

15. Thomas Friedman, *The World Is Flat: A Brief History of the Twenty-first Century* (New York: Farrar, Straus and Giroux, 2005).

16. Richard Longworth, *Caught in the Middle: America's Heartland in the Age of Globalization* (New York: Bloomsbury USA, 2008), 222–44.

2. A Map of Multiple Directions

1. Mark Chaves, *How Do We Worship?* (Herndon, Va.: Alban Institute, 1999), 7–11.

2. Arthur Koestler, *The Ghost in the Machine* (New York: Macmillan, 1967), 55, 76.

3. *The Methodist Hymnal* (Nashville: The Methodist Publishing House, 1964), #829.

4. Arlin Rothauge, *Sizing Up a Congregation for New Member Ministry* (New York: Episcopal Church Center, 1983).

5. Edwin Friedman, *Generation to Generation: Family Process in Church and Synagogue* (New York: Guilford Press, 1985).

6. Alan Klaas and Cheryl Brown, *Church Membership Initiative: Narrative Summary of Findings; Research Summary of Findings* (Appleton, Wis.: Aid Association for Lutherans, 1993), 3.

7. Gil Rendle and Alice Mann, *Holy Conversations: Strategic Planning as a Spiritual Practice for Congregations* (Herndon, Va.: Alban Institute, 2003), 6–11.

8. Mike Regele, *Associate Manual* (Costa Mesa, Calif.: Church Information & Development Services, 1990), 47.

9. www.perceptgroup.com. (Accessed July 17, 2010.)

10. Christian Scharen, "Learning Ministry Over Time: Embodying Practical Wisdom," in *For Life Abundant: Theology, Theological Education, and Christian*

Ministry, ed. Dorothy Bass and Craig Dykstra (Grand Rapids: Eerdmans, 2008), 268–86.

11. Edwin Freidman, *A Failure of Nerve: Leadership in the Age of the Quick Fix* (New York: Seabury Books), 203.

12. Richard Hirsh, *The Rabbi-Congregation Relationship: A Vision for the 21st Century* (Philadelphia: Reconstructionist Commission on the Role of the Rabbi, 2001), vi. Understanding the relationship between rabbi and congregation as ideally a sacred covenant, the report stated:

> Rabbis and rabbinical students increasingly indicate a reluctance to serve in congregational settings. They cite several common concerns: that the job is simply unmanageable; that boundaries between personal and professional time cannot be established; that the variety of roles they must fill creates unreasonable expectations and confusing standards of evaluation; that an absence of efficient and effective models of decision making, communication and leadership hinders their work.

13. www.lillyendowment.org/religion_ncr.html. (Accessed July 17, 2010.)

14. Friedman, *Failure of Nerve*, 47.

15. Walter Brueggemann, "Preaching Among the Exiles," *Circuit Rider* 22, no. 4 (July-August 1999): 22.

3. The Fourth Path of Identity and Purpose

1. Gil Rendle and Alice Mann, *Holy Conversations: Strategic Planning as a Spiritual Practice for Congregations* (Herndon, Va.: Alban Institute, 2003), 211–16.

2. Ronald Heifetz, *Leadership without Easy Answers* (Cambridge: Belknap Press, 1994), 71.

3. Judith Ramaley, "Change as a Scholarly Act: Higher Education Research Transfer to Practice," *New Directions for Higher Education* 110 (summer 2000): 76.

4. Thomas Long, *Beyond the Worship Wars: Building Vital and Faithful Worship* (Herndon, Va.: Alban Institute, 2001).

5. Roy Oswald and Speed Leas, *The Inviting Church: A Study of New Member Assimilation* (Herndon, Va.: Alban Institute, 1987).

6. Ibid., 19.

7. David Roozen, "National Denominational Structures' Engagement with Postmodernity," in *Church, Identity, and Change*, ed. David Roozen and James Nieman (Grand Rapids: Eerdmans, 2005), 617.

8. Nancy Ammerman, *Pillars of Faith: American Congregations and Their Partners* (Berkeley: University of California Press, 2005), 242–47.

9. Cynthia Woolever et al., "What Do We Think about Our Future and Does It Matter? Congregational Identity and Vitality," *Journal of Beliefs and Values* 27, no. 1 (April 2006): 54.

10. Mike Mather, *Sharing Stories, Shaping Community: Vital Ministry in the Small Membership Church* (Nashville: Discipleship Resources, 2002), 16–17.

11. Craig Dykstra, "Vision and Leadership," *Initiatives in Religion* 3, no. 1 (winter 1994): 1–2.

12. Howard Gardner, *Leading Minds: An Anatomy of Leadership* (New York: Basic Books, 1995), 14.

13. Ibid., 10–11.

14 Hugh Heclo, *On Thinking Institutionally* (Boulder: Paradigm Press, 2008), 30.

15. Meg Wheatley, *Turning to One Another: Simple Conversations to Restore Hope to the Future* (San Francisco: Berrett-Koehler, 2002).

16. Rendle and Mann, *Holy Conversations.*

17. David Bohm, *On Dialogue* (London: Routledge, 1996), 2.

18. William Isaacs, *Dialogue and the Art of Thinking Together* (New York: Random House, 1999), 252–90.

19. Thomas Long, *Testimony: Talking Ourselves into Being Christian* (San Francisco: Jossey-Bass, 2004), 44.

20. Mark Silk and Andrew Walsh, eds., *Religion by Region*, 9 vols. (New York: AltaMira Press, 2005). The Religion by Region series describes, both quantitatively and qualitatively, the religious character of contemporary America, region by region.

21. Craig Van Gelder, ed., *The Missional Church and Leadership Formation: Helping Congregations Develop Leadership Capacity* (Grand Rapids: Eerdmans, 2009), 15–32.

22. Robert Bellah et al., *Habits of the Heart: Individualism and Commitment in American Life* (New York: Harper & Row, 1985), 221.

23. Heclo, *On Thinking Institutionally*, 15–43.

24. Ibid., 33.

25. Anthony Healy, *The Postindustrial Promise* (Herndon, Va.: Alban Institute, 2005), 102.

26. Michael Hout, Andrew Greeley, and Melissa Wilde, "The Demographic Imperative in Religious Change in the United States," *American Journal of Sociology* 107 (September 2001): 468–500.

27. Roger Stump, "The Effects of Geographical Variability on Protestant Church Membership Trends, 1980–1990," *Journal for the Scientific Study of Religion* 37 (December 1998): 636–51.

28. Michael Lerner, *Surplus Powerlessness: The Psychodynamics of Everyday Life . . . and the Psychology of Individual and Social Transformation* (Oakland: Institute for Labor and Mental Health, 1986).

29. www.adherents.com/rel_USA.html. (Accessed July 17, 2010.)

30. Diana Eck, *A New Religious America: How a "Christian Country" Has Become the World's Most Religiously Diverse Nation* (San Francisco: HarperSanFrancisco, 2001), 4.

31. Barry Kosmin and Ariela Keysar, *American Religious Identification Survey* (ARIS, 2008): *Summary Report* (Hartford, Conn.: Trinity College, 2009), www.amer icanreligionsurvey-aris.org. (Accessed July 17, 2010.)

32. Lawrence Porter and Bernard Mohr, *Reading Book for Human Relations Training* (Arlington, Va.: NTL Institute, 1982), 34–36.

33. Stephen Carter, *Civility: Manners, Morals, and the Etiquette of Democracy* (New York: Basic Books, 1998).

34. Gil Rendle, *Behavioral Covenants in Congregations* (Herndon, Va.: Alban Institute, 1999).

35. Edgar Schein, *The Corporate Culture Survival Guide* (San Francisco: Jossey-Bass, 1999), xv.

36. Roozen, "National Denominational Structures' Engagement with Postmodernity," 596.

37. E. Brooks Holifield, *God's Ambassadors: A History of the Christian Clergy in America* (Grand Rapids: Eerdmans, 2007), 60–61.

38. Robert Quinn, *Deep Change: Discovering the Leader Within* (San Francisco: Jossey-Bass, 1996), 91ff.

39. Schein, *Corporate Culture Survival Guide*, 24.

40. Ibid., 117.

4. Singing the Lord's Song in a Foreign Land

1. Loren Mead, *The Once and Future Church* (Herndon, Va.: Alban Institute, 1991), 13–22.

2. Ronald Heifetz and Donald Laurie, "The Work of Leadership," *Harvard Business Review* (January-February 1997; Reprint #97106): 125–26.

3. Stephen Covey, *The 7 Habits of Highly Effective People* (New York: Simon & Schuster, 1989), 151.

4. Gil Rendle, *The Multigenerational Congregation: Meeting the Leadership Challenge* (Herndon, Va.: Alban Institute, 2002), 101–6.

5. William Strauss and Neil Howe, *The Fourth Turning: What the Cycles of History Tell Us about America's Next Rendezvous with Destiny* (New York: Broadway Books, 1997), 16.

6. Ibid., 60.

7. Jackson Carroll, "Bridging Worlds: The Generational Challenge to Congregational Life," *Circuit Rider* 22, no. 5 (September-October 1999): 23.

8. Daniel Yankelovich, *New Rules: Searching for Fulfillment in a World Turned Upside Down* (New York: Bantam Books, 1981), 7.

9. Rendle, *Multigenerational Congregation*, 55–70.

10. Roger Fisher and William Ury, *Getting to Yes: Negotiating Agreement without Giving In* (New York: Penguin Books, 1981).

11. Craig Dykstra and James Hudnut-Beumler, "The National Organizational Structures of Protestant Denominations: An Invitation to a Conversation," in *The Organizational Revolution: Presbyterians and American Denominationalism*, ed. Milton Coalter, John Mulder, and Louis Weeks (Louisville: Westminster John Knox Press, 1992), 307–31.

12. Rex Miller, *The Millennium Matrix: Reclaiming the Past, Reframing the Future of the Church* (San Francisco: Jossey-Bass, 2004), 15.

13. Kevin Armstrong, "In Search of a New Creation: Guided by the Christian Scop" (presentation given at The Oxford Institute of Methodist Theological Studies, 2002).

14. Nayan Chanda, *Bound Together: How Traders, Preachers, Adventurers and Warriors Shaped Globalization* (New Haven, Conn.: Yale University Press, 2007), 61–66.

15. Scott Thuma and Dave Travis, *Beyond Megachurch Myths* (San Francisco: John Wiley & Sons, 2007), 1–20.

16. Charles Handy, *Beyond Certainty: The Changing Worlds of Organizations* (Boston: Harvard Business School Press, 1996), 154.

17. Jagdish Sheth and Andrew Sobel, *Clients for Life* (New York: Simon & Schuster, 2000), 86ff.

18. Craig Dykstra, "The Pastoral Imagination," in *Initiatives in Religion* (Publication of the Lilly Endowment, 2001), 9, 1.

5. This Is Not Your Father's Wilderness

1. Edward Leroy Long Jr., *Patterns of Polity* (Cleveland: Pilgrim Press, 2001), 29.

2. Ibid., 31.

3. Gil Rendle, *Leading Change in the Congregation* (Bethesda, Md.: Alban Institute, 1998), 14–16.

4. Gil Rendle and Alice Mann, *Holy Conversations: Strategic Planning as a Spiritual Practice for Congregations* (Herndon, Va.: Alban Institute, 2003), 3–6.

5. Jim Collins, *Good to Great* (New York: HarperBusiness, 2001), 45–48.

6. E. Brooks Holifield, *God's Ambassadors: A History of the Christian Clergy in America* (Grand Rapids: Eerdmans, 2007), presents a full discussion of the source, forms, and limits of clergy authority in the North American experience.

7. Ori Brafman and Rod Beckstrom, *The Starfish and the Spider: The Unstoppable Power of Leaderless Organizations* (New York: Penguin Group, 2006), 50.

8. Ronald Heifetz, *Leadership without Easy Answers* (Cambridge: Belknap Press, 1994).

9. Ibid., 22.

10. Gregory Bateson, *Steps to an Ecology of Mind* (New York: Ballantine Books, 1972), 202–12.

11. John Scherer, "The Role of Chaos in the Creation of Change," *Creative Change* 12, no. 2 (spring 1991): 19–20. The contrast between managerial problem solving and the need for leadership to address appropriately pain and possibility is treated at greater length in Rendle's *Leading Change in the Congregation*, 77–100.

12. Michael Crichton, *The Lost World* (New York: Ballantine Publishing Group, 1995).

13. Heifetz, *Leadership without Easy Answers*, 14.

14. Stephen Covey, *The 7 Habits of Highly Effective People* (New York: Simon & Schuster, 1989), 239.

15. W. Edwards Deming, *Out of the Crisis* (Cambridge: Massachusetts Institute of Technology, Center for Advanced Engineering Study, 1986), 23–24.

16. Heifetz, *Leadership without Easy Answers*, 72.

17. Ibid., 75.

18. W. R. Bion, *Experiences in Groups* (New York: Basic Books, 1959), 78–86.

19. Ronald Heifetz and Marty Linsky, *Leadership on the Line: Staying Alive through the Dangers of Leading* (Boston: Harvard Business School Press, 2002), 12.

20. Donald Miller, *A Million Miles in a Thousand Years: What I Learned While Editing My Life* (Nashville: Thomas Nelson, 2009), 100.

21. Robert Quinn, *Deep Change: Discovering the Leader Within* (San Francisco: Jossey-Bass, 1996), 4–5.

22. Heifetz and Linsky, *Leadership on the Line*, 14.

23. Heifetz, *Leadership without Easy Answers*, 89.

24. Robert Schnase, *Five Practices of Fruitful Congregations* (Nashville: Abingdon Press, 2007).

25. Ronald Heifetz and Donald Laurie, "The Work of Leadership," *Harvard Business Review* (January-February 1997; Reprint #97106): 125–26.

26. Jim Collins, *Good to Great and the Social Sectors* (Boulder: Jim Collins, 2005), 5. www.jimcollins.com. (Accessed July 17, 2010).

27. Heifetz and Laurie, "Work of Leadership," 129.

28. Heifetz, *Leadership without Easy Answers*, 140.

29. Edwin Friedman, *Generation to Generation: Family Process in Church and Synagogue* (New York: Guilford Press, 1985), 208–10.

30. Joe Stephens and Lena Sun, "Subway Safety Panel Foiled by Constraints; 12-Year-Old Oversight Committee Has Little Influence on Metro Operations," *Washington Post*, August 10, 2009.

6. The Jeremiah Moment

1. Ronald Heifetz and Marty Linsky, *Leadership on the Line* (Boston: Harvard Business School Press, 2002), 11.

2. Walter Brueggemann, *Hopeful Imagination: Prophetic Voices in Exile* (Philadelphia: Fortress Press, 1986), 3.

3. Ibid., 4.

4. William Bridges, *Transitions: Making Sense of Life's Changes* (Reading, Mass.: Addison-Wesley, 1980), 89–150.

5. Ibid., 11.

6. Roy Oswald, *Running through the Thistles: Terminating a Ministerial Relationship with a Parish* (Herndon, Va.: Alban Institute, 1978).

7. http://www.youtube.com/watch?v=DBfniZuko3g. (Accessed July 17, 2010.)

8. General Board of Higher Education and Ministry, "Minutes of Several Conversations between the Study of Ministry Commission, Chairs of Orders and Boards of Ordained Ministry of Annual Conferences, Various Laity and Clergy across the Connection, and the General Conference of The United Methodist Church" (General Board of Higher Education and Ministry, 2008), 8.

9. Ibid., 33.

10. Marcus Buckingham and Curt Coffman, *First, Break All the Rules: What the World's Greatest Managers Do Differently* (New York: Simon & Schuster, 1999), 153.

11. Ibid., 57.

12. Everett Rogers, *Diffusion of Innovations* (New York: Free Press, 1995), 262.

13. Ibid., 80.

14. Richard Chait, William Ryan, and Barbara Taylor, *Governance as Leadership: Reframing the Work of Nonprofit Boards* (Hoboken: John Wiley & Sons, 2005), 15.

15. Lynne Twist, *The Soul of Money: Reclaiming the Wealth of Our Inner Resources* (New York: W. W. Norton, 2003), 49.

16. Ibid., 44.

17. Jim Collins, *Good to Great and the Social Sectors* (Boulder: Jim Collins, 2005), 11. www.jimcollins.com (accessed July 17, 2010).

18. Ibid., 13.

19. Calvin Pava, "New Strategies of Systems Change: Reclaiming Nonsynoptic Methods," *Human Relations* 39, no. 7 (1986): 615–33.

20. Wally Armbruster, *A Bag of Noodles* (St. Louis: Concordia Publishing House, 1972), 5.

21. M. Scott Peck, *The Different Drum: Community Making and Peace* (New York: Simon & Schuster, 1987), 77–85.

22. Gil Rendle, "On Not Fixing the Church," *Congregations*, May-June 1997, 15–16.

23. Michael Sheeran, *Beyond Majority Rule: Voteless Decisions in the Religious Society of Friends* (Philadelphia: Philadelphia Yearly Meeting of the Religious Society of Friends, 1983), 54.

24. Margaret Wheatley, *Turning to One Another: Simple Conversations to Restore Hope to the Future* (San Francisco: Berrett-Koehler, 2002), 3.

25. C. Jeff Woods, *Using Friendly Evaluation: Improving the Work of Pastors, Programs and Laity* (Herndon, Va.: Alban Institute, 1995), 69.

26. Collins, *Good to Great*, 5.

27. Reggie McNeal, *Missional Renaissance: Changing the Scorecard for the Church* (San Francisco: Jossey-Bass, 2009).

28. Ibid. Alternative measures more reflective of the outcome of ministry are suggested within a number of the chapters of McNeal's book.

7. Pictures of the Promised Land

1. Robert Lang and Jennifer Lefurgy, *Boomburbs: The Rise of America's Accidental Cities* (Washington, D.C.: Brookings Institution, 2007).

2. Eddie Gibbs, *ChurchMorph: How Megatrends Are Reshaping Christian Communities* (Grand Rapids: Baker Academic, 2009), 61.